GROW YOUR OWN ORGANIC
Fruit & Vegetables

GROW YOUR OWN ORGANIC
Fruit & Vegetables

An easy-to-follow directory of vegetables, fruit and herbs

Christine and Michael Lavelle

Photography by Peter Anderson

southwater

Dedication

This is dedicated to Mike Lavelle who would have loved to have seen this book.

This edition is published by Southwater

Southwater is an imprint of Anness Publishing Ltd
Hermes House, 88-89 Blackfriars Road, London SE1 8HA
tel. 020 7401 2077; fax 020 7633 9499
www.southwaterbooks.com; info@anness.com

© Anness Publishing Ltd 2005

UK agent: The Manning Partnership Ltd,
6 The Old Dairy, Melcombe Road,
Bath BA2 3LR; tel. 01225 478444; fax 01225 478440;
sales@manning-partnership.co.uk

UK distributor: Grantham Book Services Ltd,
Isaac Newton Way, Alma Park Industrial Estate, Grantham,
Lincs NG31 9SD; tel. 01476 541080; fax 01476 541061;
orders@gbs.tbs-ltd.co.uk

North American agent/distributor: National Book Network,
4501 Forbes Boulevard, Suite 200,
Lanham, MD 20706; tel. 301 459 3366; fax 301 429 5746;
www.nbnbooks.com

Australian agent/distributor: Pan Macmillan Australia,
Level 18, St Martins Tower, 31 Market St, Sydney,
NSW 2000; tel. 1300 135 113; fax 1300 135 103;
customer.service@macmillan.com.au

New Zealand agent/distributor: David Bateman Ltd,
30 Tarndale Grove, Off Bush Road, Albany,
Auckland; tel. (09) 415 7664; fax (09) 415 8892

A CIP catalogue record for this book is available from the British Library.

Publisher: Joanna Lorenz
Managing Editor: Judith Simons
Executive Editor: Caroline Davison
Designer: Lisa Tai
Additional Text: Richard Bird and Jonathan Edwards
Additional Photography: Jonathan Buckley and Michelle Garrett
Illustrator: Liz Pepperell
Editorial Reader: Janet Smy
Production Controller: Claire Rae

Previously published as part of a larger volume, *Organic Gardening*.

10 9 8 7 6 5 4 3 2 1

Contents

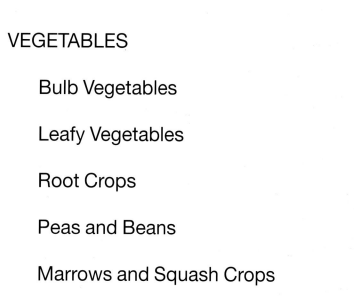

WHAT IS ORGANIC GARDENING?

The term organic means of living origin. When applied to gardening, organic has come to mean the systematic use of techniques that mirror naturally occurring systems. Put simply, it is about finding environmentally friendly ways to cultivate the land, working with rather than against nature. Organic gardening refers not just to a system of techniques, however, but also to a whole philosophy of life.

Above: *Companion plants such as these marigolds can provide welcome colour in the kitchen garden. The scent of the marigolds deters certain pests.*

THE ORIGINS OF ORGANIC GARDENING

From the point of view of gardening, the "modern" organic movement began in the late 1940s as a reaction to the increased use of pesticides and synthetic fertilizers in the years after the Second World War. In many respects, however, the principles of organic gardening have been practised for centuries. Ancient writers, among them Pliny and Virgil, commented on the importance of "good husbandry to the health of the land". Thomas Tusser, in his classic work of 1580 entitled *Five Hundred Points of Good Husbandry*, recommends crop rotation to maintain good health. The 17th-century English garden writer John Evelyn begins his *Kalendarium Hortense* with a section describing how to enrich the ground in mid-winter with "horse and sheeps dung especially, that you may have some of two years preparation".

Above: *Growing your own vegetables can be very rewarding. Here, these cabbages are being grown with companion plants.*

ORGANIC GARDENING IN THE 21ST CENTURY

Much of the current interest in organic gardening began in the 1960s, when there was increasing concern about the growing levels of environmental damage caused by pesticides and other agrochemicals. If they were causing so much damage to the natural world, then surely they must ultimately affect human beings?

The organic approach aims to reduce the effects that our gardens, farms and cities have upon the wider natural environment. Activities such as recycling, using sustainably produced materials and avoiding pesticides and other harmful agrochemicals all help in this. Organic gardening is often described as being a more natural way to garden. This can make it appear to be somehow revolutionary. In many ways, however, organic gardening could be said to be counter-revolutionary. It aims to avoid artificial inputs and gains. Instead it draws from a vast resource of wisdom and experience amassed over 10,000 years. Much of the so-called conventional wisdom is, in fact, very recent. We only have to look back as far as our grandparents to see that they were naturally organic gardeners. Organic gardening then is the marriage of good horticultural practice to an awareness of our impact upon our surroundings.

IS IT POSSIBLE TO BE WHOLLY ORGANIC?

The short answer to this would probably have to be … with great difficulty. But the purpose of this book is not to promote difficulty or set unattainable goals. The aim should always be to aspire to the ideal solution. Almost all of us face compromise on a daily basis and understand that practicalities outweigh personal ideals. With perseverance and practice, however, it is possible to become less compromised in the confines of your own garden. Simple planning and the observance of good

Left: *Organic gardens can be beautifully designed and can include plants with decorative leaf shapes.*

Above: *A well-designed and properly maintained organic garden can be both attractive and productive.*

gardening practice can steadily improve your organic credentials and, with time, a natural balance will be established in your kitchen garden. Ultimately, the aim of all organic gardeners, whether they are growing home-produced vegetables, tending a herb garden or training a few fruit trees, is to make choices appropriate to their situation. It is better to move a few steps towards the organic way than to ignore it completely.

GROWING YOUR OWN PRODUCE

Growing and eating food that is free from chemicals, such as pesiticides and fertilizers, is becoming increasingly popular. This informative guide is ideal for anyone who wishes to eat fresh, healthy, chemical-free fruit and vegetables. There are separate directories of vegetables, fruit and herbs, each explaining how to grow your produce organically. This book provides practical advice, with step-by-step photographs, on sowing, planting and harvesting, as well as choosing reliable varieties. There is also guidance on controlling pests and diseases organically and how to store your produce once it has been harvested.

ORGANIC STANDARDS

Organic standards are set out to explain the requirements that farmers, growers, processors and others must meet in order for their products or services to be marketed as organic. The standards can be extensive and cover a wide range of farming, growing and food manufacturing practices.

Are organic standards the same worldwide? No. Different countries may stipulate their own standards. IFOAM is the International Federation of Organic Agricultural Movements that represents the worldwide body of organic agriculture and provides a platform for the global exchange of information and co-operation.

Are any chemicals allowed in organic production? Yes. In line with the legal framework of the country, a very limited number of chemicals are allowed on a restricted basis. Organic standards do not allow the use of artificial herbicides or fungicides. By comparison, in non-organic farming as many as 450 chemicals can be routinely used.

If organic gardening severely restricts the use of artificial chemical fertilizers and pesticides, then how do I keep my garden healthy? Organic gardeners rely on developing a healthy fertile soil and growing a mixture of crops. By following these basic practices, organic gardeners work in harmony with nature and aim to achieve a healthy natural balance within their gardens.

Do I have to achieve any standards to become organic? No. Commercial standards are very strict and not necessarily easy to achieve for the amateur. Everyone must make choices appropriate to their own situation.

Is the organic movement just concerned with growing food? No. Going organic is not just about organic food – it should become a way of life. Today, organic wood, clothing, gardening products and even restaurants can all be found. This means that other areas of your life can be organic as well as your garden. It does not always mean completely changing your life, but it can change lives.

THE KITCHEN GARDEN

Few pleasures in life can compare with the satisfaction of harvesting and eating fresh produce from your own garden. There are many design possibilities when planning a kitchen garden. Some gardeners prefer to lay out their vegetable plot in neat rows; others choose an edible landscape that is ornamental as well as functional. There is also a seemingly endless choice of varieties in seed and nursery catalogues which can be confusing, but merely reflects the popularity of home-growing.

Left: *Kitchen gardens can provide a summer spectacle as well as a wealth of fresh, home-grown food for your table.*

Above: *Fruit such as pears and apples is one of the most welcome delights of autumn in the kitchen garden.*

Above: *Companion planting helps to keep plants healthy and also looks attractive throughout the summer.*

Above: *Kitchen-garden plants can be just as decorative as those grown for their ornamental qualities.*

PLANNING A KITCHEN GARDEN

Growing your own vegetables, herbs and fruit ensures that the food you eat is fresh, tasty and chemical-free. The healthiest food is found closest to its source, so freshly picked produce from your garden is both tastier and better for you than that which has travelled long distances by air, sea or road. Your garden will also be more appealing when it is planted with a wide selection of plants that will attract an equally diverse range of wildlife.

Above: *A well-planned kitchen garden, with companion planting, can be a feast for the eyes as well as the table.*

WHAT DO YOU WANT FROM YOUR KITCHEN GARDEN?

An ideal starting point is to make a list of all the vegetables and fruit that you eat on a regular basis, adding in a few that you are curious about and would like to try. The next stage is to look at the size of your garden and consider if there is enough room to grow everything that is on your list. Think about the quantity needed to feed your family. There is no point in planting ten apple trees for a family of four. It is a good idea to start with a few easy crops to build your confidence and progress from there.

Many edible plants, especially vegetables and herbs, are easy to grow and can be ready for harvesting in a short space of time. Children love to sow and grow less difficult crops, such as spring onions (scallions), radishes, carrots and lettuce. Growing fruit is usually a longer-term investment, as many types, such as apples, pears and blackcurrants, for example, will take several years to crop. Once they start to produce fruit, however, your investment will pay off, as they will continue to crop for many years to come and are less time-consuming than vegetables.

Furthermore, you do not need acres of space to enjoy growing your own fresh fruit and vegetables. In fact, even a small garden will support an edible crop or two. You could grow potatoes in barrels, herbs in pots and fruit trees in ornamental containers. If you live in an apartment, you can use window boxes and containers to grow fresh herbs and vegetables. Try planting hanging baskets with trailing tomatoes, herbs or fruits such as strawberries to overcome space difficulties. Edible gardening involves using any space that is conveniently available. It also promises a colourful garden and unusual ways to feed your family.

DESIGNING THE GARDEN

There are a number of points that you will need to consider in order to get the most out of your kitchen garden and to ensure that the food you produce is safe and fresh. Siting your crops next to a busy road, for instance, can mean eating produce that is polluted by cars. When siting the crops, think carefully about your own garden environment. Each garden is different and

Left: *Peas and beans can easily be trained up supports, giving height and structure to the kitchen garden.*

has specific requirements for growing various crops. Check the pH of your soil before getting underway as vegetables such as cauliflowers and cabbages will not grow well if the soil is too acidic (under pH of 6.5). As well as testing the pH level, test the soil for nutrients. The results will indicate if there is any need to improve the soil before planting.

The aspect of your garden is also critical in the siting of your plants. Fruit, for example, needs plenty of sun exposure in order to ripen properly and develop flavour. Fruit trees are also often best sited over a lawn to facilitate fruit collection.

Any design needs to consider the difference between annual and perennial crops. Annual vegetable crops, such as potatoes, carrots, cabbages and beetroot, need to be rotated within the vegetable garden to deter soil-borne pests and diseases from attacking them. Strawberries are a good example here, as they are effectively an annual, needing to be divided every year. A strawberry bed that you rotate with flowers and annual herbs (such as basil or dill) is useful for avoiding soil-borne pest problems.

Perennial crops, such as asparagus and rhubarb, may well merit their own distinct areas and are not rotated like annual crops. Raspberries and blackberries, which are both perennial, are best sited permanently on a wire trellis. Avoid putting them in a huge expanding clump that can take over your garden.

Consider, too, how difficult a particular plant (or the produce it offers) is to grow. Peaches, for example, can be challenging. They are disease-prone and require lots of care and attention. Unless you are a committed gardener with time on your hands, it may be best to purchase a few organically grown fruits from a local shop.

PLANTING THE KITCHEN GARDEN

If you have recently moved into a new home, then you will have the luxury of starting your kitchen garden from scratch. If your garden is already established, there is no need to uproot everything to grow your own produce. Gardens need not be exclusively made up of just edible or ornamental plants. You may wish to start by planting a few annual vegetables and herbs among your ornamental plants. Indeed, you can easily incorporate edible plants into the garden, even mixing fruit, vegetables and herbs in ornamental beds. This planting arrangement avoids crops grown in visually uninspiring mono-cropped rows.

If you are planting vegetables in new beds, then they can be interplanted with ornamentals and herbs. Fragrant plants such as English marigolds (*Calendula*), French marigolds (*Tagetes patula*) and oregano (*Origanum*) are excellent choices for attracting beneficial insects, and interplanting with plants such as these will help to keep pests to a minimum. Large blocks of the same vegetable are likely to attract high concentrations of pests, whereas interplanting tends to confuse and dissuade them.

If you need to remove an ornamental tree or shrub that has died or outgrown its site, consider replacing it with a fruit-bearing tree or shrub. There are many possibilities, including apples, currants, raspberries, crab apples, plums and cherries, which can all provide valuable colour and texture in the garden as well as a source of food. Apart from feeding the household, excess fruit from these trees will also provide food for a range of birds and insects.

It is worthwhile researching the eventual height of plants in the planning stages. Some will simply look out of place if they are grown in the wrong location, such as planting tall plants in front of smaller ones. Many large ones will also need some form of staking or support.

Lettuce, chives, pansies and parsley create excellent borders along the edges of raised beds. Tall plants such as dill, sunflowers, daylilies, fennel, valerian, peas and beans are best grown at the back of beds or at the centres of containers. Provide trellises and other supports where needed. Choose edible flowers such as nasturtiums and chives wherever possible because they are a natural addition to gardens and make salad bowls look and taste wonderful.

You may wish to consider an edible lawn, in which some (or even all) of the lawn is given over to a groundcover such as strawberries. Strawberries are a very attractive crop because they produce fruit for most of the summer and tolerate marginal soils and light shade. However, large patches are likely to attract pests, so they should be interplanted with strong-smelling herbs like thyme and oregano which also form good groundcover. It may be an idea to keep a permanent cover of herbs and rotate the strawberry crop on a two- or three-year cycle.

PLANTS USED AS FENCES, SCREENS AND BARRIERS

Plants can be used in a number of imaginative ways. Instead of erecting plain wooden fencing or mesh barriers why not consider planting a living one?

Above: *Ornamental alliums are good companion plants, attracting a variety of insects as well as looking impressive.*

Gooseberries, raspberries or currants are readily trained along a fence and apples can be trained as an espalier cordon or fan along a wall. Climbing plants, such as hardy kiwi fruits, trailing nasturtiums, broad beans, or sugar snap peas, can all be grown over a fence or trellis work to provide an ornate screen. Hedges can also form useful and attractive edible barriers. Shrub roses, such as *Rosa rugosa*, create an attractive, but impenetrable barrier, producing large red rose hips that contain 60 times the vitamin C of an orange. The hips can be used to make tea, jam, syrup or jelly. Currants and other fruit can also be included on the sunny side.

When designing your kitchen garden, bear in mind that the garden is for everyone in the household. Hold family discussions to involve everyone in the planning and design stage. It is worthwhile taking everyone's needs and tastes into consideration when undertaking this extremely important stage of development.

Right: *Cloches and low tunnels can increase the range of early crops that can be grown in the kitchen garden.*

CROP VARIETIES

There is a seemingly endless array of seeds available to the home gardener. Each supplier makes claims that their variety is better than all those that went before and any others currently available. Others claim to have older, more choice varieties saved from extinction and representing a time when everything was purer and more wholesome. Personal preference usually decides the best varieties for you, but an understanding of what you can expect from the seed in a packet can be very useful.

Above: *Onions come in a range of attractive colours and can be grown for their ornamental value in beds and borders.*

WHAT ARE HYBRIDS?

Often when we purchase seed, we respond more readily to the picture on the front of the packet. We may not notice whether it is marked with the terms "F1" or "hybrid". A hybrid is the result of a cross between one variety with pollen from another specific variety. The breeder chooses parent varieties that will produce first generation offspring (F1 hybrids) with known characteristics. The crossing is done in a very controlled manner so that no pollen from another variety is able to pollinate the flowers. As a result, all of the plants that are grown from the hybrid seed will be genetically identical.

Hybrids may be bred to be more widely adapted to environmental stresses such as heat, cold, disease or drought than non-hybrids. They also have more uniform characteristics, making crops more predictable in their qualities. They also have "hybrid vigour" and may grow faster or be more disease-resistant than either of the parents. They may also give better yields than open-pollinated varieties. They will not breed true, however, meaning that seed collected will not produce plants that are the same as the parent (F1 hybrids). For this reason, seed cannot be saved from F1 hybrid plants by the home gardener. Seed for hybrid varieties must be purchased year after year from the seed companies or nurseries, unless you want to gamble and grow an array of offspring.

WHAT ARE OPEN-POLLINATED VARIETIES?

Open-pollinated varieties are traditional varieties that have (in some cases) been grown and selected for desirable traits such as taste, yield or disease-resistance for many years. They often grow well in organic kitchen gardens as many were originally selected under organic conditions. These plants can mutate and adapt to the local ecosystem, as the seed is often collected and re-used by the organic gardener.

If a seed packet is labelled "heirloom", "open-pollinated" or has no special markings, then it is most likely a standard or traditional variety. The majority of lettuce, bean and pea varieties for domestic use are open-pollinated, while most cabbages, broccoli, tomatoes, cucumbers, melons and Brussels sprouts are hybrids.

Right: *Allowing a few of your crops to flower will also provide you with seed for growing next year's crop.*

Left: *Unusual crop varieties can often be grown from seed that you have collected yourself each year. This is a striking variety of kohl rabi.*

Hybrid seeds can dominate the garden seed market, but open-pollinated varieties are more or less stabilized in their characteristics, remaining fairly consistent and producing seed that will grow into plants that are more or less like the parent plants. They are a little less uniform than hybrids, but the home gardener can safely collect seed and grow plants from them that will be essentially the same as the original plants. Open-pollinated varieties either self-pollinate or are pollinated by wind or insects and they usually produce viable seed.

There have been various claims that open-pollinated varieties do not taste as good as hybrids. It is also claimed that they are smaller and not as uniform and, in many cases, this may be true. However, where matters of taste in varieties are concerned, the only real answer is to try them and see for yourself.

Right: *Old varieties of tomato tend to have varying sizes of tastier fruits that crop over a long period of time.*

WHAT ARE HEIRLOOM VARIETIES?

In the 1970s the European Community brought in regulations to encourage the breeding of new vegetable cultivars and the standardization of older ones. This resulted in a list of approved cultivars being drawn up and it became illegal to sell any cultivar that was not included on this list. It is very expensive to have a single cultivar tested in order to then register it on the list. This meant that many old cultivars were put in grave danger of being lost forever, as the funds to test each variety were not available. It was due to this legislation that HDRA, the Organic Organisation, in England, a society which was established to promote organic issues, founded the Heritage Seed Library (HSL). This seed library ensures that old or "heirloom varieties" are kept safe for posterity by distributing its seed. Although HDRA grow some of the seeds themselves, they also employ contract growers and seed guardians to make up the bulk of the seeds that are supplied.

Each year a catalogue is sent to HSL members from which they can select up to six varieties free of charge. This distribution set-up overcomes the clause of selling only approved cultivars. This service is also available to members in the United States.

The best heirloom cultivars can be traced back fifty years or longer. Many of these early varieties have been lost already, making those that remain all the more precious. A number of these cultivars have been collected and saved by families and ethnic groups dating back many years. This practice protected the genetic make-up that made each variety successful within a given environment. These base characteristics have become invaluable and the genetic strains of these vegetables are the backbone of modern disease- and drought-resistant hybrids. It is this that makes the collection and preservation of these cultivars so important.

Left: *Many heirloom varieties have been selected for the way they perform in local garden conditions, rather than for crop size or uniformity.*

CROP ROTATION

This is the practice of grouping and growing related plants together and rotating them around different areas of land in a regimented fashion from year to year. Rotating your crops in this way has many advantages, including helping to prevent pest and disease problems from arising in the first place. This method of gardening is fundamental to successful organic growing. It has been practised for thousands of years and developed into a system that is easy to follow.

Above: *The secret to achieving a thriving and healthy kitchen garden is to rotate the crops on a regular basis.*

WHY ARE CROPS ROTATED?

Continuous cropping in the same area puts both plants and soil at risk. It not only allows large numbers of soil-borne pests and diseases to build up, but, because crops require the same nutrients from the soil year after year, the practice can deplete nutrient levels. A poor infertile soil produces weak unhealthy plants, which, in turn, will be more prone to pest and disease attacks. All these problems amount to reduced yields and even complete crop failure.

When crops are rotated, the groups are divided up into closely related plants that are prone to similar pests and diseases. For example, carrots, parsnips, beetroot and potatoes are members of one group and prone to carrot fly, whereas cabbage, kale, broccoli and Brussels sprouts, which are members of another group, can be prone to clubroot and cabbage root fly. If the groups are grown in different areas on a rotational basis, it can help to prevent the establishment of soil-borne pests and diseases.

Combined with regular additions of compost and manure, crop rotation will make the soil richer, replace certain nutrients and help prevent pH imbalances that can result from repeated crops of the same type of vegetable. Companion planting will also aid a rotational plan, particularly if the species improve pest control.

MAKING A ROTATIONAL PLAN

The basic rules of crop rotation are simple. If you are planning a four-year crop rotation, the plants you have selected are split up into five groups. Group one contains the legumes (peas and beans); group two contains the brassicas (cabbages, Brussels sprouts, broccoli, kale etc); group three contains the onion family and others (onions, lettuce, garlic, sweetcorn etc); group four includes root crops (potatoes, parsnips,

BENEFITS OF CROP ROTATION

There are many benefits to be gained from rotating your crops regularly.

- Prevents the build-up of soil pests and diseases
- Helps to prevent nutrient depletion from heavy-feeding crops
- Rotated crops produce higher yields
- Results in a healthier soil

carrots, beetroot etc); and finally group five houses permanent crops such as asparagus and rhubarb.

The vegetable plot is then divided into five sections. The permanent crops are given a specific area and are not moved or included in the rotational cycle. The remaining four groups are allocated an area in which to grow. Every year each group is moved on to the next plot, making it four years before the crops are grown on the same area of land again; hence the name crop rotation.

If space is limited, crops can be grown on a three-year rotation. Quite simply, the crops are split into three groups, plus the permanent ones. The plant groups are divided up as before except group three is incorporated into group one.

There is no need to grow each crop in every year of a cycle. Remember that it is the vegetable groups that dictate the cropping cycle according to their soil needs and any associated problems. Rotating the crops helps provide the correct soil requirements for certain crops. For example, cabbages and the rest of the group grow well in soil that has been manured the previous autumn, whereas carrots and other root crops (not including potatoes) do not. Where carrots are to be grown, then the plot will need to be dug deeply in readiness for them.

It is important that you plan where the crops are to be every year, so that you know their position for the following year. A comprehensive cropping plan can help you to maximize the yield on a year-round basis by working out successional sowings and intercropping and catch cropping. The plan needs to include not only the crops that will be grown but also the companion plants and the soil amendments that are needed to support the best possible growth of your plants.

COMMON DIFFICULTIES

When planning the cycle, you may encounter certain problems. Careful planning will show that potatoes often take up more space in a vegetable bed than any other crop and finding enough room to grow them in their allocated area may prove difficult. Other problems you may come across include overwintering brassicas or plants left in the ground for seed collection. This is when you find that practising crop rotation in a small garden is difficult and that you may not be able to practise a strict rotation.

If space is proving a problem, consider some of the following strategies. Keep brassicas together as a group and never plant them in the same ground two years running. Keep potatoes together every year; if you have planned a lot of potatoes, move all the other members from group four into group three. Also bear in mind that some root crops, such as potatoes, are manure-friendly, while others, like parsnips, are not. Finally, alternating shallow-rooted plants like cabbages or lettuce with deep-rooted plants like tomatoes or squash will allow the plants' roots to do much of the soil loosening that would otherwise have to be done by hand. This will help to preserve the health of the soil, while causing minimal disturbance to its ecosystem.

FOUR-YEAR CROP ROTATION

Divide the vegetables you have decided to grow into the five groups (plots 1–5) shown in the table. Draw a plan to indicate which group of crops goes where, using a different colour for each group. (Remember plot 5 is for the permanent crops.) Next year, move the crops in each group on to the next plot.

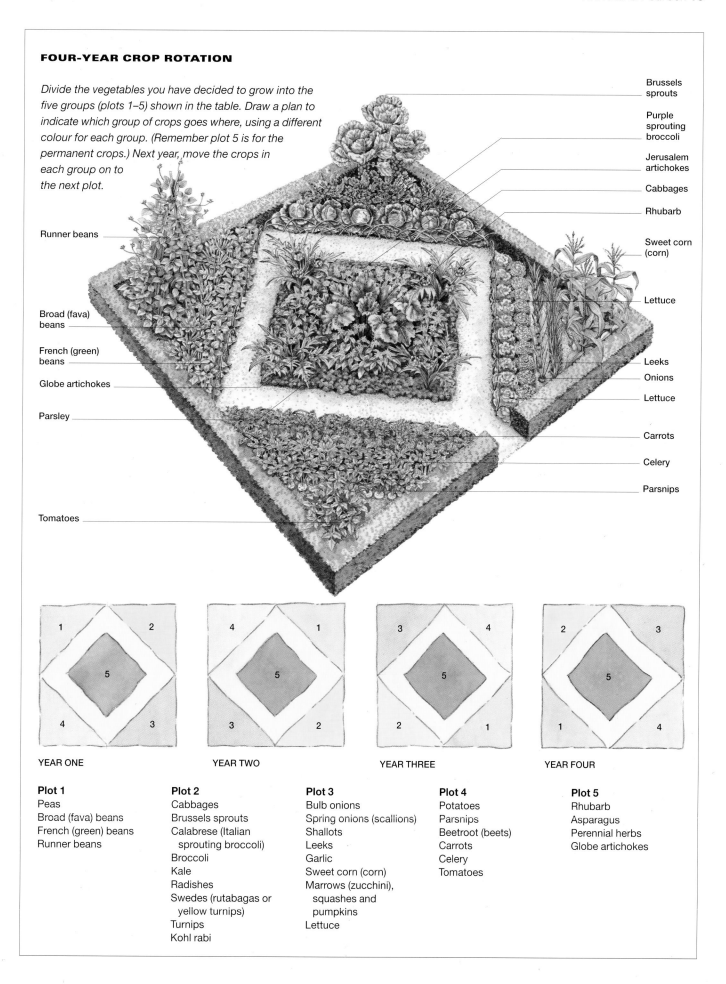

Runner beans

Broad (fava) beans

French (green) beans

Globe artichokes

Parsley

Tomatoes

Brussels sprouts

Purple sprouting broccoli

Jerusalem artichokes

Cabbages

Rhubarb

Sweet corn (corn)

Lettuce

Leeks

Onions

Lettuce

Carrots

Celery

Parsnips

YEAR ONE

YEAR TWO

YEAR THREE

YEAR FOUR

Plot 1
Peas
Broad (fava) beans
French (green) beans
Runner beans

Plot 2
Cabbages
Brussels sprouts
Calabrese (Italian
   sprouting broccoli)
Broccoli
Kale
Radishes
Swedes (rutabagas or
   yellow turnips)
Turnips
Kohl rabi

Plot 3
Bulb onions
Spring onions (scallions)
Shallots
Leeks
Garlic
Sweet corn (corn)
Marrows (zucchini),
   squashes and
   pumpkins
Lettuce

Plot 4
Potatoes
Parsnips
Beetroot (beets)
Carrots
Celery
Tomatoes

Plot 5
Rhubarb
Asparagus
Perennial herbs
Globe artichokes

GROWING METHODS

There are many different ways to grow your crops. You can try the traditionally practised method of sowing crops in rows or be more adventurous and grow them in blocks. The crops you have chosen to grow can be planted into a number of different types of vegetable bed: flat beds, raised or edged beds and no-dig beds. Each method and type of bed has its own advantages and disadvantages, which are described here, so choose the one that best suits your needs.

Above: *Twiggy sticks provide an ideal support for young climbers such as peas. They also look very decorative.*

PLANTING IN ROWS

This is the most traditionally practised and popular form of vegetable growing. It is an effective method because the spacing of the plants allows the crop to grow without excessive competition. In addition, it is relatively easy to add supports and protection such as cloches to the crops. However, this type of planting does have the disadvantage of needing relatively high maintenance. Due to the large amounts of bare earth left between the rows, the conditions are ideal for weed growth. Rows are spaced according to the optimum growth of the plants and so rows of pumpkins need to be much wider than those for carrots. Setting out rows in this way allows free movement of air along the rows. This results in fewer disease problems which can occur with more closely grown methods such as block plantings.

The rows are quite easily maintained by regular hoeing but can be wasteful of space, particularly in smaller gardens. They will produce sizeable vegetables, but this is offset by the actual yield per unit area being smaller than more intensive systems.

BLOCK PLANTING

In this method plants are grown in squares or rectangles rather than in straight rows. Blocks of plants are grown next to each other, for example in dimensions such as five plants by five plants. The numbers of plants grown can be larger or smaller than this. Block plantings use space efficiently, producing many more plants in an area than if grown in rows.

Well-tended soil can support planting that forms a close network of foliage over the soil. The soil will retain moisture extremely well underneath the canopy. It also stops weed seeds from germinating, resulting in a less weedy environment than other growing methods. However, a close canopy of leaves can have disavantages, resulting in poor air flow and high humidity which are ideal for attracting diseases such as botrytis. During dry spells watering is essential for the health of the crops. Double check all watering that has been done because water easily runs off the dense cover of the leaves and never reaches much of the root system.

Blocks can be planted and managed at ground level or in slightly raised beds. They suit modestly sized vegetables, such as root and salad crops, that are usually grown in rows. You may have to be inventive with crop protection for early-sown crops, as cloches and low polythene tunnels do not cover the area well. The blocks are edged with permanent paths for easy access to the centre from any side so you need never walk on freshly cultivated soil. As a result, the soil does not get compacted and the closely grouped plants make maintenance and cultivation easier.

Seeding a block involves sowing the furrows thinly along close rows. For example, instead of the usual 30–40cm (12–16in) distance between carrot rows, this can be reduced to 20–25cm (8–10in). Further space savings can result from growing as much as you can vertically, rather than sprawled over the ground. Wire fencing, netting or poles and tepees take up less space than blocks of climbing vegetables. This will also keep the climbing plants dry and free of disease.

FLAT BEDS

As the name suggests, flat beds are constructed at the natural ground level of your garden. They are the traditional way of cultivating ground for growing vegetables and are most suitable for gardens that have good soil. Flat beds will naturally raise the level of the soil, especially where organic matter is added on a regular basis as part of the cultivation regime, but the bed remains effectively at ground level. This form of gardening is relatively labour-intensive because all of the bed is cultivated, with large areas then being used as paths between the vegetables. With raised beds, there are no paths and only the growing areas are dug.

Left: *The close planting of crops in rows or blocks helps to retain soil moisture as well as reduce the growth of weeds.*

Above: *Plants such as beans can be trained over an arch in order to provide an ornamental and productive feature.*

RAISED AND EDGED BEDS

These can be freestanding garden beds or beds with wooden or brick walls constructed several inches above the normal ground level. Raised bed gardens not only look good but they also can help solve many problems associated with soils that are difficult to manage. Problems with soil are often aggravated in urban and suburban settings, where topsoil and vegetation may have been removed or the surface level changed during building work.

Raised bed gardens improve the environment for plants by lifting their roots above poor soil. The growing medium can be amended by the incorporation of manure and/or garden compost. Soil in these beds warms up earlier in the spring, allowing the seed sown to germinate quicker than if it is grown in flat beds. Beds should be located where they will receive full sun and with protection from prevailing winds. Do not site the beds in frost pockets or where air circulation is poor.

Drainage is important. Build the beds so that the crops will not become waterlogged, as good drainage is especially important when growing vegetables. If the bed contains clay soil, incorporate sand, grit or organic matter to improve drainage. Construct the bed so that it slopes about 2cm (¾in) per metre (yard) of horizontal distance away from any structures, or away from the centre of the bed.

NO-DIG BEDS

As the term suggests, no digging is involved in this method, which is a good way to retain good soil structure within a vegetable garden. Weeding is kept to a minimum and because the soil is not disturbed it will be alive with worms and other organisms. The bed is made on top of the ground and can be built over existing beds, lawns and even hard or rocky ground. Situate the bed in a sunny area that receives morning sun and has good drainage. It can be any size or shape, depending on your space. Start with a small bed – about 2 x 1.5m (6½ x 5ft) – but with a view to expanding in time.

When preparing the site it is not necessary to pull up the lawn or existing garden if the soil conditions are good, but if the ground is very poor, compacted or the drainage is bad, initial digging may be necessary.

Above: *Containers are an ideal way to grow a variety of crops where space is limited. These pots contain courgettes (zucchini).*

The outside wall of a no-dig bed is formed using logs, old planks, tiles, bricks or stones. Line the bed with a layer of plain wet newspaper, at least 6mm (¼in) thick. This layer should cover the enclosed area completely and overlap slightly, so as to kill off any weeds and stop new ones growing. Spread out a thin layer of hay or straw, ensuring that there are no gaps. Place a layer of good organic fertilizer, such as chicken manure, 20mm (¾in) thick, on top. Cover with a 20cm (8in) thick layer of loose bedding straw. Follow this with a 2cm (¾in) layer of good organic fertilizer and complete the bed with a top layer of garden compost, about 10cm (4in) thick. Make sure the bed is watered in well. Once it is settled you can plant out seedlings, but not seeds. Sowing seeds can begin when the bed has matured and the soil has become fine and crumbly.

No-dig beds that have been recently created are best for growing crops such as potatoes, lettuce, brassicas and cucurbits, whereas root crops grow better when the bed is mature. No-dig beds are best suited to planting vegetables in small blocks of different varieties rather than in long rows.

Left: *Vegetable beds need not be rectangular to be functional. This kitchen garden uses simple geometric shapes to provide interesting effects.*

COMPANION PLANTING

This is when two or more crops are grown together for the benefit of one or all. This technique creates a colourful landscape, made up of different species, which mirrors nature itself. Plants are grown together for several reasons, including to attract beneficial insects or to give off odours that deter or confuse pests. This is so different from large fields planted with only one crop, a monoculture that allows large numbers of pests and diseases to build up rapidly.

Above: *Nasturtiums have edible leaves and flowers as well as being a colourful companion plant.*

HOW COMPANION PLANTING WORKS

Plants have natural affinities with others of their kind. The smell of volatile oils from many plants discourages certain pests, making them excellent companion plants. A good example of this is the well-known relationship between the tomato plant and the French marigold (*Tagetes patula*). The scent of the French marigold is said to deter whitefly from entering the greenhouse and therefore avoids a whitefly attack on the tomato plant.

Plants such as yarrow (*Achillea*) and hyssop (*Hyssopus*) are just a couple of plants from a list of many that attract beneficial insects like hoverflies. The hoverflies will lay their eggs around these plants and, after hatching, the larval stage of the insect will start to eat adult aphids. So greedy are these larvae that they can eat up to 800 aphids before pupating. Many organic gardeners grow trays of single-flowered French marigolds to dot around their gardens, both in the vegetable and

Right: *Companion plants can provide welcome splashes of colour in the kitchen garden.*

BENEFITS OF COMPANION PLANTING

A mosaic of plants offers many benefits to the organic garden, some of which are outlined below.

- Creates a colourful landscape.
- Plants can attract benefical insects.
- Plant odour can deter harmful insects.
- A variety of plants together confuses pests from locating host plants.
- Plants attract birds that prey on pests.
- Flowers attract pollinators.

---

ornamental areas, in order to encourage these eating machines. This is both very effective and quite stunning to look at.

Certain distinct qualities of a plant have a proven benefit to others, such as fixing nitrogen in the soil. Clover in grass will fix nitrogen, offering the excess nitrogen produced to the surrounding grass which improves the yield. By the same token,

others are less suited as partners. It is never wise, for example, to plant two vegetables side by side that attract the same pests, as this effectively doubles the chances of attack. It is advisable to practise crop rotation or use companion planting in between them.

BENEFICIAL COMBINATIONS

There is little scientific evidence of these associations working, but if you talk to any organic practitioner, they will certainly provide plenty of anecdotal evidence. Tomatoes, for instance, like to be grown near basil and parsley plants. This is, of course, useful for cooks as well as gardeners. Separating rows of cabbages, broccoli or other brassicas with rows of onions has always been a popular combination, possibly due to the onion's strong scent confusing cabbage pests. Tomato plants also grow well next to cabbages and seem to deter caterpillars. Other beneficial combinations include leeks near carrots as they repel carrot flies, while Swiss chard thrives near carrots and beetroot. Never plant carrot and dill close by each other. This makes the carrots woodier and stronger-flavoured, and the dill milder and with weaker stems.

DECORATIVE COMPANION PLANTS

Certain flowers and flowering herbs offer potential benefits for a variety of vegetables. French marigolds (*Tagetes patula*) are cited as a wonder flower by many organic gardeners and the bright flowers make a colourful companion crop. They deter many pests, and seem to spur growth in roses. They are also said to reduce the number of soil nematodes, while attracting hoverflies and their larvae which eat aphids. French marigolds are frequently planted with pot marigolds (*Calendula officinalis*).

CROPS AND THEIR COMPANION PLANTS

While it is not an exact science, any practitioner of companion planting will tell you that individual crops have their "preferred companions".

Experience is the best guide, but the list below outlines some plant combinations that work well in most situations.

Apples Chives, foxgloves, wallflowers, nasturtiums, garlic, onions

Apricots Basil, tansy, wormwood

Asparagus Tomatoes, parsley, basil

Beans Carrots, cucumbers, cabbages, lettuce, peas, parsley, cauliflower, spinach, summer savory

Beans (broad/fava) Potatoes, sweetcorn (corn).

Beans (dwarf) Beetroot, potatoes

Beetroot Onions, kohl rabi, lettuce, cabbage, dwarf beans

Brussels sprouts Nasturtiums

Cabbages Beans, beetroot, celery, mint, thyme, sage, onions, rosemary, dill, potatoes, chamomile, oregano, hyssop, wormwood, nasturtiums, tansy, coriander (cilantro)

Carrots Peas, radishes, lettuce, chives, sage, onions, leeks

Cauliflowers Celery, beans, tansy, nasturtium

Celery Tomatoes, dill, beans, leeks, cabbage, cauliflowers

Chives Parsley, apples, carrots, tomatoes

Courgette (zucchini) Nasturtiums

Cucumbers Potatoes (early crop only), beans, celery, lettuce, sweetcorn, Savoy cabbages, sunflowers, nasturtiums

Kohl rabi Beetroot, onions

Garlic Roses, apples, peaches

Grapevines Geraniums, mulberries, hyssop, basil, tansy

Leeks Carrots, celery

Lettuce Carrots, onions, strawberries, beetroot, cabbages, radishes, tagetes

Onions Carrots, beetroot, lettuce, chamomile, kohl rabi, courgettes

Parsnips Peas, potatoes, peppers, beans, radishes, garlic

Peaches Tansy, garlic, basil, wormwood

Peas Potatoes, radishes, carrots, turnips

Potatoes Peas, beans, cabbage, sweetcorn, broad beans, green beans, nasturtium, marigolds, foxgloves, horseradish, aubergine (eggplant)

Pumpkin Sweetcorn

Radishes Lettuces, peas, chervil, nasturtium

Raspberries Tansy

Spinach Strawberries

Squash Sunflowers

Strawberries Borage, lettuce, spinach, sage, pyrethrum

Sunflowers Squash, cucumber

Sweetcorn (corn) Broad beans, potatoes, melons, tomatoes, cucumber, squash, tansy

Tomatoes Asparagus, celery, parsley, basil, carrots, chives, marigolds, foxgloves, garlic, sweetcorn

Turnips Peas, nasturtiums

White alyssum (*Lobularia maritima*), by reseeding frequently, helps to break up the soil and adds to its organic content, while chrysanthemums reduce nematodes, making for healthier soil. Mint almost always works with various types of squashes and brassicas to aid plant growth, although it can become invasive. Tansy (*Tanacetum*

Left: *Foxgloves (*Digitalis*) make excellent companion plants for growing under apple trees.*

vulgare) is said to repel ants, aphids and plant beetles although this, too, can become invasive if not regularly checked.

Chamomile (*Chamaemelum nobile*) is known as the "plant doctor" by some organic gardeners because of its alleged ability to encourage other plants to increase their production of essential oil, making plants such as rosemary and lavender taste and smell stronger. Chamomile is easy to grow and looks beautiful anywhere, although it should be kept well trimmed to avoid a straggly look. It is also thought that chamomile can help to activate the composting process if it is added to the compost heap.

Lavender (*Lavandula*) is a general insect repellent and makes an excellent small hedge. It is a great addition to the garden, attracting bees and numerous white and blue butterflies.

Plants that produce berries such as cotoneaster and the rowan tree (*Sorbus*) will attract birds into the garden. Birds, in turn, eat many pests, such as protein-rich

aphids, caterpillars and various flies. Thrushes are the unsung heroes of the garden because they decrease the snail population quite considerably.

Be prepared to experiment before committing to a companion species. Nasturtiums have been cited as an effective aphid control, although many wonder if they do this by attracting all the aphids to themselves. What works in one area may not always work elsewhere and experimentation is the key to success in this interesting yet uncertain area of organic gardening.

CROPS AND THEIR ANTAGONISTS

Some plants are highly antagonistic to one another. You should always avoid planting the following combinations.

Asparagus Onions and potatoes

Beans Chives, fennel or garlic

Carrots Dill

Carrots, cauliflower or potatoes Tomatoes

Peas Onions, garlic and shallots

Potatoes Pumpkins, summer squashes

MAKING THE MOST OF YOUR SPACE

There are three basic growing techniques that you can use to make the most of your space. These are known as intercropping, catch cropping and successional sowing. By adopting the latter two practices, you will extend the cropping season instead of harvesting a crop all at once. You will also make use of the available space, therefore increasing yields. All that is needed is careful planning to work out which crops to sow and when.

Above: *Close planting in blocks makes the most of available space and allows more crops to be raised in a season.*

INTERCROPPING

This kitchen-garden technique increases productivity and also helps to keep the numbers of weeds down. It refers to the practice of planting a fast-growing crop, such as carrots, radishes and lettuce, between main crops that are slower growing. These include vegetables such as cabbages, peas and potatoes.

Intercropping involves harvesting the quicker-growing crop first before the slower-growing one achieves total foliage cover of the soil or shades out the area. A good example of intercropping is to grow a crop of spring onions or lettuce between tomatoes. Similarly, spinach or radishes can easily be planted out early between sweetcorn or, alternatively, radishes can be planted between cabbages.

Intercropping can also be used to increase productivity. It ensures that no space is left unused and makes the most efficient use of light, nutrients and moisture. It will also reduce the amount of weeds in the vegetable patch by maintaining a continuous plant canopy over the soil.

One slight variation on the theme is to combine the benefits of a green manure with a crop. This can be useful in the case of winter crops because the green manure doubles up as a cover crop, protecting the soil from erosion and leaching as well as stabilizing soil temperatures. If a leguminous green manure is planted in late summer or early autumn in a bed along with leafy crops such as Brussels sprouts, it can provide nitrogen throughout the remaining growing season. It will also provide a boost for early

crops that will be planted out after the green manure crop has been dug into the soil. While intercropping requires careful planning, it can increase the productivity of even a relatively small vegetable plot.

CATCH CROPPING

This technique is when fast-maturing vegetables, such as radishes and lettuce, are grown in an area of ground that has just been cropped and has a vacancy until the next crop is either sown or planted. The sowing of the catch crops can be done in between the main ones or after harvesting at the end of the season if there is time. It is important to know how long a crop takes to mature when planning catch cropping so that you do not sow anything that takes too long to mature in between the main crops.

Left: *Successional sowing in rows allows the same space in the vegetable plot to be kept productive throughout the growing season.*

FAST-GROWING CROPS SUITABLE FOR INTERCROPPING AND CATCH CROPPING

Use all the available space by sowing vigorous growing crops in between rows of the main crops. The list below shows the time it takes some fast-growing crops to mature.

Carrots	9 to 20 weeks
Endives	7 to 13 weeks
Lettuce	4 to 14 weeks
Radishes	4 to 8 weeks
Rocket (arugula)	3 to 5 weeks
Salad leaves	4 to 14 weeks
Spinach	5 to 10 weeks
Spring onions	8 to 10 weeks

SUCCESSIONAL SOWING

This is the practice of sowing the seeds of fast-maturing vegetables at regular intervals several times during the growing season. This practice will ensure that you have a continuous supply of crops such as lettuces, carrots and spinach throughout the season. Successional sowing is also useful where crops are sown directly outdoors early in the season where they may be prone to frost damage. Early crops

Above: *The close spacing of rows and successional sowing of new rows allows the maximum use of space on your plot.*

such as lettuce and radish can be sown under the cover of, for example, a cloche where they will begin to develop earlier than would otherwise be possible. Subsequent sowings outdoors will mature later, thus extending the growing season for harvesting.

Gardeners with small plots can use this method by sowing only a half a row at any one time. This process is then repeated a week or so later, with further sowings as often as you like. This way you will have fresh vegetables for several weeks and will avoid a sudden glut.

CROPS SUITABLE FOR SUCCESSIONAL SOWING

The technique of successional sowing can ensure a continuous supply of fresh vegetables. It also increases the productivity of the garden and avoids harvest gluts.

Beetroot	Spring to summer
Broccoli	Spring to summer
Cabbages	Spring to summer
Carrots	Spring to summer
Endives	Spring to summer
Kohl rabi	Winter to summer
Lettuce	Winter to summer
Parsnips	Winter to spring
Peas	All year round
Potatoes	Spring
Radishes	Winter to summer
Salad leaves	Spring to autumn
Rocket (arugula)	Spring to autumn
Spinach	Spring to summer
Spring onions (scallions)	Spring to autumn
Swedes	Spring to summer
Swiss chard	Spring to summer
Turnips	Winter to spring

Above: *Sweetcorn (corn) is a late-maturing crop that can be intercropped with fast-growing, early salad crops. This enables you to make the most of your growing space.*

SOWING IN THE OPEN

There can be nothing more satisfying than sowing seeds and watching in anticipation for them to germinate. Watching the seedlings grow in your kitchen garden, making it come alive with leaves, flowers and insects is a fantastic experience. One of the drawbacks of sowing out in the open is that you are at the mercy of the weather, but you can manipulate your garden environment by using cloches, small plastic bottles and polythene tunnels to increase your chances of success.

Above: *A dibber (dibble) is a very helpful tool to use when you are planting crops such as garlic or seedlings outside.*

SITE REQUIREMENTS

If you are a novice kitchen gardener, be assured that sowing seed is easier than you may think. In order to germinate successfully seeds need water, air, a suitable temperature and a place into which they can root in order to support the top growth that will follow. For this reason, good soil preparation is everything to organic success. Most garden soils are able to supply all the necessary elements and only slight modifications are usually necessary. However, it is important that the ground is prepared in a way that will enable the seed to germinate evenly and grow in a uniform environment. The prior preparation of a seedbed can provide the seed with the environment that it needs and has the added bonus of making the task of seed sowing easier.

Preparing a seedbed is simple. Following cultivation, the ground is levelled using a rake, held at a shallow angle, to break down any large clods. The art of levelling is to keep the rake angle shallow and move the high spots over into the low spots with even strokes. Hold the rake firmly at the rear and let the shaft run smoothly through the front hand. All stones and large objects, including organic matter such as twigs or previous crop debris, should be removed by combing them out with the teeth of the rake, while holding the tool in a near vertical position. The soil is then firmed with light treading. A light shuffle across the bed is best. Once firmed, lightly rake the soil again at a shallow angle to produce a light "fluffy" surface that runs freely through the teeth of the rake. This is the perfect environment for sowing and growing seeds.

SEED REQUIREMENTS

The conditions that seeds require to germinate are easy and straightforward to create. A well-aerated moist soil environment is almost all that the seed needs. Most seeds will germinate quite successfully once the temperature gets above 7°C (45°F). Seeds carry their own food supply that provides them with everything they need for those first crucial days following germination. Once the plant begins to establish and grow, it needs soil-borne nutrients. This means that the soil in which it is growing needs to be of the right fertility for the plant. Poorer soils can benefit from the addition of a base dressing with fish, blood and bone prior to sowing to give the boost that the developing plant needs, although loamier soils need only be properly dug and prepared to support germination.

SOWING SEEDS OUTDOORS

1 *Set a tight string line where you intend your crop row to be and make a shallow drill with the edge of a swan-necked hoe.*

2 *Water dry soil using a watering can fitted with a fine rose about an hour before sowing and allow to drain.*

3 *Sow the seed thinly along the length of the row. Larger seed may be station sown at regular intervals.*

Some seeds can benefit from being soaked for a short period in tepid water just before planting to help them take on the water they need for germination. This is especially true of beets, but other large seeds also benefit from this treatment.

SOWING IN ROWS

Seed is usually sown in rows. Using a tightly drawn garden line as a guide, draw the corner of a swan-necked hoe along the line to create a shallow drill of about 1–2cm (⅜–¾in) depth, depending upon the seed's individual requirements. Dry ground can be watered after the drill is made. Sow the seed thinly and mix fine seed with silver sand to make it easier to distribute evenly. Mark the end of each row with a label before moving on to the next.

STATION SOWING

Seeds of larger growing plants, particularly those with seed that is large enough to handle, benefit from station sowing. This involves sowing two or three seeds at intervals that will be the eventual crop spacing. If all three germinate, then the two weaker ones are removed or transplanted to gaps where none has germinated.

WIDE ROWS

Certain seeds, particularly peas and beans, benefit from being planted in wide rows. Two rows are effectively station sown at

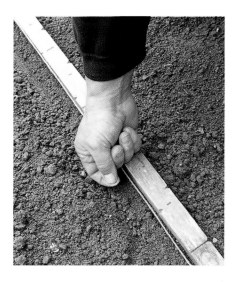

once, one on each side of a drill that is 15cm (6in) across. The drill is made with the flat of the hoe and after sowing the soil is carefully raked back. Make sure that you do not disturb the seeds from their stations.

BROADCASTING (BLOCKS)

Broadcasting is an ancient method of seed sowing that was used to sow large areas of crops. It involves a "broadcasting" action that separates the seed to an even spacing. The easiest way to do this in small vegetable plots is to split the seed into two halves, mixing small seed with fine sand. Scatter the seed carefully, letting it run from your hand in even arcs as you move your arm from side to side. Sow each half of the

Left: Station sowing is ideal for larger seeds or seedlings that resent disturbance. Use a marked stick to set the spacing of the seed.

seed at a 90-degree angle to the other, thereby assuring an even distribution. Gently rake the seed in once sown and lightly water if needed.

PROTECTING SEEDLINGS

Seedbeds, with their fine "fluffed" earth, act as magnets to birds and animals. Some may take the seed from the ground, but, in truth, most will find it more attractive as a dust bath or litter tray. Once the seedlings emerge, however, some birds find them irresistible. They must be kept out with some form of barrier. One of the easiest methods is to form a low tunnel of chicken wire, supporting this on hoops. For larger areas, a series of stakes in the ground can be covered with netting to keep birds at bay. Sticks with thread or string stretched between them are also effective, but less easily removed for you to tend the crop.

LABELLING

When you sow a row or area of seeds, label it straightaway. Re-usable plastic labels are the best option. Each label should have the name and variety of the plant sown. You may also wish to record the sowing date and if the seed was pre-treated.

4 *Place a label at the end of each row, showing the crop name, variety and the sowing date, before you start a new one.*

5 *Gently cover the seed using a rake. Take care not to disturb or move the seed in the row when you cover it.*

6 *Alternatively, seed can be covered using a soil and potting mix. This is useful on heavy soils and avoids capping (surface hardening).*

SOWING UNDER GLASS

Sowing seed under glass extends the growing season and enables you to raise tender crops that only survive outside in warmer months. It is also ideal for rapidly establishing plants to use as catch crops and as early companion plants. In short, it offers variety and choice for your cropping regimes. Plants raised under glass can be grown on until they reach a size where they are better able to resist pest attack. They can also be planted out at their final spacing, thereby avoiding thinning or gaps in rows.

Above: *A propagator is a useful piece of equipment for raising your seed in ideal growing conditions.*

HEAT REQUIREMENTS

Most seeds have a preferred temperature range within which they will grow. A heated greenhouse, a conservatory or even a warm living room will often provide this, although seeds needing a constant high temperature may need a propagator. Such seeds are mercifully rare among vegetables, although cucumbers, tomatoes and peppers are good examples of crops that will benefit if they are first started off in a propagator.

CHOICE OF CONTAINER

There are a variety of containers that may be used to sow seed under glass. The most common form is the plastic seed tray which has now largely replaced the wooden seed tray. Although more attractive, wooden trays are difficult to keep clean and may harbour plant diseases. Plastic trays can be made of durable polyurethane or sometimes a more flimsy, thin, moulded plastic which is intended for single use. They are available in a variety of sizes, although small 9cm (3½in) pots may be more suitable when you are raising only a few plants.

Modular seed trays are another option. These are made up of individual cells, and a single seed is sown into each one. Seeds that are sown in these trays have the advantage of not suffering any root disturbance when they are planted out in their eventual position. The same is true of some biodegradable pots, which are formed out of paper and coir. These are better (environmentally speaking) than those made from peat, but any recycled material used for these trays is acceptable in the organic kitchen garden.

Inventive recycling can also provide an array of useful sowing containers. Re-using plastic cups, vegetable packing trays and

any other throw-away items that might otherwise end up on a landfill site are all possibilities worth exploring. Old plastic bottles make good individual propagation cowls for small pots and plastic bags can also be used to cover the tops of pots and trays in order to maintain humidity.

PROPAGATORS

These are, in effect, mini-hothouses that help to keep the seed in a warm, moist, stable environment both above and below the soil line. Expensive propagators involve the use of electric soil-warming cables and some have thermostats to control the soil temperature. Many are designed for use in the greenhouse, but

Above: *Modular trays are ideal for planting large seeds and avoid disturbance to roots when planting out or potting on.*

Left: *Many propagators have ventilators on the top in order to aid the flow of fresh air to the seedlings.*

some models are narrow enough for use on a windowsill inside the house. Alternatively, instead of buying the whole propagator, you can purchase a heating mat on which the seed trays can stand in order to receive heat at the bottom. This system has the advantage of being mobile and easily moved about from area to area. Another cheaper method is to buy soil-heating cables to bed into sand. The seed trays sit on the bed of heated sand to receive an even supply of bottom heat.

AFTERCARE OF SEEDLINGS

Once seeds begin to germinate, they can be moved gradually into a less humid environment. The trays are freed of plastic covers, or the propagator vents or lids are opened and, after a few days, the lid is removed completely. As soon as the seedlings reach a size at which they can be handled, they are carefully pricked out into individual pots or larger boxes and trays. Always handle the seedlings by the leaves,

Above: *Individual pots can be used for large seeds. Plant two seeds per pot and remove the weaker seedling.*

SOWING IN TRAYS

1 *Fill a seed tray with propagation potting mix that has been thoroughly mixed. Fill the tray to overflowing and do not firm in the potting mix.*

2 *Using a straightedged piece of board, level the surface of the potting mix by carefully moving the board across the top of the tray.*

3 *Water the tray and leave to drain for about 20 minutes before sowing the seed on the moist surface of the potting mix.*

4 *Larger seed can be placed on the surface of the potting mix at regular intervals. Regular spacing will prevent overcrowding.*

5 *Once the seed has been sown, use a sieve to cover the surface with a fine layer of potting mix.*

6 *Do not cover the seeds of plants that require light for germination. Always check the growing requirements of plants before sowing the seed.*

---

gently lifting each one from beneath, using a dibber (dibble). Never hold them by the stems because this can cause a great deal of damage to the developing plant. They should be spaced at least 5cm (2in) apart to allow for subsequent development. Water

Above: *Growing vegetables in pots under glass can extend the growing season and also provide a colourful greenhouse display.*

the transplanted seedlings with a fine upturned rose attached to a watering can that has been filled with water overnight, thus bringing it up to room temperature and not giving the transplants a shock of cold water. Keep the seedlings on a warm and sheltered windowsill or in a greenhouse or conservatory. A constant temperature will promote healthy growth.

HARDENING OFF

Plants that have been grown in a greenhouse cannot be put straight outside because their growth is too soft to withstand the cold. They must be gradually hardened off and acclimatized to outdoor conditions. The young plants are hardened off by moving them from the greenhouse and into a cold frame, planted out under cloches, low polythene tunnels or horticultural fleece. Open up the cloches and cold frames or remove the fleece

during the day and replace at night for a week or two before planting out or removing the cloches completely. Remove low polythene tunnels after a couple of weeks depending on the weather conditions. If these are severe, leave in place for longer.

Above: *Watering from below by pouring the water into the base of the seed tray will prevent damage to newly emerging seed.*

THINNING AND TRANSPLANTING

Thinning seedlings not only allows the plants left in the soil to develop and mature into their natural shape and habit, but it is an essential process for good plant health. Thinned seedlings can be transplanted into bare areas or more often special seedbeds are set up or crops are grown under glass and the whole batch of seedlings are transplanted into their final destination within the vegetable garden.

Above: *Growing plants from seed is one of the most satisfying ways of producing new stock for the kitchen garden.*

WHY THIN SEEDLINGS?

All plants need space to develop and grow. Plants that are growing too closely compete not only for space, but also for light, water and important nutrients. In addition to this competitive stress, they also become prone to a variety of fungal diseases, as the air is not able to move around them. Thinning the seedlings helps to counteract these problems and will result in larger, stronger and healthier plants.

HOW TO THIN SEEDLINGS

Thinning is essentially two processes in one. Firstly, you are removing all the plants that are excess to requirements and at the same time you are selecting the biggest, healthiest and strongest plants that will be retained to form the crop.

Before starting to thin, dry ground must be watered, preferably the night before you intend to thin. A measuring stick, marked with the appropriate crop distance, can be used to show the approximate position of

Above: *Rows of seedlings are often too crowded and need to be thinned when the plants are young.*

the individual plants. Remove all the plants in between each of the markers, selecting the healthiest plant at or near the mark on the stick. If there are no plants at the marked point, then you can transplant one of the seedlings that is excess to requirements into this position. When you are removing the excess plants, place a finger on the soil at either side of the seedling that is being kept. This protects it from root disturbance. Once you have finished, water the remaining seedlings with a fine rose on a watering can to re-firm the soil around the plants. The seedlings that have been removed can be put on the compost heap.

Avoid thinning with this method on hot dry days or in windy conditions, as the remaining seedlings may become water-

Left: *Seedlings grown elsewhere in the garden can be lifted and replanted in their eventual positions. This method is good for crops that need wide spacing.*

stressed if their roots are disturbed. The alternative, in this case, is to snip off the seedlings at ground level with a pair of sharp scissors, thereby avoiding root disturbance.

THINNING DISTANCES

Thinning seedlings ensures that you have the strongest, healthiest plants. The following measurements are the distances that need to be left between thinned seedlings.

Beetroot	7.5–10cm (3–4in)
Broad beans	
(fava beans)	23cm (9in)
Carrots	7.5cm (3in)
Dwarf French beans	
(bush green beans)	20cm (8in)
Florence fennel	25cm (10in)
Kohl rabi	20cm (8in)
Lettuce	23cm (9in)
Parsley	15cm (6in)
Peas	5cm (2in)
Parsnips	15–20cm (6–9in)
Radishes	2.5–5cm (1–2in)
Runner beans	25–30cm
	(10–12in)
Spinach	15cm (6in)
Spring onions	
(scallions)	5cm (2in)
Swedes (rutabaga	
or yellow turnip)	30cm (12in)
Swiss chard	30cm (12in)
Turnips	15–20cm
	(6–8in)

TRANSPLANTING SEEDLINGS

1 *Water your row of seedlings at least an hour before transplanting and preferably the night before if no rain has fallen.*

2 *Using a fork to loosen the soil, gently lift the seedlings. Take care to handle them by their leaves and never touch the stems.*

3 *Using a tight line, straight edge or notched planting board, replant the seedlings at the appropriate spacing for that crop.*

4 *Gently water the seedlings immediately after sowing. Never let roots dry out at any stage during transplanting.*

COMMON PLANTING DISTANCES

It is important that you always allow the correct spacing between crop plants so that they will grow into strong, healthy specimens. You can use a garden line and a measuring stick in the vegetable plot in order to work out the correct position for each plant in a row.

Asparagus	30–38cm (12–15in)
Aubergines (eggplant)	60cm (24in)
Broccoli	60cm (24in)
Brussels sprouts	50–75cm (20–30in)
Cabbages	30–50cm (12–20in)
Calabrese (Italian sprouting broccoli)	15–23cm (6–9in)
Cauliflowers	50–75cm (20–30in)
Celery	23–30cm (9–12in)
Courgettes (zucchini)	60cm (24in)
Cucumbers	60cm (24in)
Garlic	15cm (6in)
Globe artichokes	75cm (30in)
Kale	60cm (24in)
Leeks	15cm (6in)
Marrows (zucchini)	60cm (24in)
Onion sets	10cm (4in)
Peppers	45–60cm (18–24in)
Potatoes	30–38cm (12–15in)
Pumpkins	90–180cm (3–6ft)
Rhubarb	75–90cm (30–36in)
Runner beans	25–30cm (10–12in)
Shallots	15–18cm (6–7in)
Sweetcorn (corn)	30cm (12in)
Tomatoes	60cm (24in)

TRANSPLANTING SEEDLINGS

The most common way of transplanting seedlings involves planting container-grown plants into open ground. Early vegetable crops can easily be raised in this way. The other method is to raise seedlings in open ground near to where they are to be planted out. Transplanting outdoor seedlings means that a smaller area of the vegetable plot is needed for sowing and, in consequence, a smaller seedbed is required. Transplanting seedlings is a good way of growing plants such as lettuce that are to be used in catch-cropping beds or where plants are to be planted out in no-dig beds.

The ideal time for transplanting outdoor seedlings is during damp overcast weather because this helps to prevent the seedlings' roots drying out. As is the case when thinning the plants, the seedlings will need watering the evening before. It is best to dig up only a few plants at a time, discarding any that are weak, damaged or appear to be sick. Seedlings can be placed in a plastic bag to maintain humidity around them while they are out of the ground.

A garden line can be set out in the vegetable patch in a similar manner to the way in which it is placed for preparing a seed drill. The position of the plants can then be determined using a measuring stick. Use a dibber (dibble) or thin trowel to plant the seedlings, firming lightly around the base before moving on to the next transplant. Once the row is completed, it is important that you water them in.

For catch cropping or planting among other plants, the surrounding crop may well determine the spacings between the transplants, although the procedure remains exactly the same.

AFTERCARE

The aftercare that your crops require is essential to ensure healthy plants that produce high yields. There are a number of different techniques that are listed below to help you on your way. Just remember that the more effort you put in then the better they will taste. As well as judicious watering and feeding, you will also have to weed the vegetable plot and provide some form of plant protection and support. But the reward of such care and attention is delicious home-grown produce.

Above: *Regular cropping of vegetables such as this ruby chard will encourage the development of new growth.*

WATERING

Vegetables need watering if there is no significant rainfall. This is especially true when the crops are young and only have shallow roots. If your soil is very light, or free-draining, you can enrich it to help water retention by digging in organic matter, growing green manures or by continuous mulching.

If you have a large garden, mulching around the crop with straw, farmyard manure, garden compost or another similar substance can help to limit water loss. When you water, it is best to give the plants a thorough soaking, allowing the water to penetrate deeply. Giving a light watering will just encourage shallow surface roots that are easily damaged by prolonged drought. Prolonged dry periods also encourage plants to bolt, thus ruining the crop.

Certain plants such as cabbages and lettuces are naturally shallow rooted, whereas others such as tomatoes and squash are naturally deep rooted. Shallow rooters especially benefit from mulching and may need watering often in hot summers.

FEEDING

As long as a regular crop rotation and soil enrichment programme is followed, feeding is unnecessary for most crops. Tomatoes, pumpkins, courgettes and marrows (zucchini) are hungry crops and do need a regular liquid feed, and others may sometimes need a tonic. Good (but smelly) liquid feeds can be made by filling a barrel or bucket with comfrey leaves or nettles, covering with water and steeping for a few days; or use a sack of sheep manure soaked in water. Dilute these feeds 1:10 with water. If you have a wormery, the liquid from this is also an excellent feed.

Above: *The effort you put into protecting and caring for your crops will be rewarded at harvest time.*

Apply these feeds once every week or two. Many plants are given their main feed annually. This type of feeding is normally applied to fruit trees and bushes in the spring and is best applied in the form of a slower-release fertilizer such as bonemeal.

WEEDING

Check your plants regularly and try to keep them as weed-free as possible. Remember that weeds compete with your plants for light, space, water and nutrients. It is better to weed a little and often than to weed irregularly. Even areas that have been mulched or have close cropping regimes need regular checks and weeds removed.

PLANT PROTECTION

Pests and diseases come in many different forms. Over time you will learn which specific problems your garden is prone to. Keep a yearly notebook of all the things that affect your crop each season, noting what control measures you used and how effective they were. In time you will have a record of how and when to manage pests and other problems in your own garden.

Above: *The careful harvesting of crops is essential if they are to store well. Here, carrots are being lifted with a garden fork.*

Above: *The regular harvesting of peas and beans will help to extend the length of the harvest period.*

Above: *Taller plants and climbers will need some form of support. Canes or sticks with twine tied between them provide ideal temporary supports.*

PROVIDING SUPPORT

Plants may need supporting, especially climbers such as peas and beans. This support must begin at an early age, using twiggy pea sticks or hazel sticks, both of which can look ornate. Bamboo canes can be used for a host of climbing plants, but it is more ethically correct to use local materials rather than to use a product that has been transported thousands of miles. Squashes can be grown up fancy supports made from stakes and strong string or rope, making a curious garden feature. Other plants such as globe artichokes and Florence fennel can benefit from individual supports for their stems.

Above: *Marrows and pumpkins are easily stored in trays that should then be kept in a cool dark place.*

HARVESTING AND STORING

When harvesting, it is tempting to pick the good specimens and leave the rest, but remember to pick and compost poor or rotten ones as well as the best of the crop. Diseased or damaged crops can begin to rot and may infect the remaining harvest.

Freshly picked vegetables are higher in nutritional value than stored ones. So, during the growing season, pick what you need and store the surplus. Choosing when to pick a certain vegetable is a matter of taste. Some prefer to pick produce such as beans when they are young, small and succulent, whereas others prefer the beans to be more mature.

Crops can be stored in a number of ways. Root crops can be left in the ground in all but the coldest winters, lifting them as they are needed. Some crops, such as parsnips, actually develop a better taste after they have been subjected to frost. Alternatively, root crops can be stored in a cool dark place. They should be cleaned and stored in sand and a sterile organic substance such as coir, untreated sawdust, fine leaf mould, fine bark or sterilized soil.

Store other vegetables on shelves or boxes, ensuring that they do not touch. Onions and garlic are best kept in open sacks or in strings. Cabbages can be kept in nets until needed for up to two to three months. Other brassicas such as Brussels sprouts and swedes are best kept outside in the ground, harvesting them as needed.

Freezing is another storage option. Some vegetables, such as asparagus, beans and cauliflowers, are best blanched in boiling water for a couple of minutes before freezing. Alternatively, you can cook the vegetables and then freeze them, as is the case for marrows, pumpkins and rhubarb.

Above: *Store root crops such as carrots in a cool dark place and cover them in sterile sawdust, leaf mould or coir.*

CROPS FOR STORING OVER WINTER

Harvest time often brings the problem of a crop glut. Storage can enable you to enjoy this bounty for longer.

Asparagus Best consumed fresh. Cook or blanch before freezing
Aubergines (eggplant) Cook before freezing
Beetroot (beets) Shelf storage or pickling
Broad (fava) beans Freezing or drying
Brussels sprouts Freezing. Leave on plant until needed
Cabbages Freezing or shelf storage. Leave in ground in mild conditions
Carrots Leave in ground in mild conditions. Shelf storage
Cauliflowers Blanch before freezing. Shelf storage if hung upside down in dark and misted
Celery Cook before freezing. Limited shelf storage
Courgettes (zucchini) Cook before freezing. Limited shelf storage
Dwarf French beans (bush green beans) Freezing
Garlic In sacks or strung
Kale Harvest through winter
Kohl rabi Leave in ground if mild or protected, medium shelf storage
Leeks Freezing, leave in ground in mild conditions, shelf storage
Marrows (zucchini) Cook before freezing, shelf storage
Onions In sacks or strung
Parsnips Leave in ground until needed or late winter
Peas Freezing or drying on plant
Peppers Blanch before freezing. Pickle or dry
Potatoes Store in paper sacks once cleaned and dried
Pumpkins Cook before freezing. Good shelf storage if fully ripe
Rhubarb Cook before freezing
Runner beans Freezing
Shallots In sacks or strung
Spinach Cook then freeze
Swedes (rutabaga or yellow turnip) Leave in ground until needed (may go woody by late winter)
Sweetcorn (corn) Freezing or pickling
Tomatoes Cook before freezing. Pickle
Turnips Leave in ground until needed

GROWING HERBS

Herbs are valued for their culinary, medicinal, decorative and aromatic properties. They come in a diverse range of sizes, shapes and habits, ranging from ground-creeping thyme through to the tall architectural stems of angelica. The choice of herbs is so great that there is always something to offer a gardener with only a window box, hanging basket or a small space. A herb garden offers a treat for the senses and these fragrant plants are also easy to grow in the organic garden.

Above: *Herbs are easy to grow given the right growing conditions. They provide an attractive, often fragrant, display.*

WHERE TO GROW HERBS

Herbs can be grown in a range of settings, such as custom-designed herb gardens and ornamental borders. They can also be grown as companion plants in the vegetable garden and are eminently suited to growing in containers, hanging baskets and window boxes. They are especially useful if grown near the kitchen.

Herbs range from tall showy herbaceous plants such as fennel (*Foeniculum vulgare*) and tansy (*Tanacetum vulgare*) to ground-hugging cushion plants such as thyme (*Thymus vulgaris*). The majority of herbs originate from dry sunny environments and so need sunshine to help them develop their essential oils. It is best to site herbs in an open, sunny spot in the garden where they will thrive.

SOIL PREPARATION

Drier sites suit most herbs, and the sunnier and hotter the site the better they will taste. The taste and smell of herbs is usually due to the production of essential oils within the plants. If they are grown in hot conditions, then the concentrations of essential oils will be greater. Growing herbs in very moist rich soils can accelerate their growth, but will result in a milder flavour. They will also look better and flower less than their "hot-site" counterparts and be easier to harvest.

Herbs are, however, best grown in a soil that is loamy with some added organic matter. The ideal pH is 6.5 to 7.0, which means that herbs can easily be planted among vegetables in the kitchen garden.

Above: *You can restrict the spread of invasive plants such as mint (*Mentha*) by planting them in pots or buckets that are then buried in the ground.*

SOWING HERB SEED

Herbs may be sown directly in the soil outdoors, just like vegetables. The preparation of the seedbed and the sowing techniques are exactly the same, and they can easily be interplanted or block planted among other vegetables.

Alternatively, herb seeds may be planted under cover, raising them in the same way as early vegetables and bedding plants and then hardening them off before planting out in the garden. This method is especially useful for more tender, leafy herbs such as basil or coriander (cilantro).

Above: *Pinching out newly planted herbs such as this bay (*Laurus*) will encourage bushy, leafy growth.*

Basil (*Ocimum basilicum*), for example, associates well with outdoor tomatoes, both in the garden and in the kitchen. These can be planted out together from an indoor sowing and the crop will be mutually complementary. Indoor sowing can also provide you with herbs that can be cropped earlier in the season, effectively extending the useful life of your organic herb garden.

Left: *Herbs are an important element in both ornamental and kitchen gardens, being decorative as well as useful.*

PLANTING HERBS

1 *Excavate a planting hole that is about a quarter to half as big again as the plant's rootball. Make sure it is deep enough.*

2 *Ensure that the top of the compost is the same level as the surrounding soil. Refill the gap around the rootball and firm the soil.*

3 *Water the plant immediately after planting. Keep the plant well watered until it is fully established into the surrounding soil.*

PLANTING HERBS IN THE GARDEN

Herbs can be sited anywhere in the garden as long as it is sunny. They have a range of forms and colours and often make valuable additions to the ornamental garden. Foxgloves (*Digitalis*), sage (*Salvia officinalis*) and the curry plant (*Helichrysum italicum*) are a few examples of herbs that can be used in annual and herbaceous borders as well as in the kitchen garden. Some herbs, such as mint (*Mentha*) and lemon balm (*Melissa officinalis*), can become very invasive if they are not contained in a pot or sunken sink when growing among other plants in an ornamental border. Remove the flower-heads from the mint before they have had a chance to seed, as the seed will germinate all over your border.

PLANTING HERBS IN CONTAINERS

Herbs make excellent subjects for use in pots and containers and are wonderful for patio gardens that catch plenty of summer sun, although you need to make sure that the potting mix never dries out. Raised beds, which provide good drainage, are also good areas for growing herbs. Always plant them in a free-draining potting mix that will not become waterlogged. There are numerous cultivars of culinary herbs that can be used for ornamental purposes, and groups of pot-grown herbs can be extremely decorative as well as supplying you with a range of fresh flavourings. Thyme, rosemary, lavender and sage are all good choices to grow in pots, either outdoors or on your windowsill.

Above: *Herbs are easily grown in a container which will provide an excellent focal point in the kitchen garden.*

Herb pots require little maintenance, save for watering and the occasional feed during the growing season. Most are rarely long term and are best restarted yearly or every other year. Herbs that are permanently in pots, such as bay trees, will need repotting every year. Spreading subjects like thyme can be lifted and both top-pruned and root-pruned prior to repotting.

Mint and other spreading herbaceous subjects may need dividing and repotting from time to time. This is done by splitting the crown of the plant into smaller pieces and then repotting one of these back into the container with some fresh potting mix. Dividing in this way is best performed annually for very vigorous herbs. Harvesting on a regular basis is often enough to control the growth of many potted herb arrangements (where a number are planted in one container), but a light trim may also be necessary from time to time.

Potted herbs may also be grown in the greenhouse to ensure a supply both earlier and later in the season. Try growing basil (*Ocimum basilicum*), coriander (cilantro; *Coriandrum sativum*), chives (*Allium schoenoprasum*) and dill (*Anethum graveolens*) in pots because this will save money if you spend a lot on fresh herbs. Pots raised under glass can be brought into the kitchen for ease of use. A series of successional sowings under glass will ensure that you have fresh herbs for most or even all of the year, both indoors and out.

Above: *Planting spreading herbs such as thyme (*Thymus*) in pots will help to control them and can also be decorative.*

HARVESTING AND STORING HERBS

Many commonly used culinary herbs such as basil, coriander (cilantro), chives and parsley can be grown indoors on a windowsill or conservatory during the cooler winter months if you have space. If you are not able to spare growing room for these, most are easily stored for use later. Herbs are easily harvested and most of the storage techniques are simple and straightforward.

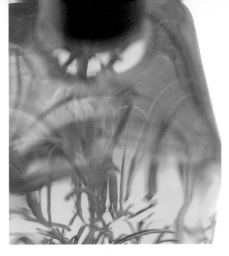

Above: *Aromatic herbs such as rosemary (*Rosmarinus officinalis*) can be used to flavour bottles of olive oil.*

HOW TO HARVEST HERBS

Various parts of herbs, including the leaves, flowers, fruits and seeds, are gathered at different times, depending upon the plant and the part that provides the desirable properties. Annual leafy herbs such as basil (*Ocimum basilicum*) and parsley (*Petroselinum crispum*) should be carefully picked, never taking more than about 10 per cent of the growth in a single picking.

The same is true of perennials such as sage (*Salvia officinalis*), thyme (*Thymus vulgaris*) and rosemary (*Rosmarinus officinalis*) because severe pruning or over-stripping of the leaves will weaken the plant. It is important that you not remove more than one-third of the growth at any one time. If you harvest carefully, you will get a more vigorous leaf growth that will result in healthier plants.

As a general rule, pick herbs just before the plant is about to flower, which is when they have the strongest flavour. Pick the leaves when they are fresh and at their sweetest, selecting blemish-free, upper leaves. Collect the leaves in early morning or late evening, provided they are dry, rather than in bright afternoon sun when the plant's sap is rising. This is when the aroma of herbs is at its strongest and is easily lost if picked during this time of day. Flowers such as borage (*Borago officinalis*) and lavender (*Lavandula*), however, are best picked just before they reach full bloom and once they begin to open in the heat of the day.

Rhizomes, like ginger and turmeric, are collected in autumn, just as the leaves begin to change colour and the maximum amount of nutrition has been stored. Use a fork to gently free the roots from the soil and always avoid "hand-pulling" them. Choose only the best ones and use a vegetable brush to gently loosen any dirt. If you do need to wash them, do so quickly in cold water and avoid soaking them, as this can result in lost flavour.

Harvesting seeds tends to vary from plant to plant. Some seeds, like those of borage, simply fall to the ground as soon as they are ripe. Thyme seeds are very small and hard to see. Parsley and coriander seeds shake off very easily, and frequently the plants will have sown next year's crop for you before you realize they have gone to seed. One method of harvesting any seed that is difficult to collect is to tie a small paper bag over the flower head when the seeds start to form, ensuring that you can collect the seed without losing any. It would be advisable to use this method for collecting from plants with small seed as they can drop off when ripe or sometimes spring from the plant.

Above: *The best time to harvest herbs is usually just before they flower. This is when they have their strongest flavour.*

Above: *Herbs can be dried for later use by hanging them in bunches in a dry place out of direct sunlight.*

DRYING HERBS AND FLOWERS

Store herbs in a cool, dry place with minimum exposure to air and sunlight. One of the most popular methods of preserving them for use during the winter months is drying. This method can actually improve the flavour of some herbs, particularly the leaves of bay trees (*Laurus nobilis*). Herbs may be dried in bundles secured with a rubber band or string and hung upside down from a rack in a dry location such as an airing cupboard or shed.

When drying the herbs, the temperature of the area should not exceed 30°C (86°F) because the plants' essential oils will evaporate at or above this temperature. Do not dry your herbs in the kitchen where they will be spoiled by the humidity caused by cooking.

Fresh herbs can also be placed in brown paper bags. Remember to label the bags because it will be hard to distinguish between the herbs once they have dried. Store in a dry, dark, cool place until the herbs inside are dry, shaking the bags occasionally so that the plants dry evenly. Remove any stems and store the dried herbs in airtight jars. Keep the jars away from light to protect the colour and flavour of the herbs. Roots are best chopped into small pieces and dried in an oven. In general, you can expect those that you have grown and dried yourself to last at least two years.

STORING HERBS

Herbs can also be preserved in other ways, so that you can use them in cooking throughout the year.

Herb salts In a cool oven, spread a layer of ground salt on a sheet of greaseproof (waxed) paper. Sprinkle the chopped fresh herbs on top of the salt and bake for 10–20 minutes. When the herbs are dry, let them cool and place in a jar. Chives, oregano, thyme, lemon balm, lemon thyme, parsley, rosemary and basil can all be treated this way.

Puréeing This method involves mixing approximately 60ml (4tbsp) of olive oil with 2l (8 cups) fresh basil leaves which have been washed and dried. These are blended in a processor until puréed before being transferred to a jar. Stir each time you use it and top with a thin layer of oil afterwards. The purée should keep for up to one year in a refrigerator.

Above: *After herbs have been hung up to dry, separate the seeds from the dry flower heads before storing in tightly sealed jars.*

Freezing herbs Herbs such as dill, fennel, basil and parsley freeze well. The herbs should be cleaned and put into separate, labelled freezer bags. Alternatively, chop the leaves and freeze them with a little water in ice-cube trays. Chop the herbs finely, filling each cube, half with herbs and half with water, before freezing. Transfer the frozen cubes to plastic bags and label. Frozen herbs are best used within six months.

HERBAL INFUSIONS

You can also make a hot infusion of leafy herbs by placing the herb and any fine-quality olive oil in a glass bowl. This is then placed over a pan of gently simmering water and heated gently for about three hours, ensuring that the water in the pan does not dry out. The strained oil, once it has cooled, should be stored in airtight bottles or jars.

A cool infusion of flowery herbs involves using fresh herbs such as chamomile which are ground with a pestle and mortar and packed into a large jar and covered with oil. The sealed jar is then left in a warm, sunny place for two to three weeks and shaken occasionally. It is then strained and placed into airtight jars or bottles where it can be stored for up to a year.

A simple way of creating aromatic olive oil is to simply add a large sprig of your chosen herbs – rosemary and mint are good choices – to a bottle of olive oil. Store the bottle in a cool dark place for about ten days before using.

You can also make you own herbal vinegars by adding fresh herbs such as tarragon or rosemary or cloves of garlic, slices of ginger, chillies or peppercorns and all-spice powder to white vinegar. Crush about a quarter litre volume (1 cup) of loosely packed fresh herbs for each litre of vinegar. If you are using dried herbs, use half the amount of herb stated above. It is important that you use only commercially prepared vinegars, as homemade vinegar may not have a low enough pH to prevent bacterial growth. Place the vinegar in a pot on the stove and heat, but do not boil. Place the herbs in a clean, sterilized jar and slightly crush them. Pour the vinegar over the herbs and cover the jar tightly. Let the herb-vinegar mixture steep in a dark place at room temperature, shaking the jar every couple of days. After a week, strain the vinegar and place in bottles and store for up to six weeks.

DRYING AND FREEZING HERBS

1 *Pick seed just as it is ripening. Place the seeds on a tray or in a paper or muslin bag. Leave in a cool, dark place for a few days until the seed is completely dry.*

2 *Herb seeds that have been dried can be stored in old glass jars with an airtight lid. Store the jars in a cool, dry, dark place and label them for future reference.*

3 *Herbs can be frozen in ice-cube trays. Fill the trays with water after you have added the herbs to make ready-to-use cubes. Herbs can also be packed into freezer bags.*

GROWING FRUIT TREES AND BUSHES

Freshly picked fruit from the organic garden tastes absolutely delicious. The warm taste of a juicy sweet raspberry or the crisp flavour of a tree-ripened apple would tempt many a gardener into growing their own fruit produce. The tastes can be quite different from shop-grown produce where storage, handling, packing and off-the-tree ripening all take their toll on the quality and taste of the fruit.

Above: *A sunny wall provides an ideal location for growing fruit trees, such as this pear, that need warmth.*

WHERE CAN FRUIT BE GROWN?

Fruit trees and bushes can be grown wherever there is space. Strawberries can be used in hanging baskets or tubs, dwarf apple trees can be planted in ornamental containers and a number of fruits, such as cherries and white and red currants, can all be grown against walls. Fruits not only provide produce for the kitchen table but many of them have ornamental qualities and can blend well with other plants in the decorative garden.

CHOOSING A SITE

The best site for fruit, both indoors and out, is a sunny one. Sunlight is essential, not just for the ripening of the fruit itself but also for flower bud formation and flowering. In addition, fruit trees and bushes often appreciate a sheltered spot where even exotic fruit can be raised. Within the garden a sheltered sunny wall can provide the ideal place to grow peaches and apricots. If cold winters are a problem, then provide winter protection in the form of a portable frame or, alternatively, grow the plants in a greenhouse. It is worth noting that providing your plants with the ideal conditions for healthy growth will reap its rewards in the

end. Not only will you harvest heavier yields, but, more importantly, your plants will be less prone to pest and disease attacks, which is an obvious advantage when growing organically.

SELECTING THE RIGHT PLANTS

Variety selection should not be based purely on hardiness but on personal preference. You may also wish to consider how easy the fruit tree or bush is to grow, fruit size, taste and the time of harvest. Selecting more than one variety can result in having fresh fruit over a longer period due to a succession of ripening.

Some fruit trees combine the best qualities of two plants. Grafting utilizes the qualities of the variety as top growth (scion) and other desirable qualities from a rootstock that may be absent from the variety. The scion is the fruiting variety that is budded or grafted on to the rootstock which is selected for certain characteristics such as dwarfing, nematode insect resistance, soil type, cold hardiness and disease resistance.

The most commonly grown rootstocks for amateur gardeners are the apple semi-dwarfs and dwarfs. Grapes are also grafted on to clonal rootstocks, although they are often supplied on their own roots. Olives and various types of berry are also usually supplied as plants on their own roots.

Dwarf apple trees are very useful in small gardens and are eminently suited to container growing. They produce fruit of the same size, colour and quality as larger standard trees and require the same pruning, nutritional and care regimes as a standard-size tree.

Left: *Most fruit bushes will benefit from a generous application of well-rotted manure or compost early in the year.*

Dwarf trees fruit much sooner after planting and bear less fruit per tree. When harvesting the fruit, you can reach all parts of the tree from the ground without using a ladder and the trees are easier to train and prune on an annual basis. Grafting the desired variety on to special clonal rootstocks "dwarfs" apples. The most popular dwarfing rootstocks for apple were developed in England and are designated as either EM or M (for East Malling) or MM (for Malling Merton). Dwarfed trees must be pruned annually or size control may be lost. In addition, loss of fruit by frost or pests will also increase growth so necessitating summer pruning.

PLANTING FRUIT TREES AND BUSHES

As with any other type of tree, good ground preparation and careful handling are essential steps to successfully establishing your fruit trees and bushes. The cheapest option when buying fruit trees is to purchase bare-rooted plants. The disadvantage is that they are only available during the dormant season. The most important factor in handling bare-rooted plants is not to let the roots dry out. When you buy trees always check the condition of the roots and packing material. Heel in plants by covering the roots with moist soil in a cool environment outdoors if they are not to be planted immediately.

Dig a hole slightly wider and deeper than the spread and length of the root system, making sure the sides of the hole are not "glazed" over as this will result in a root girdling. After trimming diseased, dead, broken or extra long roots, place the tree in the hole and spread out the roots. For larger trees, place the stake in the hole and drive it in (remembering to first remove the tree and cover the roots). Place the tree back into

PLANTING A FRUIT TREE

1 *Dig a hole in the ground that is at least half as large again as the rootball of the fruit tree. Loosen the sides and the base of the planting hole with a garden fork.*

2 *Remove the pot and check the rootball for girdling roots. Tease these out by hand or with a garden fork.*

3 *Use a straightedge to make sure that the plant is at the right depth in the hole. Fill around the roots with soil, firm it down and water well.*

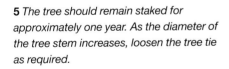

4 *Hammer in a stake at an angle of about 60° in order to avoid the rootball and place a tie on the tree. Saw off the end of the stake. Nail the tie to the stake to secure it.*

5 *The tree should remain staked for approximately one year. As the diameter of the tree stem increases, loosen the tree tie as required.*

the hole and return the soil, firming in layers of about 30cm (12in) as you go. This avoids large air spaces being left around the roots and ensures that it is set firmly. Trees should be planted at the same depth as they were grown in the nursery. Make sure the bud union (for trees on rootstocks) is about 5–7cm (2–2¾in) above the soil line. Do not place fertilizer in the planting hole as this can be added later. Mulch the newly planted tree with well-rotted manure or compost to suppress weeds. Container-grown nursery stock can be transplanted any time of the year. Site preparation is the same as for bare-rooted stock. Make sure that you check the roots as they can become distorted or root bound if they are grown in containers for a long period of time. Teasing these roots out can help avoid root girdling, but the best way to do this is to use field-grown (bare-rooted) stock.

PRUNING NEWLY PLANTED STOCK

Fruit trees must be pruned when they are planted for a number of reasons. If planting bare-rooted stock, the top of the tree must be pruned to counter-balance the loss of the root system which would have been severed in the nursery during lifting. Pruning also forces the growth of laterals from which the future framework of the fruit tree will be selected. Branches that are desirably located can be retained as part of the framework whereas undesirable branches are removed.

FRUIT TREE POLLINATION

Pollination is the transfer of pollen from the male part of the flower to the female part of the flower (the stigma) to allow fruit to set and seeds to develop. Seeds cause the fruit to develop properly. If both the pollen and stigma are from the same flower or from another flower from the same variety, the process is called self-pollination. Fruit trees that set fruit as the result of self-pollination are called self-fruitful, whereas those relying on pollen from a different variety are called self-unfruitful. The latter needs two varieties near to each other for fruit set to occur. This is called cross-pollination.

Apples Apples generally need two varieties for good fruit set. This can be another apple variety or a crab apple that blooms with the edible crop.
Apricots Self-fruitful
Berries (all types) Self-fruitful
Cherries Sweet cherry is self-unfruitful and needs two varieties for good crop set. Sour cherry varieties are self-fruitful.
European plums Self-fruitful
Japanese plums Self-unfruitful as a rule with the exception of Santa Rosa which will set fruit fairly well without cross-pollination.
Nectarines Self-fruitful
Peaches Self-fruitful with the exception of 'J.H. Hale' which has to be pollinated by another variety.
Pears These always need two varieties to ensure good fruit set.

SUPPORTING FRUIT TREES AND SHRUBS

Many of the fruits that we grow, such as free-standing apple or plum trees, require support only in the early stages, whereas other fruits, like the raspberry, need this throughout their lives. Supports benefit the plants in a number of different ways. They help in establishing strong roots and can prop up trained specimens such as cordons and espaliers. This helps to maintain healthy vigorous growth and increase fruit yields.

Above: *Apples can easily be grown in rows as cordons that are supported by a framework of stakes and wires.*

WALL AND FENCE FRUIT

The training of fruit on a wall or a fence is carried out to gain the maximum production of high-quality fruit in a limited space. As well as being ideal for a small garden, this can also look extremely decorative. Numerous training systems, based on the art of espalier which originated in France and Italy about 400 years ago, have been devised. The most useful training systems used in gardens today are the fan, espalier and cordon. Apples, pears and plums are all suited to this method of training, which is usually supported by a wall, fence or wire trellis. The plants are normally held to the wall or fence using wires which are held in place by vine eyes, positioned 60–90cm (2–3ft) apart. The wire is led through the holes in the vine eyes and secured at both ends. The wires should be no more than 30–45cm (12–18in) apart.

FREESTANDING WIREWORK

Raspberries, blackberries and other hybrid berries are all grown on a permanent framework. They are usually grown on a freestanding structure that supports the loose growth of the plants. To build such a structure, insert a post at least 60cm (24in) into the ground at the end of each row. Brace each end post with another post set at a 45-degree angle. Insert intermediate posts between the two end ones at a distance of every 2m (6½ft). They are set in at the same depth as the end posts, but no bracing posts are needed. Fix the wires on to the posts so that they run the length of the support. Place the first wire 60cm (24in) from the ground, pull tight and attach to the posts using staples or eye-bolts. The other wires are attached at 30cm (12in) intervals until they reach the top of the support. The final height depends on the height of the fruit.

INDIVIDUAL SUPPORT

When they are first planted, all free-standing trees require support to help them to establish a strong healthy root system. You can use a stake to support a fruit tree, ensuring that the stake is placed on the windward side of the tree. The stake is inserted before the tree is planted and is driven well into the ground. The general rule is to have a stake that is one-third the height of the tree showing above the ground. The tree is then tied to the stake using a tree tie. Do not use string or rope because this can damage the bark. A low stake such as this will allow the top part of the tree to move about freely and so help the tree to thicken and strengthen its trunk. For most fruit trees the stake should only be left in the ground for approximately one year and not for several years as is commonly practised.

STAKING A FRUIT BUSH

1 *Using a large mallet, drive a strong wooden post into the ground at the end of a row of the fruit bushes to a depth of about 60cm (2ft).*

2 *Fix another strainer post at a 45-degree angle in order to support the upright. Place this on the side the wire is to run and nail it firmly.*

3 *Fix the wires to one of the posts and then stretch these tightly along the row, stapling them at each post along the row as you go.*

4 *The fruit bushes can be fastened to or trained along these wires. Take care not to tie stems too tightly as this will damage them.*

PROTECTING FRUIT

There can be few more frustrating events in the kitchen-garden calendar than losing your fruit crop (or a fair portion of it) to birds. However, we have to remember that birds are a strong ally in the fight against pests in an organic garden and should be encouraged into fruit-growing areas when the bushes are not fruiting. Protection for the fruit crops will therefore need to take the form of moveable cloches or fruit cages where the netting can be removed after fruiting has taken place.

Above: *Cloches can be used to protect young strawberries from bad weather and also to keep pests at bay.*

FRUIT CAGES

This is perhaps the easiest way to protect tall fruit crops such as blackcurrants, raspberries and gooseberries because these plants can all be grown under the one structure. This makes it easy to maintain and harvest the fruit.

A permanent fruit-cage structure with removable netting is the ideal scenario because the netting can be put in place just before the crop ripens and then is taken down again after fruiting has occurred. This allows the birds to roam freely around the area at all other times, but without jeopardizing the crop at fruiting time. Alternatively, a series of small cages can be constructed over crops that ripen at different times, netting each of them individually as the fruit begins to ripen. This is a wildlife-friendly way of protecting the fruit, but it is also time-consuming.

Above: *A tunnel of wire netting is ideal for protecting ripening strawberries from pests such as birds.*

LOW-LEVEL PROTECTION

Smaller- or lower-growing crops, such as strawberries, can also benefit from a barrier to protect them from birds. This is easily achieved, as the structure does not need to be large, permanent or even particularly sturdy. One simple method is to form a low tunnel of chicken wire, supported on hoops that are bent into an inverted U-shape. For larger areas, a series of stakes hammered into the ground can be covered with netting to keep the birds at bay. Plants growing on wire trellises can be protected with netting draped over the stakes and top wires and weighted at the base with stones.

Left: *Fruit trees growing against a wall can easily be protected with a cost-effective frame that is covered with netting.*

Right: *Fleece stretched over a frame can help protect the blossom of wall specimens from late frosts.*

Larger bush fruit can be covered with netting and weighted down with stones. A little of the crop may be accessible to birds, but most will be protected.

PROTECTION WITHOUT BARRIERS

Most bird deterrents depend upon shocking the birds or mimicking something that they are naturally afraid of. Scarecrows are an age-old favourite. Other deterrents mimic the shape of hawks or make noises that will startle the birds. A relatively recent "innovation" has been to hang compact discs from wires stretched through the crop. Most of these deterrents tend to work very well at first until the birds get used to them. However, the only drawback is that when the birds get used to them, they resume their onslaught with a vengeance. The only way to overcome this is to keep changing the deterrents every few days.

PRUNING FRUIT TREES AND SHRUBS

The general purpose of pruning fruit trees is to regulate growth, increase crop yields and to improve fruit size and quality. The fruit trees also need to have all the dead, diseased and damaged wood removed as well as overcrowded areas thinned out. Pruning is also performed in order to establish a tree with a strong framework that is capable of supporting heavy crops without causing damage to the plant.

Above: *The careful pruning of trained specimens, such as this pear, will result in good blossom and improve fruit yields.*

WHEN TO PRUNE FRUIT TREES

If a fruit tree is pruned in spring, all the effort that the tree has put into bud production is wasted. The best time to prune is in winter when the plants are dormant and the sap has not yet started to rise. This applies to all fruit except for plums and cherries which are susceptible to silverleaf disease at this time and are best pruned in summer.

Summer pruning is also recommended if you wish to control vigorous growth in formally trained fruits such as fans, cordons and espaliers.

When pruning is underway, older fruit-bearing trees should be pruned first. Young, non-bearing apple trees and stone fruits can be pruned later to minimize the risk of winter injury.

BASIC PRUNING CUTS

Although there are different methods of pruning and training, the pruning cuts are the same. Always make the pruning cut just above a bud, ensuring that the cut is angled away from the bud. This will allow rainwater

---

BENEFITS OF PRUNING

Pruning fruit trees and bushes has many advantages, some of which are outlined below.

• Increased fruit yields.
• Can aid ripening of the fruit.
• Maintains healthy growth.
• Regulates growth.
• Improves fruit size and quality.
• Controls the spread of diseases.

---

to drip down the other side of the stem and away from the bud, thus protecting the top of the cut from rotting.

Larger branches will need to be cut with a saw. If the branch is very heavy, you will need to remove the branch in three separate stages. Cut underneath the branch first, 20–25cm (8–10in) away from where the final cut will be. Make the second cut on the top of the branch just behind the first undercut. Follow this through until the

weight of the branch makes the wood split and it falls off cleanly at the undercut. You will then need to make a third cut at the branch collar, cutting straight from the top to the bottom of the branch as there is no weight left to tear the bark.

Above: *Training can give rise to a variety of ornamental shapes. These pear trees have been trained into a cylindrical shape.*

PRUNING LARGE BRANCHES

1 *Make a cut about 20–25cm (8–10in) out from where the final cut will be on the underside of the branch. Cut about a third of the way into the branch.*

2 *Make a cut about 10cm (4in) nearer the position of the final cut, cutting until the branch snaps. The initial undercut prevents the wood splitting or bark from stripping.*

3 *Position the saw for the last cut to avoid damaging the swollen area at the base of the branch. The cut will heal in a couple of seasons. No wound painting is necessary.*

SUCCESSFUL FRUIT TREE AND SHRUB PRUNING

Pruning fruit trees is a very complex subject and, like so many areas of organic gardening, is the subject of opinion and hot debate. Despite this it is possible to apply certain guiding principles that can enable you to prune your fruit trees and bushes successfully.

1 Remove root suckers arising at the base of the tree
These compete with the upper growth for water and essential nutrients and their dense habit can harbour pests.

2 Always cut out dead, dying, damaged or diseased limbs first
Helps to maintain the plant's health and enables you to see precisely what needs doing next.

3 Remove low, drooping limbs
These will not bear fruit and will often be heavily shaded by growth above. They are an unproductive drain on the tree.

4 Remove upright growth or outward growth in the case of wall-trained bushes
Upright growth will produce a flush of growth at the end and will not fruit well. Branches growing away from the wall will shade the fruit behind causing poor ripening.

5 Remove crossing or dense parallel growth
Crossing growth will rub and can cause bark damage that will allow disease entry. Dense growth will also shade the developing fruits. This will slow and limit the ripening of the fruit.

6 Freestanding trees should have upper limbs cut back further than lower limbs
This will result in the development of a conical shape that will allow light penetration all the way down the side. Fruit will ripen more evenly.

7 Remove water sprouts as they develop
Water sprouts can quickly develop and cover the developing fruits, causing poor ripening and harvesting difficulties. They can be easily removed by hand. This is best done early in the season when the growth is soft and is therefore easily removed. Carry out regular inspections throughout the season to control the water sprouts.

8 Once the larger cuts have been made, thin out the smaller branches
Removing thick branches first allows you to see what remains to be done and also makes it easier to get to the remaining pruning work. Removing older wood encourages young growth to fill the gap. Remember to stand back and view what you have pruned as you go along.

9 Always make clean cuts above a leaf bud or close to the stem
Pruning cuts that are not performed cleanly or that leave a long stub will damage the plant tissue and encourage the entry of pests and diseases.

10 Avoid feeding with nitrogen for a season before and following heavy pruning
Both pruning and high nitrogen fertilizers promote the development of rapid growth flushes that can result in the poor development of the crop.

Above: *This well-established pear tree has been trained into an espalier on wire supports. Many fruit trees can be grown and supported in this way.*

Above: *This pear tree has been grown as a fan. Fans are an ideal way to train many species of fruit tree and are well suited for growing against a wall.*

HARVESTING AND STORING FRUIT

When harvesting your fruits, you will find that there is only so much you can eat fresh or give away. There is always surplus fruit left over and you are faced with the question of what to do with it. Leaving some on the plant to help feed the wildlife in your organic garden is a good idea, but storing the rest of the excess fruit using a variety of methods will ensure that you can eat your home-grown produce over a longer period of time.

Above: *An apple is ready to be picked if it can be removed from the tree with only a single twist of the fruit.*

HARVESTING

The key to successfully storing fruit begins well before harvesting commences. Your first objective should be to grow fruit that is as healthy as possible because it will be the best for storage. Harvesting immature crops or attempting to save those that are in poor condition – due perhaps to a lack of water or nutrients or to pest and disease damage – can lead to many storage losses.

There are several ways that fruit can be stored and the condition of the picked crop will usually be the deciding factor as to which of these you should use. Top fruit such as apples and pears can often be stored fresh through most of the winter, whereas stone fruits and berries, such as peaches, strawberries and raspberries, must be quickly consumed, turned into a preserve or frozen.

Careful handling, both during and following harvesting, is essential because, from the moment they are harvested (and in many cases well before), crops have no means of repairing any physical damage that they may suffer. Even firm, strong-looking fruit such as apples can easily be bruised, although the damage may well not show up immediately.

As well as good handling, a careful selection of the fruits during harvesting is essential for successful storage. You should inspect the picked fruits and select only those of the best quality for fresh storage. Reject any that have a broken skin or show any sign of pest or disease damage. Do not throw them on the compost heap yet, however, because damaged fruit may well be useful for making preserves such as jellies and jams or for freezing.

It is also a good idea to leave a small percentage of mature fruit on the plants when you are harvesting to help feed the wildlife in your organic garden.

STORING

In general, the storage area for fruit must be frost-free, safe from pests, rainproof and ideally kept at a constant temperature.

STORING FRUIT

To store surplus fruit and avoid the risk of rotting, make sure that you use the appropriate method.

Apples, pears and quinces
Store in a cool place for up to 12 months, depending on the variety.
All other fruit Eat immediately or freeze. Alternatively, preserve fruit by bottling or making into jam. Fruit can be kept for up to 12 months, depending on the method of preservation that has been used.

The long-term storage of any fruit calls for cool conditions with adequate ventilation. If you have space, consider having a separate refrigerator specifically for fruit storage, or choose an area with a low temperature that does not go below freezing. A garden shed or garage can be ideal, in many cases, but even these

Far left: *Pick soft fruits, such as strawberries, raspberries and gooseberries, carefully to avoid bruising the fruit.*

Left: *Pears can last for up to 12 months, depending upon the variety. Lay them in a recycled box, ensuring that the fruits do not touch and air can circulate around the fruit.*

Above: *Fruit trays, recycled from supermarkets, make ideal storage boxes for surplus fruit. The trays should be kept in a cool dry place such as a garage or shed.*

Above: *Soft fruit is best placed in small individual containers as it is picked to prevent it being squashed and spoiling. Store in a refrigerator or other cool place.*

spaces may need extra insulation if winter weather conditions become severe. Some houses have a basement, cellar or unheated room that may be ideally suited for the task. Attics are not recommended for fruit storage because of their wide temperature fluctuations and variable humidity.

It is worthwhile trying out a variety of different storage methods. This can be done by splitting the crop up and then trying out different locations in your home. You will soon find which are the best places to store fruit, and what areas are best for storing a particular kind of fruit.

Ensure that you check the stored fruit regularly, at least weekly, removing any that show signs of decay. Remember the old adage that "one bad apple spoils the whole barrel"? This can be true for your crop too unless you prevent rots from spreading. The unblemished parts can often still be used for eating or cooking. If lots of fruits begin to rot simultaneously, it could be that the storage conditions are not suitable, the crop has reached its maximum "shelf-life" or the fruit was not of sufficiently good quality to start with.

FREEZING AND PRESERVING

Freezing is an excellent way of storing all the surplus fruit that has been produced in your garden. Unfortunately, fruit tends to lose its firmness once it has been frozen,

although the taste will remain more or less the same. Raspberries, for example, are best used for making pies or flans after they have been frozen and will be of very poor quality if they are eaten raw. Most fruits can be frozen after they have been stewed or puréed; this is true of fruits such as apples and plums.

Fruits like strawberries and blackcurrants that are not suited to long-term storage can be made into jams, pickles and chutneys. You can find recipes for these in good cookbooks.

Above: *One of the simplest ways of preserving fruit is to freeze it, although once frozen most fruits are only good for cooking.*

Above: *Adding a favourite fruit such as these cranberries to good wine vinegar can produce interesting flavours.*

Right: *Bottling fruit in alcohol is an ideal way to preserve soft fruits such as peaches, nectarines and apricots.*

VEGETABLES

Growing disquiet with the quality and safety of commercially produced food has encouraged many people to grow their own vegetables. Eating home-grown vegetables that have been cultivated naturally is perhaps one of life's great pleasures. For these reasons, it is very easy to understand the growing popularity of organic kitchen gardening. You do not need a large-scale kitchen garden to grow a selection of favourite vegetables. Many crops, such as tomatoes and aubergines (eggplants), can be easily cultivated in containers in a small courtyard or patio.

Left: *The bright yellow flowers of courgettes (zucchini) are edible as well as highly decorative.*

Above: *Lettuces are available in a variety of different colours, making a valuable decorative addition to the vegetable plot.*

Above: *Onions can be obtained in a wide range of different shapes, sizes and colours. They are relatively easy to grow.*

Above: *The delicate red flowers of runner beans look spectacular in the kitchen or ornamental garden.*

BULB VEGETABLES

ONIONS

Allium cepa

Onions are available in a wide range of shapes, sizes and colours: oval, cylindrical, red, white and golden brown. They are easy to grow and need little care throughout their growing period. By using different growing methods to obtain a fresh supply, and through careful storage, it is possible to achieve an all-year-round supply of home-grown onions.

SOIL

Grow in fertile soil with good drainage. Do not plant in ground that has been freshly manured. Dig and manure the previous autumn. Add compost to the ground to improve the soil structure. Crop rotation can prevent a number of pests and diseases.

ASPECT

An open, sunny site, but sets will tolerate some shade.

PLANTING SETS

The majority of onion sets are planted out in early spring. Plant in rows, with 10cm (4in) between each set and 25cm (10in) between the rows, so that the tip of the bulb peeks above the surface. Firm around the sets to remove any air pockets. To harvest an early crop, plant out Japanese onion sets in early autumn. These will be ready for lifting in mid-summer of the following year.

Above: *Once harvested, onions can be stored in open sacks or hung up in strings in a well-ventilated room or shed.*

SOWING SEEDS OUTSIDE

If you have room, sow directly outside in rows in late summer. Sow thinly, as there will be less waste when thinning. The odour, which is exuded when the stems are crushed during thinning, will not be too strong, so there will be less chance of attracting onion fly. Thin out when the soil is moist. The onions will not be ready for harvesting until late summer to autumn of the following year. To spread out the maturing of the onions, sow direct outside in rows in late winter and early spring. This will produce a crop ready to harvest in early autumn. Protection may be given in colder areas.

SOWING SEEDS UNDER GLASS

Sow seeds in trays in mid-winter. Harden off the seedlings in a cold frame and in mid-spring plant out in rows, 10cm (4in) apart, leaving 25cm (10in) between each row.

AFTERCARE

A weed-free area enhances the yield. Hand weeding is preferable to hoeing as hoes can cut into the bulbs. Water the maturing crop only if the season is dry and stop watering after the onions have swollen. Mulching with compost helps to retain moisture in the soil and suppress weed growth.

HARVESTING AND STORAGE

Harvest throughout the growing season. Onions for storing must be fully mature before lifting. When the onions are mature, and the leaves start to turn yellow and flop over lift each bulb slightly with a fork, thus preparing the bulb for lifting. After that, it is best to leave them in the soil for a week or so, especially if the weather is dry and sunny. Harvesting can then be done in a dry period two weeks later. Remove all the soil and dry in a sunny place (if left outside bring indoors during wet periods).

PESTS AND DISEASES

The main pest is the onion fly. The maggots eat the bulbs, resulting in yellow drooping leaves. Onion fly usually affects onion seeds rather than sets. Onion eelworm causes swollen and distorted foliage, kills young plants and softens bulbs on older plants. Destroy any affected plants. Onions are also susceptible to neck rot and white rot.

CULTIVATION

SETS

Planting time Early spring; early autumn (overwintering varieties)

Planting distance 10cm (4in)

Planting depth Tips of onions just showing through soil

Distance between rows 25cm (10in)

Harvesting Late summer (most varieties); mid-summer (over-wintering varieties)

SEED

Sowing time Mid-winter (under glass); late summer outside

Sowing distance Sow thinly

Sowing depth 1cm (½in)

Distance between rows 25cm (10in)

Thinning distance 5–10cm (2–4in)

Harvesting Late summer to autumn

VARIETIES

FROM SEED

'Ailsa Craig' An old variety with globe-shaped bulbs and golden skin.

'Hygro F1' A high yielder which stores well. Round-shaped bulb, slim neck and pale-coloured skin.

SETS FOR SPRING PLANTING

'Jet Set' A recent introduction which tastes delicious. Round and smooth skinned. Matures readily.

'Sturon Globe' A large-sized onion with excellent storage qualities.

SETS FOR AUTUMN PLANTING

'Radar' Hardy and early maturing. Mild flavour and a crunchy texture.

'Senshyu' Yellow, flat bulb with a mild flavour.

red onion

brown onion

small brown onions

white onion

SPRING ONIONS (SCALLIONS)

Allium cepa

These slender plants with a white or red shank have a small bulbous base, which can be eaten either raw or cooked. Unlike bulb onions, however, spring onions must be eaten fresh. Sow continuously throughout the growing season and harvest eight weeks after sowing.

SOIL

Like most onions, spring onions prefer a light soil, but they will grow in most soils that are rich in organic matter. Crop rotation helps prevent infection from pests and diseases. They can also be grown in tubs or window boxes in a peat-free potting mix.

ASPECT

Spring onions grow best in an open sunny site, but can tolerate some shade.

SOWING

Sow every three weeks from early spring to late summer for a continuous crop from spring through to early autumn. To harvest an early spring crop, sow 'White Lisbon Winter Hardy' or any other hardy variety in late summer or early autumn. This crop will overwinter and be ready for picking in early spring. Sow crops thinly in rows 1cm (½in) deep with 10cm (4in) between each row.

AFTERCARE

Water in dry conditions and weed during the growing season. Protect overwintering spring onions with a cloche in cold weather.

Above: *Thin out congested rows of spring onions. Larger thinnings can be used to add interest to summer salads.*

Above: *If the spring onions are difficult to lift, use a small fork in order to avoid breaking the stems.*

HARVESTING AND STORAGE

From sowing to harvesting takes around seven to eight weeks. Use a small hand fork to loosen ground before pulling. Thin out the crop when harvesting, taking out every other plant and leaving the remaining plants to grow on.

PESTS AND DISEASES

Onion fly is the main pest, turning the leaves yellow as the bulb is eaten by the maggots, eventually killing the plants. Onion eelworm is another major pest, killing young plants and severely damaging older plants by softening the bulbs. Destroy affected plants. Diseases such as onion white rot and onion downy mildew can also affect the plant. This is not a severe problem, however, as their lifespan is so short. Move to another growing site if symptoms appear.

Left: *Spring onions produce small bulbs that are little more than a slight swelling at the base of the plant.*

CULTIVATION

Sowing time Early spring to early autumn
Sowing distance Thinly, around 1cm (½in)
Sowing depth 1cm (½in)
Distance between rows 10cm (4in)
Thinning distance Sow correctly to avoid thinning, otherwise thin out rows when harvesting
Harvesting 8 weeks after sowing

VARIETIES

'White Lisbon' Excellent variety for successional sowing.
'White Lisbon Winter Hardy' Good for autumn sowing; hardy throughout the winter.

spring onions (scallions)

SHALLOTS

Allium cepa Aggregatum Group

Shallots are very closely related to onions, but they have smaller bulbs with a milder flavour. They usually taste sweeter than onions and the leaves can be used as a substitute for chives in a range of dishes. Shallots will grow clusters of bulbs instead of the single bulb that we are used to with onions. They vary in size and shape. Some varieties are torpedo-shaped, whereas others are rounded, with colours varying from light brown to red.

SOIL

Shallots thrive in a light soil. Plant in ground manured the previous autumn or, if not, add garden compost to the soil before planting. Do not plant in freshly manured soil as this will cause bulb rot.

ASPECT

An open sunny site, but they will tolerate a little shade.

PLANTING

Higher yields are obtained from planting sets rather than by sowing seeds. Seeds will produce a single bulb for harvesting whereas sets will cluster up to produce many bulbs per plant. Planting can begin in early winter in mild areas that have a well-drained soil, but, in general, shallot sets are best planted out in late winter or early spring. Plant sets individually, using a dibber or trowel, in rows 15cm (6in) apart and with 25cm (10in) between the rows. The tip of the set should be just showing above the surface of the soil.

AFTERCARE

After planting look out for any sets that may have been lifted by the frost and replant. Weed throughout the growing season and water the crop during dry spells.

HARVESTING AND STORAGE

Lift the bulbs in mid-summer, when the leaves have turned yellow, and separate the clusters. Leave the shallot bulbs to dry out on a rack of wire netting. They will be ready to store when the leaves have shrivelled. Remove the dead leaves and any dirt on the bulbs. Store the shallots in a cool dry place on trays or in netting bags.

PESTS AND DISEASES

Although they are generally trouble free, shallots can occasionally be attacked by the same pests and diseases as onions.

Left: *This is a healthy young crop of shallots with the bulbs beginning to form. They will soon be ready for harvesting.*

CULTIVATION

Planting time Late winter to early spring
Planting distance 15cm (6in)
Planting depth Tips showing through
Distance between rows 25cm (10in)
Harvesting Mid-summer

Left: *Plant shallots using a dibber (dibble) or a trowel to insert the bulb. Only the tips of the bulbs need to be showing above the surface of the soil.*

Above: *Place harvested shallots on wire racks or trays in order to dry them before putting them into storage.*

Onion fly and onion eelworm attack the leaves and the bulb. Destroy affected crops. Diseases such as neck rot can also be a problem, especially in hot dry summers.

VARIETIES

'Delvad' Stores well and has an excellent flavour.
'Longor' Elegant elongated bulb, with a mild flavour.
'Sante' Large round bulb, high yield.

shallots

LEEKS

Allium porrum

If a range of leek varieties are grown, this traditional winter vegetable can be harvested over a long period of time. The long white shafts have many culinary uses, while the green or blue foliage looks very decorative in the vegetable garden.

SOIL
Grow in a rich fertile soil. Dig thoroughly in autumn, adding well-rotted manure or garden compost. Although leeks prefer moist soil, they perform poorly on waterlogged or compacted soil. Crop rotation discourages diseases such as leek rust.

ASPECT
Require an open sunny position.

SOWING
In early to mid-spring, sow very thinly in rows, 1cm (½in) deep, with 15cm (6in) between the rows. Transplant when the seedlings are 20cm (8in) tall and as thick as a pencil (normally after two to three months). If the soil is dry, water the evening before transplanting to avoid tearing the plants when lifting. Dig out the leeks in batches and transplant out into rows, 30cm (12in) apart, with 15cm (6in) between the

Above: *Earthing up leeks is essential in order to blanch the stems. You can also plant the leeks in trenches and fill these in.*

plants. Use a dibber to make a hole 15cm (6in) deep and drop a single plant into the hole, leaving 5cm (2in) of foliage showing. Do not firm around the base of the plant, but gently water the plant and the soil will settle in around the base.

AFTERCARE
Earth (hill) up the leeks as they grow, moving the soil up around their stems to blanch them. Keep the rows of leeks weed-free and water the plants if dry, especially when they are young.

HARVESTING AND STORAGE
Leeks will be ready to harvest from early autumn to late spring. Lift the leeks with a fork when needed, as they will keep fresh in the soil for many weeks until they are required. Autumn varieties will not survive winter frosts and therefore need to be harvested before mid-winter.

PESTS AND DISEASES
Leek rust can occur in warm dry weather, causing bright orange pustules to form on the leaves. It often disappears when cooler wetter weather arrives in autumn. Destroy plants if they are severely affected.

Leeks can very occasionally be prone to the same pests and diseases as onions. Destroy any affected plants.

Left: *The green-blue architectural foliage of leeks provides a striking decorative effect in the organic vegetable garden.*

Above: *Leeks will stay fresh in the ground for many weeks. Lift when required with a fork as they tend to snap off if pulled.*

CULTIVATION
Sowing time Early to mid-spring
Sowing distance Sow very thinly
Sowing depth 1cm (½in)
Distance between sown rows 15cm (6in)
Transplanting time When seedlings reach 20cm (8in)
Planting depth 15cm (6in)
Distance between planted rows 30cm (12in)
Harvesting Early autumn to late spring

VARIETIES
AUTUMN AND MID-SEASON
'King Richard' Good early cropper.
'The Lyon' Thick white stems, with a mild flavour.

WINTER
'Alvito RZ' Resistant to rust and not prone to bolting.
'Giant Winter' Produces well in extremely cold climates.
'Musselburgh' A reliable and versatile favourite.

leeks

GARLIC

Allium sativum

This aromatic bulb is used to season many cooked dishes. Its strong flavour is more prominent in home-grown crops. Garlic does not produce seed, so it must be grown from bulbs, which are available from garden centres or seed merchants. Choose a variety that suits your soil and climate. Garlic bulbs bought at supermarkets can often fail or produce distorted plants.

SOIL
Garlic grows better in light sandy soils, especially if planting takes place in autumn. It does best in soils manured for the previous crop. Do not plant in freshly manured soil.

ASPECT
Garlic will flourish in an open sunny site.

PLANTING
Plant out in mid- to late autumn if your soil is light and free-draining. Break the bulbs up into individual cloves just before planting. Plant the cloves in rows, using a dibber or trowel, to 5cm (2in) below the soil surface. Leave 7.5–10cm (3–4in) between the cloves and 30cm (12in) between the rows. If your soil is heavy and retains water easily, plant out in early to mid-spring. Starting your individual cloves off in pots under glass or in cold frames three to four weeks before planting will benefit the maturing of the crop.

Above: *Wet springs can rot off newly planted garlic bulbs. This can be overcome by starting off the bulbs under glass.*

Left: *The garlic bulbs form below the surface, unlike those of its close relative, the onion, which mainly form above ground.*

AFTERCARE
Weed throughout the growing season and water in spring during dry periods.

HARVESTING AND STORAGE
The leaves will turn yellow when the bulbs are ready for lifting, usually in mid- to late summer. Remove any soil or long roots before spreading the bulbs out on trays or wire staging to dry out. Remove the leaves as well if you are not intending to plait (braid) them later. Store by threading the bulbs on a string or stiff wire, or by tying or plaiting the leaves together. Hang in a cool, frost-free area such as a garage or shed.

PESTS AND DISEASES
Garlic is generally trouble free, although it may be affected by onion white rot and leek rust.

CULTIVATION
Planting time Mid- to late autumn in light soils, early to mid-spring in heavy soils
Planting distance 7.5–10cm (3–4in)
Planting depth 5cm (2in)
Distance between rows 30cm (12in)
Harvesting Mid- to late summer

Above: *Plant bulbs using a dibber (dibble) or trowel 7.5–10cm (3–4in) apart. Use a line of string to keep the rows straight.*

Right: *Store garlic by threading a stiff piece of wire through the dry neck of the bulbs. You can also tie them together with string.*

VARIETIES
'Long Keeper' Good storage qualities. Often just listed as garlic.
'Printanor' Best planted in early to mid-spring.
'Thermidrome' Suits early planting.

garlic

LEAFY VEGETABLES

SWISS CHARD

Beta vulgaris Cicla Group

Swiss chard is easier to grow than spinach and much less prone to bolting. Swiss chard is also known under the names of chard (rhubarb, red or ruby) and seakale beet. Spinach beet or perpetual spinach is a type of Swiss chard which is categorized within this section.

SOIL

Swiss chard and perpetual spinach require a soil that is fertile and does not dry out easily. Dig in plenty of well-rotted manure or garden compost in the autumn.

ASPECT

Prefer an open site, but will also tolerate light shade.

SOWING

Sow seeds in late spring 10cm (4in) apart in rows 2.5cm (1in) deep. Keep 38cm (15in) between the rows. When the seedlings have germinated, thin them to a distance of 45cm (18in) for Swiss chard and 38cm (15in) for perpetual spinach.

A sowing can be done in late summer to prolong the season. This crop will harvest until the following summer. Provide winter protection throughout the cold months.

AFTERCARE

Water during dry spells and keep the bed weed-free. Mulching with garden compost will help retain moisture in the soil and suppress weed growth. Remove any flower heads if they appear.

Above: *Swiss chard grown in colder areas benefits from protection in the winter months. Cloches or low tunnels are ideal.*

HARVESTING AND STORAGE

Harvest when the leaves are small; if they are picked when they have matured the flavour of the leaf will be bitter. Always pick around the outside of the plant, leaving the inner area to regrow. To avoid damage, cut with a sharp knife. Both crops do not store well and are best eaten fresh.

PESTS AND DISEASES

Swiss chard and perpetual spinach are generally trouble free. Slugs are the only major enemy that they might encounter. Spacing plants correctly discourages the overcrowding which causes the humid conditions in which slugs as well as diseases such as downy mildew thrive.

CULTIVATION

SWISS CHARD AND PERPETUAL SPINACH

Sowing time Late spring

Sowing distance Sow 10cm (4in) between the seeds

Sowing depth 2.5cm (1in)

Distance between rows 38cm (15in)

Thinning distance To 45cm/18in (Swiss chard); to 38cm/15in (perpetual spinach)

Harvesting Late summer to spring

Left: *Many varieties of Swiss chard produce brightly coloured stems that make for a very decorative display in the vegetable plot.*

Below: *Harvest the crop by cutting off the stems when needed. Cut from the outside inwards to allow the inside to regrow.*

VARIETIES

SWISS CHARD

Often simply listed as Swiss chard.

'Bright Lights' Very ornamental containing a mixture of red, orange, cream, pink and yellow stems.

'Charlotte' This has an unusual combination of purple leaves and red stems.

'Fordhook Giant' A very attractive variety with large green leaves and white stems.

Perpetual spinach is normally listed simply as Perpetual Spinach or Leaf Beet.

Swiss chard

red-leaved Swiss chard

KALE

Brassica oleracea Acephala Group

Kale is one of the hardiest vegetables and can withstand wet and poor soil conditions. Coupled with the fact that kale does not have the same problems with pests as cabbages, for example, it is surprising that more people do not grow this delicious winter green. This may be due to the fact that kale has a strong flavour and a bitter taste if it is not cooked properly. Try one of the new cultivars and harvest the young succulent leaves. Many varieties of kale are grown solely for ornamental purposes.

Above: *The foliage of curly kale has a wonderfully textural effect in the organic vegetable garden.*

SOIL

Kale thrives on fertile well-drained soil and will tolerate poorer soils that other brassicas, such as cabbages and cauliflowers, will not. Dig the soil in autumn, incorporating some well-rotted manure or garden compost. Kale does not grow well in acidic conditions, so you will need to lime the soil after cultivation.

ASPECT

Grow in an open sunny situation.

SOWING

Begin sowing kale thinly in rows in late spring in the open ground. The rows should be 1cm (½in) deep with 20cm (8in) between the rows. When the seedlings have germinated, thin to a distance of 5cm (2in). Lift and transplant the seedlings when they are 13cm (5in) high and plant them in their final location. Water the seedlings the night

before lifting in order to make this operation easier. Plant out in rows, with 45–60cm (18–24in) between the plants, depending on the variety grown. Keep a distance of 60cm (24in) between the rows.

AFTERCARE

Weed throughout the growing season and water the kale crop if it is dry, especially in the summer. Mulching with garden compost will help to retain moisture in the soil and also to suppress weed growth.

HARVESTING AND STORAGE

Kale has a long harvesting period, from autumn through to mid-spring. Remove a few leaves from each plant, starting with the crown. This will encourage new succulent side-shoot growth which can be harvested in spring. All growth is best removed with a sharp knife.

PESTS AND DISEASES

Kale is not prone to the worst of the cabbage family pests such as cabbage root fly and club root. However, whitefly, cabbage caterpillar and cabbage aphid can all be troublesome.

Left: *When harvesting kale, select the younger, more succulent leaves. Remove only a few leaves from each plant because this will help the plants to recover and produce more.*

CULTIVATION

Sowing time Late spring
Sowing distance Sow thinly
Sowing depth 1cm (½in)
Distance between sown rows 20cm (8in)
Thinning distance 5cm (2in)
Transplanting time When 13cm (5in) high
Planting distance 45–60cm (18–24in) apart
Distance between planted rows 60cm (24in)
Harvesting Autumn to mid-spring

VARIETIES

'Darkibor F1' Densely curled medium green leaves of uniform habit. Harvest in early winter.
'Nero di Toscano' Extremely dark green leaves which have a blistered appearance. Has a strong peppery taste.

curly kale

CAULIFLOWERS

Brassica oleracea Botrytis Group

The soil requirements and aftercare of cauliflowers are demanding. Failure to provide the right conditions can result in small button-headed plants and low yields. The effort is well rewarded, however, with beautiful white or purple heads (also known as curds) that taste delicious.

SOIL
Cauliflowers need a well-consolidated soil, which is deep, fertile and moisture-retentive, so dig several months before planting, incorporating well-rotted manure or garden compost. Alternatively, plant after a crop of nitrogen-fixing green manure.

ASPECT
Cauliflowers like an open sunny site. It is important to avoid frost pockets if growing winter varieties.

SOWING
Sow the seeds of summer varieties in a cool greenhouse in mid-winter for an early crop. Prick out the seedlings when they are large enough. When they reach 13cm (5in), harden off for a couple of weeks and plant out in cloches in early spring. Plant in rows, 55cm (22in) apart, with 60cm (24in) between the rows. Firm around the plants.

Autumn and winter varieties can be sown outdoors in late spring. Sow thinly in nursery beds before planting in a permanent site. Sow in rows, 1cm (½in) deep, with 20cm (8in) between rows. Thin to 5cm (2in) apart. Transplant seedlings when they are

Above: *Protection from the sun is needed for the developing heads. Snap the outside leaves over the heads.*

Above: *Harvest the firm heads of cauliflower by cutting with a sharp knife just below the first set of leaves.*

13cm (5in) tall and bearing 5 to 6 leaves, watering in well and taking care when lifting them. Plant out between 60–70cm (24–28in) apart, depending on the variety, in rows 70cm (28in) apart. Firm in well.

AFTERCARE
After planting, mulch the crop with garden compost. Water in dry periods and feed occasionally. Cover with netting or wire mesh in order to protect leaves from birds. In winter, tie up or fold the leaves around the head to protect from rain and frost. Protect from sun in the same way. Use felt or plastic collars around the plants to protect from cabbage root fly.

HARVESTING AND STORAGE
Start harvesting when the heads are small so that not all of the crop is harvested at the same time. When the florets separate or turn brown, they are too mature. Hang upside down in a cool dark shed for up to three weeks; mist the heads now and then.

PESTS AND DISEASES
Susceptible to the same pests and diseases as cabbages.

CULTIVATION
SUMMER CAULIFLOWER
Sowing time Mid-spring (outdoors); mid-winter (under glass)
Sowing distance Sow thinly
Sowing depth 1cm (½in)
Distance between rows 20cm (8in)
Thinning distance 5cm (2in)
Transplanting time Spring (seedlings sown outdoors); early spring (seedlings sown under glass)
Planting distance 55cm (22in)
Distance between planted rows 60cm (24in)
Harvesting Late summer (if sown outdoors); mid-summer (if sown under glass)

AUTUMN CAULIFLOWER
Sowing time Late spring
Sowing distance Sow thinly
Sowing depth 1cm (½in)
Distance between rows 20cm (8in)
Thinning distance 5cm (2in)
Transplanting time Early summer
Planting distance 60cm (24in)
Distance between planted rows 70cm (28in)
Harvesting Autumn

WINTER CAULIFLOWER
Sowing time Late spring
Sowing distance Sow thinly
Sowing depth 1cm (½in)
Distance between rows 20cm (8in)
Thinning distance 5cm (2in)
Transplanting time Summer
Planting distance 70cm (28in)
Distance between planted rows 70cm (28in)
Harvesting Late winter to early spring

VARIETIES
SUMMER
'All the Year Round' A heavy yielder, producing heads all through the summer.
'Idol' This mini cauliflower is ideal for growing in a small garden. Good for successional sowing.

AUTUMN
'Stella F1' Suitable for all soil types and less demanding than other varieties. High-quality heads produced.

'Violet Queen' Purple-headed and maturing from late summer to mid-autumn.

WINTER
'Purple Cape' Bears rich purple heads with an excellent flavour. Harvest in early spring.
'Wainfleet' Good frost resistance.

cauliflower

CABBAGES

Brassica oleracea Capitata Group

Cabbages come in a variety of different shapes, colours and sizes. Due to the range of varieties available, it is now possible to harvest this crop fresh all the year round. They are invaluable in winter when there is a limited range of fresh vegetables available. Cabbages can be cooked or eaten raw in salads or coleslaw.

SOIL

Cabbages thrive in firm, well-consolidated soil that is not freshly manured. Therefore, cultivate the land several months prior to planting, adding well-rotted manure or garden compost. Cabbages do best in a soil with a pH of 6.5–7 – if the soil is too acidic, lime after digging and before planting. The fungal disease clubroot thrives in damp acid soil, so improve any drainage problems. Crop rotation helps to prevent an infection.

ASPECT

Likes an open sunny site and will tolerate exposure.

SOWING OUTDOORS

For all varieties start off by sowing cabbage seeds in a nursery bed. Sow thinly in rows 1cm (½in) deep, with 15cm (6in) between rows. After germination thin out the seedlings in the rows to 8cm (3in) apart to prevent the seedlings becoming weak and spindly. Transplant the young cabbage plants to their permanent position when they are 10cm (4in) tall and have grown 5 or 6 leaves. Water the rows the day before lifting. This will aid lifting and minimize root and stem damage. Apply a general organic fertilizer a week prior to planting for all varieties except spring cabbage. Plant in their final rows, 35cm (14in) apart for spring and summer cabbage and 50cm (20in) for autumn and winter cabbage. Leave 60cm (24in) between the rows for spring and summer cabbages and 65–70cm (26–28in) for autumn and winter varieties. Plant firmly for all varieties. Water thoroughly after planting.

SOWING UNDER GLASS

To grow an early crop of summer cabbage sow in seed trays, pots or modules in a cool

Left: *Cabbages are prone to the fungal disease clubroot. You can reduce the risk of this disease occurring by practising crop rotation.*

VARIETIES

SPRING
'Flower of Spring' Large pointed heads that are ready in mid-spring.
'Spring Hero F1' Good-sized heads that are ready in late spring to early summer.
'Wintergreen' Spring greens that are ready from late winter or hearting up in late spring.

SUMMER
'Golden Acre' Has lovely round firm heads. Great for cooking or used raw in coleslaw.
'Minicole F1' A white compact type that stores well.
'Stonehead F1' Shows some resistance to mildew and is not prone to splitting. Also stores well.

AUTUMN
'Cuor di Bue' Light green pointed leaves and with plenty of flavour.
'Hardora F1' A red cabbage which produces a good uniform crop. Excellent storage qualities.

WINTER CABBAGE AND SAVOYS
'Best of All' An early maturing Savoy which can be harvested from early to late autumn.
'Christmas Drumhead' An old blue dwarf variety with flat solid hearts.
'January King' Excellent frost resistance, crisp with a sweet flavour.
'Vertus' A Savoy which can withstand severe frosts.

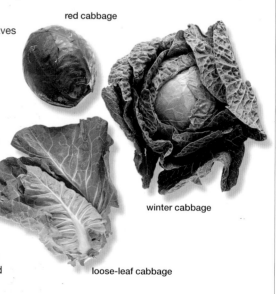

red cabbage

winter cabbage

loose-leaf cabbage

Left: *Blue varieties of cabbage are unusual, but very striking in the vegetable plot.*

Below: *This healthy crop of cabbages is growing well and will soon be ready for harvesting.*

greenhouse in mid-winter. When the seedlings are large enough prick out into individual pots or modules. Grow on and harden off before planting outside under cloches in early spring. Follow the same spacing as for transplants (see opposite). Small plants can also be bought from a nursery or garden centre, but always buy from a reputable source as introduced plants may contain clubroot.

AFTERCARE
Water young plants, especially transplants, until established. Keep the beds weed free. Mulch beds with garden compost to help retain moisture and suppress weed growth. If your vegetable patch is prone to attracting cabbage root fly, apply a felt or plastic collar around the base of the cabbage to stop the fly laying its eggs.

HARVESTING AND STORAGE
Cut the hearts when they have become hard and dig up the stalks. Spring cabbage stalks can be left and cut on top with a knife in a cross shape. This will produce another four smaller cabbages.

PESTS AND DISEASES
Cabbage root fly is one of the major pests. Place a collar of felt or plastic around the base of the plant to stop the fly laying its eggs near the plants.

Caterpillars, mainly from the small white butterfly, can munch their way through a considerable amount of leafage. Pick them off by hand or erect a cage around the crop to keep out the adult butterflies. If you see small holes in the young leaves of cabbages it is almost certainly flea beetles. Slugs and snails will also cause damage to the leaves.

Protect from pigeons by erecting netting or wire mesh cloches. Cabbages are prone to the soil-borne fungal disease clubroot. The roots of the plant begin to swell and the plants become stunted with all growth severely affected. Destroy any infected plants.

CULTIVATION
SPRING CABBAGE
Sowing time Late summer
Sowing distance Sow thinly
Sowing depth 1cm (½in)
Distance between sown rows 15cm (6in)
Thinning distance 8cm (3in)
Transplanting time When 10cm (4in) tall
Planting distance 35cm (14in)
Distance between planted rows 60cm (24in)
Harvesting Spring

SUMMER CABBAGE
Sowing time Early to mid-spring
Sowing distance Sow thinly
Sowing depth 1cm (½in)
Distance between sown rows 15cm (6in)
Thinning distance 8cm (3in)
Transplanting time When 10cm (4in) tall
Planting distance 35cm (14in)
Distance between planted rows 60cm (24in)
Harvesting Mid-summer onwards

AUTUMN CABBAGE
Sowing time Late spring
Sowing distance Sow thinly
Sowing depth 1cm (½in)
Distance between sown rows 15cm (6in)
Thinning distance 8cm (3in)
Transplanting time When 10cm (4in) tall
Planting distance 50cm (20in)
Distance between planted rows 65–70cm (26–28in)
Harvesting Autumn

WINTER CABBAGE
Sowing time Late spring
Sowing distance Sow thinly
Sowing depth 1cm (½in)
Distance between sown rows 15cm (6in)
Thinning distance 8cm (3in)
Transplanting time When 10cm (4in) tall
Planting distance 50cm (20in)
Distance between planted rows 65–70cm (26–28in)
Harvesting Winter

Left: *Protect young cabbage seedlings from cabbage root fly by placing a felt or plastic collar around the base of the plant.*

BROCCOLI

Brassica oleracea Cymosa Group

Broccoli is also known as purple sprouting broccoli or sprouting broccoli and is closely related to calabrese. The two can be easily confused because calabrese, which has green heads, is often sold in the supermarkets under the name of broccoli. As the common name suggests, most varieties of broccoli have purple heads, but you can also grow varieties with creamy white heads that look rather like small cauliflowers. The harvesting of broccoli fills a period in which there are very few other vegetables maturing.

SOIL

Manure the soil in autumn, as rich soil is required for good growth. Apply a general organic fertilizer before sowing or alternatively sow a nitrogen-fixing green manure as the previous crop. Broccoli requires a pH of 6.5–7. Lime if necessary to bring the pH up to the recommended level.

ASPECT

Broccoli requires an open sunny position free from strong winds.

Above: *Harvest the shoots of broccoli when they have begun to bud up and before they have come into flower.*

SOWING

During spring sow seeds thinly in rows to a depth of 1cm (½in) with 15cm (6in) between the rows. After germination, thin to 5cm (2in) apart within the rows. When the plants reach 13cm (5in) high, lift them and transplant to their final location. Water the young plants the day before transplanting to soften up the soil which will make them easier to move. Plant out in rows 60cm (24in) apart with 75cm (30in) between the rows. Plant deeply (with the first leaves sitting on the soil surface) to discourage cabbage root fly and to help stabilize the plant. Firm in well around the base of the plants, again to help stabilize the transplants and to remove any air pockets.

For an early crop, sow broccoli in seed trays or modules under cover from mid- to late spring. Harden off for two weeks in a cold frame before planting out.

AFTERCARE

Keep well watered during dry periods to allow healthy growth throughout the growing season. Mulching the rows with garden compost will help the soil retain moisture and keep weeds in check. Weed the rows throughout the season. Use crop covers of fleece to protect the plants from

Left: *Purple sprouting broccoli is one of the most colourful and decorative of vegetables for the kitchen garden.*

cabbage root fly in the early stages or protect the plants individually by putting a cabbage root fly mat around each one.

HARVESTING AND STORAGE

Start harvesting in late winter and continue through to mid-spring, depending on the varieties grown. Harvest the shoots before they flower. Cut the shoots when they have begun to bud up and are 15cm (6in) long. Cut the shoots from all around the plant; regular cutting encourages new shoots. Pick off any flowering shoots – if they are left on, the plant will become exhausted and cease to produce new shoots for picking.

PESTS AND DISEASES

Broccoli is prone to the same pests and diseases as cabbages.

BRUSSELS SPROUTS

Brassica oleracea Gemmifera Group

This hardy vegetable is delicious if cooked correctly. Try growing some of the tasty new F1 hybrids, which freeze very well. If a range of varieties is grown, harvesting can begin in late summer and finish in early spring.

SOIL

Dig the ground and incorporate well-rotted manure or garden compost in autumn. Brussels sprouts do not grow well in acidic soil conditions, so add lime if necessary to bring the pH up to 6.5–7.

ASPECT

Brussels sprouts thrive in an open sunny position that is protected from strong winds.

SOWING

Sow outside in a nursery bed from early to mid-spring. Start by sowing the early varieties and successively sow mid-season and late varieties in turn. Sow thinly in rows 1cm (½in) deep with 15cm (6in) between rows. After germination, thin out the seedlings to 8cm (3in) apart. Transplant when the seedlings are 13cm (5in) high, watering the previous evening to make lifting easier. Plant in rows, 75cm (30in) apart, with 75cm (30in) between the rows. Firm well to remove any air pockets. You

Below: *Many gardeners believe that Brussels sprouts are best harvested after the first frost because this improves the flavour.*

can intercrop between the rows at this early stage. For late-summer picking start the sowing off under glass in late winter. Harden off and plant outside when the young plants are 13cm (5in) high. Use cloches to protect the early stages of growth.

AFTERCARE

Use wire-mesh cloches to deter pigeons. Weed throughout the growing season and water in dry periods. Apply a foliar feed during the summer. Stake any plants if needed and, as early autumn approaches, draw up the soil around the stems to steady the plants against wind. Apply felt or plastic collars around the base of the plants to prevent cabbage root fly from laying its eggs.

Left: *As these Brussels sprouts develop, the bottom leaves will turn yellow. Remove these as they do so.*

HARVESTING AND STORAGE

Start harvesting from the bottom of the plant, picking the sprouts when they are still tight, after the first frosts as this improves flavour. Crop only a few from each plant. Every time the crop is harvested work further up the stem. When all the sprouts have been harvested, cut off the top of the plant and cook as a cabbage.

PESTS AND DISEASES

Prone to the same problems as cabbages. The main problem is clubroot, a soil-borne fungal disease. Destroy infected plants. Small white butterfly caterpillar and aphids may also affect the crop. Remove caterpillars by hand and spray aphids with an insecticidal soap.

VARIETIES
'Braveheart F1' One of the sweetest flavoured sprouts. Matures in early winter to early spring.
'Oliver F1' An extremely early variety, cropping from late summer if sown under glass. Produces large sprouts.
'Trafalgar F1' This will provide sweet sprouts in early winter. It has a good root system.

Brussels sprouts

CALABRESE (ITALIAN SPROUTING BROCCOLI)

Brassica oleracea Italica Group

There is often confusion over the difference between broccoli and calabrese. This occurs because the green spearheads of calabrese are misleadingly sold under the name of broccoli in supermarkets. Calabrese normally has green-headed spears, whereas broccoli has purple or white. Calabrese has a taste similar to asparagus and a succulent texture when it is steamed, rather than boiled.

SOIL

Calabrese grows well in a firm rich soil, which has been well manured in the autumn or for a previous crop. They do not mature well in poor soil.

ASPECT

Calabrese thrives best in a sunny location that is sheltered from wind.

SOWING

Calabrese does not transplant well, so sowing directly in rows outside is the best method of growing. Position seeds in groups of two or three in drills 30cm (12in) apart. Rows are best positioned 30cm (12in) apart. After germination, select the strongest seedling and thin out the others.

Above: *Calabrese (Italian sprouting broccoli) does not transplant particularly well and so it is best to sow the seed in situ and then thin the seedlings.*

AFTERCARE

The young growth of calabrese is susceptible to "pecking" by pigeons and other birds. Protect the crop by using netting or other barrier methods. Keep the crop well watered throughout the summer. Apply a mulch of garden compost during the growing season in order to help conserve moisture. Regular weeding will also help to do this. Plants that are grown for harvesting towards the end of the season may require staking to stabilize them from autumn winds.

HARVESTING AND STORAGE

Harvest from late summer to mid-autumn depending on variety. Cut the heads (spears) and side shoots while the flower buds are closed. Once the flowers have opened the heads become woody and unpalatable and the production of new ones will cease. Cut the central flower head first to promote the growth of side shoots. Always spread harvesting of the crop, never completely stripping a plant. Cutting of a plant may continue under favourable conditions for up to six weeks.

Left: *Harvest calabrese from late summer to early autumn. Cutting the central flower head first promotes the growth of side shoots.*

PESTS AND DISEASES

Calabrese is prone to the same pests and diseases as cabbages.

CULTIVATION

Sowing time Successional sowing from mid- to early summer

Sowing distance Sow 30cm (12in) apart in groups of two to three. Thin to strongest plant later

Sowing depth 1cm (½in)

Distance between rows 30cm (12in)

Harvesting Late summer to mid-autumn

VARIETIES

CALABRESE (ITALIAN SPROUTING BROCCOLI)
'Corvet' Matures 60 days after planting out. Good large heads that produce well after cutting.

'Express Corona' Produces a succession of spears after the main head is cut. Quick to mature.

'Green Comet' A good early cropper with large heads. Little spear production after the main head is cut.

'Green Sprouting' Spears are ready for harvesting in mid-summer; good flavour.

'Italian Sprouting' An excellent flavour with a long cropping season.

ROMANESCO (ROMAN BROCCOLI)
'Romanesco' A large headed variety that is yellow-green in colour. A good substitute for cauliflower.

calabrese (Italian sprouting broccoli)

CHINESE CABBAGE

Brassica rapa var. *pekinensis*

Although this vegetable has been grown in Asia since the 5th century, it is relatively new elsewhere, having arrived in Europe in the 20th century. With its tall erect habit and slender leaves, Chinese cabbage could easily be mistaken for cos (romaine) lettuce. It has a mild flavour and can either be cooked, stir-fried or eaten raw as a salad leaf.

SOIL

Chinese cabbage prefers a fertile soil that retains moisture. Dig in plenty of well-rotted manure or garden compost in the autumn as it performs poorly on denuded soils.

ASPECT

Likes an open position and will tolerate a little shade in summer.

SOWING

It is best to sow in situ because they do not transplant well. Sow in rows 1cm (½in) deep with 10cm (4in) between the seeds and 25cm (10in) between the rows. Once large enough, thin out seedlings to 30cm (12in) apart. If starting off inside, sow into modules or small pots to avoid disturbance during transplanting.

AFTERCARE

Water liberally in dry conditions. Mulch with garden compost to help retain moisture and suppress weed growth.

HARVESTING AND STORAGE

Chinese cabbage is quick growing, maturing 7–10 weeks after sowing. Cut the heads off and leave the stump in the ground to sprout new leaves. Chinese cabbage needs to be eaten fresh.

PESTS AND DISEASES

Older varieties can be prone to bolting; there are a number of varieties on the market that are more resistant to this problem. Slugs, snails and cabbage caterpillars can be a problem. Although Chinese cabbage can be prone to other cabbage pests and diseases, they are not a major problem.

Below: *This young crop of Chinese cabbage is flourishing. The variety is 'Green Rocket F1'.*

CULTIVATION
Sowing time Early to mid-summer
Sowing distance 10cm (4in)
Sowing depth 1cm (½in)
Distance between rows 25cm (10in)
Thinning distance 30cm (12in)
Harvesting Late summer to late autumn

Left: *Chinese cabbage grows very quickly and is ready to harvest in just seven to ten weeks after sowing. Remove the heads and leave the stump in the ground to sprout new leaves. If successional sowing is practised, harvesting can take place until late autumn.*

Above: *The yellow flowers of this Chinese cabbage look very striking against the dark green leaves.*

VARIETIES
'Kasumi' Has a loose habit with extremely good resistance to bolting.
'Jade Pagoda' Extremely tall and thin heads.
'Tip Top' Shows resistance to bolting.

Chinese cabbage

CHICORY

Cichorium intybus

Chicory has a bitter taste that you either love or hate. It is split into three main types: witloof (Belgian chicory), sugarloaf and red chicory (radicchio). Witloof is the traditional forcing type that produces tight leafy heads called chicons. These are produced in winter when the roots are lifted and blanched. Sugarloaf looks rather like a cos (romaine) lettuce, with its large outer leaves encompassing the inner leaves, therefore blanching naturally. Red chicory is self-blanching, but can be forced to produce red and white leaves. They are all a welcome addition to the winter salad bowl.

SOIL

Chicory will grow in most fertile soils. Manure or incorporate garden compost the previous autumn.

ASPECT

Thrives in an open sunny position.

SOWING

Start to sow chicory from spring through to mid-summer, depending on the type grown. Sow thinly in rows to a depth of 1cm (½in). Keep a distance of 30cm (12in) between the rows. Thin to a distance of 15–30cm (6–12in), depending on the variety. For later sowing protect the crop with a cloche.

FORCING CHICORY

To blanch chicory, cut off the leaves in late autumn to just above the level of the soil. Cover the stump with 15cm (6in) of a

Above: *Red chicory (radicchio) does not need the same care as Belgian or witloof chicory. This variety is 'Alouette'.*

mixture of compost and grit. The leaves will grow in the darkness under the soil, becoming blanched. Alternatively, lift the chicory roots and plant five in a large pot of free-draining potting mix so the cut tips are just showing. Cut the roots so they fit into the pot. Cover with a pot or a bucket and place inside in a warm dark place. The chicon will be ready to harvest in 2–3 weeks. Cut and re-start the process.

AFTERCARE

Water throughout dry periods and weed during the growing season.

HARVESTING AND STORAGE

Witloof forcing type They will be ready to cut 3–4 weeks after the start of the forcing process. Cut the chicons just above the

Below: *Chicory should be sown in rows from spring to mid-summer. Allow 30cm (12in) between the rows.*

crown, when the tips of the plants start to show through the potting mix. Leave the roots in, water the compost and a smaller secondary crop may be harvested.
Sugar and red chicory – non-forcing type Cut the chicons when they are 15cm (6in) long. The stumps may shoot again.

PESTS AND DISEASES

Generally trouble free, although slugs can be a problem in mild, damp weather. Do not plant too close together to allow for maximum air movement. This reduces hot moist conditions that slugs thrive in.

CULTIVATION

Sowing time Spring to mid-summer
Sowing distance Thinly
Sowing depth 1cm (½in)
Distance between rows 30cm (12in)
Thinning distance 15–30cm (6–12in)
Harvesting Autumn into winter

VARIETIES

WITLOOF
'Brussels Witloof' Good for winter forcing.
'Normanto' No soil layer needed when forcing.

SUGARLOAF
'Crystal head' A modern variety which has improved hardiness.
'Sugarloaf' Sweeter than other varieties. Good drought resistance but will only tolerate mild frosts.

RED CHICORY
'Pallar Rossa' Good taste. Green leaves turn dark red. Needs winter protection.
'Rossa di Treviso' Deep red leaves and is non-hearting. Becomes pink and white when it is blanched.

chicory

LETTUCE

Latuca sativa

There are many different types of lettuce to choose from now – cos (romaine), butterhead, crisphead and loose-leaf. These different types come in various shapes, sizes and colours, and are often used in the ornamental garden. With careful planning, it is possible to crop lettuce nearly all the year round, with the help of a cloche or two.

SOIL

A good quantity of organic matter is needed in the soil, which will help retain moisture. Dig plenty of well-rotted manure or garden compost into the soil in the autumn. Lettuce does not grow well on acidic soil, so lime if necessary after digging.

ASPECT

Lettuce likes an open sunny position, but will welcome partial shade if grown in the heat of the summer.

SOWING

EARLY CROP For early crops start by sowing under glass in trays or modules in late winter to early spring. Plant these under cloches to protect against frost.
MAINCROP Start sowing outside from early spring onwards. Sow in rows 1cm (½in) deep with 30cm (12in) between the rows. Thin to 15–30cm (6–12in) apart, depending on the variety grown. Thinnings can be used as transplants for other rows, although this is not usually successful during the hot summer months due to excessive heat.
LATE CROP Late-summer sowings will mature from autumn and early winter. Provide protection for these crops by covering with cloches in mid-autumn. Selected varieties will overwinter under cloches or can be grown under glass.

AFTERCARE

Planted areas need to be weeded throughout the growing season. Keep the crop well watered. It is better to do this in the morning rather than in the evening. The plants will use up the water during the day and the planted area will not be damp in the evening. This will discourage slugs and cause less fungal disease. If slugs are a problem, protect young plants with plastic bottle cloches until well established.

Above: *Many varieties of lettuce are extremely decorative and can be planted out to enhance decorative borders.*

HARVESTING AND STORAGE

HEARTED LETTUCE This is ready for cutting when the heart is firm. If left long after this, they are likely to bolt.
LOOSELEAF Pick leaves as needed or cut the whole plant.

PESTS AND DISEASES

Slugs relish lush green vegetation and lettuce is no exception. If slugs are a severe

Above: *A hearted lettuce is ready for harvesting when the heart (middle) feels firm. If left longer the plant is likely to bolt.*

problem, grow on in modules before planting out, as they are less likely to severely damage established plants. Aphid attacks are common too. Other pest attacks can come from cutworms and root aphids. If the lettuces are planted too close together or are overwatered, fungal diseases such as downy mildew and grey mould may occur. Careful planting and watering can alleviate much of this.

> **CULTIVATION**
> **Sowing time** Late winter (under glass) to early spring onwards
> **Sowing distance** Thinly
> **Sowing depth** 1cm (½in)
> **Distance between rows** 30cm (12in)
> **Thinning distance** 15–30cm (6–12in)
> **Harvesting** Early summer onwards

VARIETIES

COS
'Little Gem' Extremely quick maturing. A compact little plant with a sweet flavour.
'Winter Density' Sweet variety which is excellent for overwintering to crop in spring.

BUTTERHEAD
'Avondefiance' Resistant to root aphid and mildew, and slow to bolt.
'Buttercrunch' Dark green in colour with a compact habit.

CRISPHEAD
'Floreal RZ' A firm heart with bubbled leaves. Resistant to bolting and tipburn as well as mildew and root aphid.
'Roxette RZ' An iceberg with a superior flavour. Fast growing, with a solid heart.

LOOSE-LEAF
'Malibu RZ' A vigorous red-leaved lettuce which is resistant to mildew. Uniform in habit.
'Salad Bowl' Green leaves with serrated edges. Harvest for a long period.

hearted lettuce

iceberg lettuce

loose-leaf lettuce

cut-and-come-again lettuce

SPINACH

Spinacia oleracea

Spinach is a close relative of the beetroot and not the lettuce as might first appear. This crop contains an extremely high iron content, similar to that found in peas. It is a relatively hard crop to grow because it requires a high content of organic matter in the soil and needs copious amounts of water throughout the summer. If the conditions are not ideal, the plants tend to bolt and the crop will be lost. Spinach tastes delicious steamed with fresh crushed garlic or when used in quiches or egg florentine.

SOIL

Incorporate plenty of garden compost or well-rotted manure in the autumn. This will aid moisture retention in the soil during the following summer, which is a must for healthy growth.

ASPECT

Spinach is best grown in light shade in summer, making it a good choice for intercropping. This also reduces the chance of the crop running to seed. Spinach will grow just as well in an open sunny site if the soil remains moist and the area is not too hot.

Above: *This well-maintained vegetable plot includes a thriving crop of spinach. Spinach needs large amounts of water in summer.*

Above: *Spinach is prone to bolting, so choose resistant varieties or site summer crops in light shade to reduce the risk.*

SOWING

Start by sowing in early spring and successional sow until late spring. Sow thinly in rows to a depth of 1cm (½in), with 30cm (12in) between the rows. Apply a general organic fertilizer prior to sowing. When the seedlings are large enough, thin them to 15cm (6in) apart. They will be ready to harvest in early to late summer.

A crop can be sown in late summer or early autumn. Cover with cloches for protection during the winter. This crop can be harvested over winter and spring.

AFTERCARE

Water throughout dry periods. Weed throughout the growing period. Mulch with garden compost to help retain moisture.

HARVESTING AND STORAGE

Start by harvesting the outer leaves when they have reached a reasonable size; it is possible to remove half of the foliage at any one time. Pick more sparingly with winter varieties. Cut and harvest continually to promote new growth.

PESTS AND DISEASES

The main problem is bolting. This is when the plant grows quickly and starts to flower and set seed, making the crop inedible. This condition is encouraged by hot, dry weather. Site the crop carefully before sowing and choose less prone varieties. Spinach is susceptible to downy mildew, but there are plenty of resistant varieties. Spinach blight can also affect the crop. In both cases destroy infected material.

Above: *When harvesting select young fresh outer leaves. Do not remove more than half the foliage or this will weaken the plant.*

CULTIVATION

Sowing time Successional sow from early spring to late spring
Sowing distance Thinly
Sowing depth 1cm (½in)
Thinning distance 15cm (6in)
Distance between rows 30cm (12in)
Harvesting Early to late summer

VARIETIES

'Avanti RZ' An early maturing variety, suitable for greenhouse production or summer sowings outside. Resistant to powdery mildew.
'Giant Winter' Very hardy and ideal as a winter crop.
'Medinia' A good vigorous summer variety which is slow to bolt and resistant to mildew. A good all-rounder.

spinach

SALAD LEAVES

As salad has become more popular in recent years, alternatives to lettuce are becoming more widely grown. Crops such as endive (*Chichorium endivia*), rocket (arugula; *Eruca vesicaria*) and lamb's lettuce (mache; *Valerianella locusta*) are all delicious salad leaves. Rocket is particularly worth growing as it has a rich spicy flavour. Nowadays many different leaves can be included in one salad bowl, therefore it is not unusual to choose all of the above when preparing a salad. Rocket and lamb's lettuce are mainly grown for winter use when other salad crops are scarce, but can also be grown in the summer.

SOIL
Salad leaves thrive in moisture-retentive soil.

ASPECT
All grow best in cool conditions, so partial shade in summer is ideal. Bolting can occur if the plants get too hot. They are ideal for intercropping.

SOWING
Sow rocket and lamb's lettuce in late summer. Rocket can also be sown through to early autumn. Sow thinly in rows 1cm (½in) deep with 30cm (12in) between the rows. Thin the seedlings when large enough to 15cm (6in) apart for rocket and 10cm (4in) apart for lamb's lettuce. Early sowings can take place for both crops in spring. These will be ready to harvest in summer.

Endives can be sown from spring until late summer. Sow thinly in rows 1cm (½in) deep with 38cm (15in) between the rows. Once the seedlings have germinated, thin out to a distance of 30–35cm (12–14in), depending on the variety. Harvest in summer to winter.

AFTERCARE
Cover with cloches in late autumn or early winter. Water liberally in dry weather. Mulching with garden compost will help to conserve soil moisture as well as suppress weed growth.

HARVESTING AND STORAGE
Individual leaves can be cut off as required. Endives will re-sprout from cut stalks. All

Above: *Broad-leaved endives are more tolerant of cold conditions than the curly-leaved varieties.*

salad leaves need to be eaten fresh as they do not store or freeze.

PESTS AND DISEASES
Generally trouble free, although rocket may occasionally be attacked by flea beetles. Slugs and snails may pose a problem for all types of salad leaves.

Right: *Curly-leaved endive can be used in salads or cooked. Unblanched leaves like these are more bitter than blanched ones.*

CULTIVATION

ROCKET AND LAMB'S LETTUCE
Sowing time Spring (early sowing); late summer to early autumn (later sowings)
Sowing distance Thinly
Sowing depth 1cm (½in)
Distance between rows 30cm (12in)
Thinning distance 10–15cm (4–6in)
Harvesting Summer to winter

ENDIVE
Sowing time Spring to late summer
Sowing distance Thinly
Sowing depth 1cm (½in)
Distance between rows 38cm (15in)
Thinning distance 30–35cm (12–14in)
Harvesting Summer to winter

VARIETIES

ENDIVE
'Monaco RZ' A curly-leaved type, with a blanched heart and large green outer leaves.
'Stratego' A broad-leaved type. Compact, slow to bolt and resistant to tip burning.

ROCKET
More commonly sold under one of its common names, rucola or salad rocket, rather than varieties.

LAMB'S LETTUCE
Sometimes sold under the common name of corn salad.
'Verte de Cambrai' An old French variety with a good flavour.

endives

lamb's lettuce

rocket

ROOT CROPS

BEETROOT (BEETS)

Beta vulgaris

For many of us, the word beetroot conjures up a picture of a small, round, red vegetable pickled in a jar. However, this delicious vegetable comes in a range of colours, such as white, yellow, the commonly grown red and a variety with concentric rings of pink and white. Shapes range from round through cylindrical to tapered, depending on the variety grown. Extremely easy to grow, beetroot can be eaten fresh from early summer to mid-autumn. Pickling excess crops will ensure a supply all year round.

SOIL

Grows in most soil types (except acid soils) and thrives on rich moist soils. Adding organic matter to the soil in autumn or early winter will increase water retention, but is only necessary if none was incorporated the previous year. Never sow or plant in newly manured ground. Cylindrical and tapered varieties keep their shape and mature better in sandy soil.

ASPECT

An open sunny site is preferable for growing beetroot. It thrives in seaside locations

Above: *Harvesting can begin seven weeks after sowing by pulling the smaller beetroot (beets) out. Continue to pull as required.*

due to its tolerance to salt, the wild ancestor of beetroot being native to coastal situations.

SOWING

Sow the seeds in drills 2.5cm (1in) deep with 20cm (8in) between the rows. Sow 8cm (3in) apart. Some thinning may be required as the seedlings begin to develop. Sow from early spring through till early summer, sowing at two-week intervals. Excess cropping and late sowing can be used for pickling. If earlier crops are desired, then these may be sown under cloches.

AFTERCARE

Thin out seedlings if necessary, leaving the healthiest in situ. Keep any thinnings for the compost heap. Keep the crop weed-free, taking care if using a hoe as they are easily damaged. Beetroot needs a moist soil and should be watered every two weeks in dry periods to avoid "hardening" of the crop. Consistency in watering is essential as successive wet and dry conditions will make the roots split. Mulching with compost will help the soil retain moisture.

Left: *Beetroot grows best in light soils. Growing in raised beds allows you to choose the growing medium best suited to the crops.*

CULTIVATION
Sowing time Early spring through to early summer. Successional sow every two weeks
Sowing distance 8cm (3in) and thin out after germination
Sowing depth 2.5cm (1in)
Distance between rows 20cm (8in)
Harvesting Late autumn to early spring

HARVESTING AND STORAGE

The first crop will be ready to pick about six to seven weeks after sowing. Pull as required, twisting the leaf off rather than cutting. Store autumn-harvested beetroot in boxes, covering the crop with moist peat-substitute or sand. These boxes should then be placed in a cool dry place.

PESTS AND DISEASES

Usually trouble free.

VARIETIES
'Barabietola di Chioggia' Rosy pink skin and white flesh with concentric pink circles.
'Carillon' A cylindrical, long red variety with resistance to bolting.
'Detriot Globe' Good uniform shape and flesh free from rings. Large roots are good for exhibiting.
'Egyptian Turnip Rooted' Early and quick-growing.
'Libero' Good resistance to bolting; fast growing with high yields.

purple beetroot

white beetroot

golden beetroot

SWEDES (RUTABAGAS OR YELLOW TURNIPS)
Brassica napus

Swedes are very similar to turnips, but their skin is normally yellow and they have a sweeter, milder flavour. Although this vegetable is grouped within root crops, it is botanically a member of the cabbage family. Crop rotation must therefore be planned carefully, grouping swedes in with cabbages because they suffer from the same pests and diseases.

SOIL
Although they will grow on heavy soils, swedes prefer a light soil that contains plenty of organic matter. Dig in the autumn, incorporating plenty of well-rotted manure or garden compost. Adding organic matter increases the moisture retention of the soil in summer, which is essential for good growth.

ASPECT
Thrive in an open sunny location.

SOWING
In late spring to early summer sow thinly in rows 1cm (½in) deep. Keep the rows 40cm (16in) apart. Once the seedlings are large enough, thin out to 25cm (10in) apart.

AFTERCARE
Swedes must be well watered throughout the summer months, otherwise they will turn woody and split. Mulch rows to retain moisture in dry periods. Keep well weeded throughout.

HARVESTING AND STORAGE
Harvest from autumn into the winter months. Lift when they are large enough to use – you do not need to wait until they are maximum size. The crop can stay in the soil until spring, lifting only when required. Alternatively, lift and cut off the leaves and store in boxes filled with dry sand. Keep in a cool shed or garage.

PESTS AND DISEASES
Prone to the same problems as cabbages. Flea beetles are a frequent pest. To help prevent infestations, prepare the soil well by incorporating plenty of organic matter. Watering in dry periods and mulching will also help. Mildew and clubroot are another problem. Resistant or tolerant cultivars are available.

Above: *Swedes are usually round, but can vary in shape according to the variety and growing conditions.*

CULTIVATION
Sowing time Late spring to early summer
Sowing distance Thinly
Sowing depth 1cm (½in)
Distance between rows 40cm (16in)
Thinning distance 25cm (10in)
Harvesting Autumn onwards

VARIETIES
'Acme Purple Top' Medium-sized roots with a good flavour.
'Joan' Good for early sowings. Has a moderate resistance to clubroot and mildew.
'Marian' A fairly new variety with excellent texture and flavour. Moderately resistant to clubroot and mildew.

swedes

Right: *Swedes can be harvested from autumn onwards. You can leave the crop in the soil until spring, lifting it as required. Cut off the leaves and store in boxes filled with dry sand.*

KOHL RABI

Brassica oleracea Gongylodes Group

This curious vegetable is a member of the cabbage family. It is the swollen stem, found at the base of the plant, that is eaten. Tasting something like a cross between a cabbage and a turnip, kohl rabi can be eaten raw or cooked. Although not widely grown, it has a number of good qualities. It grows very well on shallow soils and performs well in hot dry weather, whereas its culinary rival, the turnip, needs a firm, fertile soil. The green varieties are used for cropping in summer, while the purple types are mainly grown to harvest in autumn and early winter.

Above: *This extremely healthy crop of kohl rabi has been grown in a free-draining soil in an open sunny position.*

Right: *This perfect specimen of kohl rabi has been watered throughout any dry periods to prevent the swollen stem from splitting.*

SOIL
Thrives in light soil conditions, but will grow on heavier soils. Dig the soil in the autumn, incorporating well-rotted manure or garden compost if this has not already been done in the previous autumn.

ASPECT
Grow kohl rabi in an open sunny site.

SOWING
Sow the seeds thinly in rows 1cm (½in) deep. Keep 30cm (12in) between the rows. Start sowing under cloches in late winter and outside in early spring. Successionally sow kohl rabi at three-week intervals until late summer. This will provide a fresh supply of tender globes. Thin out the rows when the seedlings are large enough to 15cm (6in) apart.

AFTERCARE
Weed regularly throughout the growing season, taking great care not to damage the shallow roots if you are using a hoe for weeding. Mulching with garden compost will also help to prevent the germination of any weed seedlings. Watering in dry periods will help to prevent the stems of the kohl rabi from splitting, although they are less likely to split than turnips.

HARVESTING AND STORAGE
Pull kohl rabi from the ground when they are about the size of a tennis ball because they tend to become woody if they are left to grow much bigger. Harvest as and when

required because they do not store well and tend to shrivel. Later crops will keep in the ground until winter. Cut back the leaves and shorten the roots before taking them indoors to prepare.

PESTS AND DISEASES
Kohl rabi is prone to the same pests and diseases as cabbages. Flea beetles are the main problem. Symptoms of an attack include small holes in the leaves and stems during summer. To avoid an attack, do not let the plants dry out and encourage quick seedling growth.

CULTIVATION

Sowing time Late winter (under cloches); early spring to late summer (outdoors)
Sowing distance Thinly
Sowing depth 1cm (½in)
Distance between rows 30cm (12in)
Thinning distance 15cm (6in)
Harvesting Summer through to early winter

VARIETIES

'Azur Star' Purple-blue bulbs with white flesh. A quick-maturing variety.
'F1 Cindy RZ' An early maturing variety which is slow to bolt. Large white bulbs with strong green foliage.
'Green Delicacy' An extremely old variety. Pale green globes with white flesh.
'Green Vienna' Green-skinned with white flesh. Good for early sowings.
'Purple Vienna' Purple-skinned globes with white flesh. Good for late sowings.
'Rowel' Lovely sweet flesh. Tends not to become woody if picked after it becomes the size of a tennis ball.

kohl rabi

TURNIPS

Brassica oleracea Rapifina Group

Turnips are a very easy crop to grow. Like carrots, home-grown turnips are much tastier than shop-bought specimens. Although the root is normally round, cylindrical root shapes are not uncommon in the early varieties. Turnip roots usually have a white skin that is coloured green, purple or yellow at the top. Inside the root, the flesh colour can vary from white to yellow. Group turnips in with cabbages when planning crop rotation as they are closely related and suffer from the same pests and diseases.

SOIL

Turnips thrive in firm, fertile soil that retains moisture. Dig in the autumn and incorporate plenty of well-rotted manure or garden compost to help retain moisture. If the soil is acidic, lime after digging. Practise crop rotation to avoid soil-borne diseases.

ASPECT

Grow best in a sunny position, but can take some degree of shade.

SOWING

For an early crop, start by sowing under cloches in late winter. Sow direct outside from early spring onwards. Sow thinly in rows 1cm (½in) deep, with 25cm (10in) between the rows for early crops. After germination, thin to 15cm (6in) apart. Successional sowing during spring and summer will ensure a steady supply of turnips. For turnips to be harvested in autumn and winter, sow in late summer. Sow to the same depth, but allow for 30cm (12in) between the rows and thin seedlings to 20cm (8in).

Right: Harvest early and summer varieties as soon as they are the size of golf balls for optimum flavour.

Below: Do not allow turnips to turn woody. If lifted when young, the crop will not only taste better but be easy to pull.

AFTERCARE

Regular watering is required, otherwise they run the risk of bolting. Weed throughout the growing season.

HARVESTING AND STORAGE

Pick turnips harvested in summer when they are the size of a golf ball. Varieties for picking in autumn and winter are harvested when required, or lift and store in trays of moist sand and keep in a shed or garage.

PESTS AND DISEASES

Prone to the same pests and diseases as cabbages, mainly flea beetle. Keep watered and prepare soil well to avoid attack. Violet root rot and clubroot are also a problem. Destroy all diseased material. Practise crop rotation to help avoid clubroot.

Left: Turnips belong to the cabbage family and can suffer from clubroot. Practise crop rotation in order to prevent infection.

CULTIVATION

Sowing time Late winter (under cloches); early spring and summer (outside)

Sowing distance Thinly

Sowing depth 1cm (½in)

Distance between rows 25–30cm (10–12in)

Thinning distance 15–20cm (6–8in)

Harvesting Summer to winter

VARIETIES

'Golden Ball' A relatively old variety with excellent storage qualities. Round golden roots with tender flesh.

'Market Cross F1' A quick grower. White roots that have an excellent flavour.

'Snowball' Fast maturing and best eaten small; lovely white skin.

'Veitch Red Globe' Roots are two tone, a red top and white bottom. Quick to mature.

turnips

PARSNIPS

Pastinaca sativa

Parsnips are a good vegetable for the inexperienced gardener as they require very little work and are easy to grow. It is the underground swollen root that is eaten. The root looks similar to a carrot but is creamy white in colour and slightly longer. Parsnips taste great used in stir-fries, mashed up with carrot or as an accompaniment to fish or roast meats.

SOIL

Do not grow on freshly manured ground, but on ground that has already been manured for the previous crop. Ideally, the soil needs to be dug over during the winter and be stone-free to produce good-quality parsnips. Compost from your heap may be added to improve the soil structure.

ASPECT

Parsnips like an open sunny site, but will tolerate light shade.

SOWING

It is essential to sow fresh seed every year. Sow in late winter through to late spring in drills 1cm (½in) deep and space seeds

Above: *It is advisable to sow fresh parsnip seed every year because even one-year-old seed is unlikely to germinate successfully.*

15cm (6in) apart. Alternatively, sow sparingly and thin out at the seedling stage. Rows are spaced 30cm (12in) apart. Germination can be slow, sometimes taking up to three weeks. This allows for intercropping between rows by sowing radish or lettuce.

AFTERCARE

Thin out rows of seedlings (where necessary) to 15cm (6in) apart. Throw thinnings on to your compost heap as they do not transplant easily. Water the crop during dry periods, never allowing the soil to dry out. Carry out regular weeding, taking care not to damage the crowns of the new plants.

HARVESTING AND STORAGE

Start harvesting when the foliage starts to die down in mid-autumn. The best-tasting parsnips are lifted after the first frosts. Lift only when required; the remainder can be left in the ground through to late winter. A certain number may also be lifted and stored in a box of moist sand to ensure supplies throughout the winter.

PESTS AND DISEASES

Generally trouble free, but parsnip canker can affect the crop. Do not plant in freshly manured ground. Instead, sow later or use canker-resistant varieties. Acidic soil conditions can also cause canker. Carrot fly and celery fly may attack parsnips.

Left: *Parsnips can be left in the ground and harvested as they are required. The best-tasting parsnips are lifted after the first frost.*

Above: *Parsnips are hardy plants and so they are best left in the ground until ready for harvesting. Lift with a fork in order to avoid damaging the root.*

CULTIVATION

Sowing time Late winter to late spring
Sowing distance 15cm (6in) or sow sparingly and thin out at seedling stage
Sowing depth 1cm (½in)
Distance between rows 30cm (12in)
Thinning distance 15–20cm (6–8in)
Harvesting Mid-autumn to late winter

VARIETIES

'Avonresister' Resistance to canker.
'Half Long Guernsey' Heavily tapered roots with a sweet flavour.
'Tender & True' Excellent flavour, good resistance to canker.
'White King' A heavy yielding variety with delicious, well-textured roots.

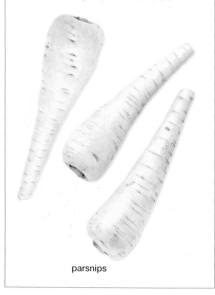

parsnips

RADISHES

Raphanus sativus

This extremely fast-growing vegetable has a wider crop diversity than is commonly known. Along with the familiar round red radish commonly used in salads, there are also varieties with pink, yellow or white roots. Winter varieties can have roots the size of carrots and other types are grown for their pods. Due to their attractive roots, which sit slightly above the soil, they are often grown among decorative plants in the ornamental garden.

SOIL

Radishes will grow in most soils, but thrive in soil that is rich in organic matter and is moisture retentive. Dig in plenty of garden compost before sowing if the ground was not manured for a previous crop.

ASPECT

Thrive in an open sunny site, but will welcome some dappled shade at the height of summer. This makes radishes ideal for intercropping during this period.

SOWING

Summer crops can be started by sowing outside under cloches in late winter and in early spring. Sow thinly in rows 1cm (½in) deep with 15cm (6in) between the rows. Thin to 2.5cm (1in) apart. Successional sowing will prevent a glut at harvest time.

Above: *When harvesting radishes, discard any that have become large or old, as they will be too woody and hot to eat.*

Sow in small rows every two weeks. Sow winter varieties in mid-summer. They are larger than the maincrop varieties, so the rows should be spaced 25cm (10in) apart and the crop thinned to 15cm (6in) apart.

AFTERCARE

Keep weed-free throughout the season and water in dry periods.

HARVESTING AND STORAGE

Pick before they get too old and woody. Select the larger roots first and leave the rest of the crop to grow. Winter cultivars can be left in the soil with a layer of straw

Below: *For small quantities of radishes, it is best to sow short rows every two weeks to obtain a succession of crops.*

over the top for protection. Harvest when required; otherwise lift the radishes and store them in trays of sand until needed.

PESTS AND DISEASES

Radishes are related to cabbages and are prone to the same pests and diseases. Flea beetle and slugs are normally the main problems. If more problematic pests or diseases take hold, destroy plants and grow in an alternative location.

VARIETIES

'**Berosa**' Grown for winter use. Grows up to 15cm (6in) long. Ideal for slicing.

'**Rondeel RZ**' A bright red round radish. Good uniformity.

'**Sirri RZ**' Excellent root colouring with strong foliage. Stores well.

'**Sparkler**' A spring variety that has a red base to the root with a white tip.

radishes

POTATOES

Solanum tuberosum

This native of South America is one of the easiest vegetables to grow. Potatoes are split up into two main groups: earlies and maincrop. Earlies are harvested in summer, offering the welcome taste of new potatoes, whereas maincrop potatoes are harvested later and can be stored for use during the winter.

SOIL

Potatoes thrive on sandy soil that is slightly acidic, but will grow almost as well on nearly every other type of soil. However, they grow best on a fertile soil that is rich in nitrogen. Plant in soil that has had organic matter added in the autumn; they should never be planted on freshly manured ground.

ASPECT

A warm sheltered site is best. Always avoid frost pockets, which can damage the foliage of early varieties emerging from the soil.

PURCHASING SEED POTATOES

Seed potatoes are not actually seeds, but swollen tubers from the potato plant. They can be purchased from mid-winter to mid-spring. It is important to purchase certified seed potatoes, as this will ensure a healthy virus-free stock.

CHITTING

Before planting outdoors, place seed potatoes with the seeds' eyes (the dormant buds on the surface) facing upward on a 2.5cm (1in) layer of potting mix in trays or egg boxes. They should be left indoors in light warm conditions to encourage the

Above: *It is only the tubers of the potato plant that are edible. All other parts such as the leaves and fruits are poisonous.*

sprouting of small shoots. This is called chitting. In six weeks the shoots will have grown to 2.5cm (1in), the ideal length to plant. Chitting is essential for earlies but not necessary for maincrop potatoes, although this can still prove beneficial in colder years.

PLANTING

Planting is normally carried out in trenches 10–15cm (4–6in) deep with 30–40cm (12–16in) between the tubers. Keep 45cm (18in) between the rows for first earlies and 65–75cm (26–30in) for second earlies and maincrop varieties. Always plant the seed potatoes with their "eyes" facing upwards, taking care not to break off the new growth. An alternative to hoeing out the trenches is to plant the potatoes individually (to the same specifications) using a trowel or potato dibber. Once planted and covered with soil, create a small mound above them.

If you cannot face digging over a vegetable bed, why not try the "no-dig bed system"? Cover the soil with well-rotted manure or compost and simply place the seed potatoes on top, 30–40cm (12–16in) apart. Cover the seed potatoes with a 10cm (4in) layer of old straw. Alternatively, if you are gardening in a confined space, try planting the seed potatoes in pots. This

Above: *Before planting out potato tubers, place them in a tray in order to "chit" them. This is essential for early potatoes.*

Above: *Earth up the potatoes in order to increase yields and prevent light reaching the new potatoes. Light will make them turn green and they will be poisonous.*

method can allow people with even the smallest gardens to experience home-grown, pesticide-free new potatoes.

AFTERCARE

PROTECTION FROM FROST

Cover the young growth with straw or fleece if there is any risk of frost.

EARTHING UP

This task is essential if large yields are to be obtained. Earthing up also stops light getting to the new potatoes, which makes them turn green and poisonous. Another

Above: *When harvesting maincrop potatoes, leave them on the surface for an hour or two to let them dry out and to harden the skins.*

benefit of this is that it makes the soil easy to work for crop rotation. Earth up when the foliage is 20cm (8in) tall. Hoe up the earth around the foliage until only a small amount of leaf is still showing at the top. This process is carried out again just before the foliage between the rows joins up.

WATERING

Potatoes need copious amounts of water throughout their growing period in order to develop plenty of good-sized tubers. It is essential to water heavily in the early stages of development. Watering every 10 days during dry periods is a good guide to follow.

HARVESTING AND STORAGE

EARLIES These are ready to lift when the potato plant is flowering – usually towards the end of early summer or the beginning of mid-summer for first earlies, and late summer for second earlies. Harvest the potatoes using a potato fork (with balls on the end of the tines) or a flat-tined fork to reduce damage to the crop.

MAINCROP These are harvested in early autumn, 10–14 days after the withered brown foliage has been removed and put on the compost heap. Lift the potatoes on a warm dry day and leave on the surface for several hours to dry out. Store only perfect potatoes in a sack or in trays in a cool, dark, frost-free place. Diseased potatoes do not store well and must be used at once.

PESTS AND DISEASES

The potato's worst enemy is blight. This is particularly bad in wet summers where the weather is hot and humid. The first sign of

the disease is brown patches on the leaves. These should be cut off to prevent the spores being washed off into the soil to infect the tubers. Choose resistant varieties if possible. Scab disfigures the tuber by cracking and brown discoloration. Water the crop heavily to help overcome the problem and do not grow on ground that has been recently manured. Potatoes are also damaged by diseases such as violet root rot and blackleg. Slugs, eelworms and cutworms are the worst pests, all of them eating and damaging the tubers.

CULTIVATION

FIRST EARLIES
Planting time Early spring
Planting distance 30–40cm (12–16in)
Planting depth 10–15cm (4–6in)
Distance between rows 45cm (18in)
Harvesting Early summer

SECOND EARLIES AND MAINCROP
Planting time Mid- to late spring
Planting distance 30–40cm (12–16in)
Planting depth 10–15cm (4–6in)
Distance between rows 65–75cm (26–30in)
Harvesting Summer onwards

VARIETIES

FIRST EARLIES
'Accent' Attractive yellow skin and flesh, high yielding.
'Premiere' Resistant to blight and high resistance to common scab.
'Red Duke of York' Superb texture and flavour.
'Swift' Resistant to golden eelworm and tolerant to blackleg.

SECOND EARLIES
'Cosmos' Resistant to blight and common scab.
'Kestrel' Great flavour, ideal for baking. Performs well in drought conditions.
'Marfona' Good for baking, stores well.
'Wilja' Good resistance to disease and drought.

MAINCROP
'Cara' Stores well, good blight resistance.
'Désirée' Distinctive flavour and a superb roaster.
'Milva' Good flavour with resistance to blight.
'Valor' Good overall disease resistance together with high eelworm resistance and high resistance to blight.

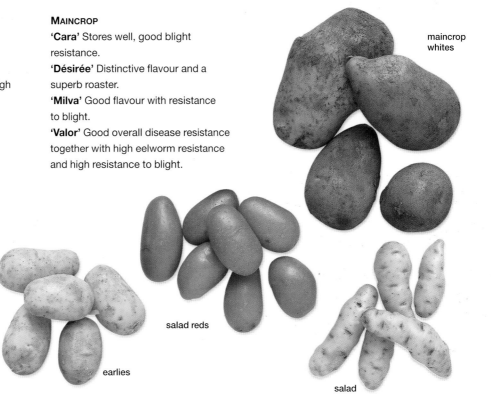

maincrop whites

salad reds

earlies

salad

CARROTS

Daucus carota

If there is a vegetable that tastes incomparably better if it has been grown in your own garden, it must be the carrot. Home-grown carrots have a sweet, juicy flavour compared with the bland, watery taste of those sold in supermarkets. The edible part of the carrot is the root, which is usually orange, although there are also pale yellow and white varieties. Root shapes vary from round to long and tapered. Carrots that are planted within an ornamental area and left in the ground over winter will flower in their second year. The flowers are ideal for attracting beneficial insects into the garden.

SOIL

Although carrots will grow in heavy clay soils, they do best on light sandy soils where the drainage is good and root growth is not impaired. The soil should be free of stones and fresh manure, as both will cause the carrot roots to fork. Do not manure the soil in the season before sowing.

ASPECT

Carrots require an open sunny site.

SOWING

Sow outside from early spring, or under cloches from late winter. Sow thinly in rows 1cm (½in) deep with 15–20cm (6–8in) between the rows. Sow successively until

early summer. If your soil is very heavy, use a crowbar to make holes, fill with a compost-and-grit mix and then sow into these holes. Thin the young seedlings to 5–8cm (2–3in) apart. Try to thin on a still evening to avoid attracting carrot fly. Bury the thinnings in the compost heap or wormery to avoid dispersing the smell.

AFTERCARE

Weed the crop regularly, making sure not to disturb the roots or shoots too much. Mulch the crop to help retain moisture and suppress weed growth. It is important to water during dry periods.

HARVESTING AND STORAGE

Start to harvest from late spring onwards, usually seven to eight weeks after sowing. Lift with a fork, especially when the soil is dry. Maincrop carrots can be left in the ground and harvested when required. In colder areas, cover over with straw until harvesting. Alternatively, carrots can be lifted in mid-autumn. After cleaning the roots and trimming the foliage to 1cm (½in), they can be stored in boxes containing a mixture of dry potting mix and sand. The carrots must not touch each other. These will keep until early spring.

PESTS AND DISEASES

The main pest is carrot root fly which lays its eggs on the plant and can destroy the crop in severe cases. There are several methods to deter the fly from laying eggs. By delaying sowing until early summer, you will miss the first batch of egg laying in late spring. The second batch is in late summer until early

Left: *Plant carrots near onions or chives. This helps mask the smell of the carrots to deter its main pest, the carrot root fly.*

CULTIVATION
Sowing time Early spring (under cloches) and successively to early summer
Sowing distance Very thinly
Sowing depth 1cm (½in)
Distance between rows 15–20cm (6–8in)
Thinning distance 5–8cm (2–3in)
Harvesting Late spring onwards

Left: *You can start harvesting carrots from late spring onwards.*

autumn. Lift your early summer crop before risk of infestation. Another effective method is to erect a barrier of fleece or fine mesh around the crop. Companion planting can also help. Onions, for example, will mask the smell of carrots. Plant four rows to every row of carrots or plant in a mosaic pattern.

VARIETIES

EARLY
'Amsterdam Forcing' Small roots that are ideal for freezing.
'Nantes 2' Matures quickly. Has a lovely sweet flavour.
'Parabel' Small and spherical root that is sweet flavoured.

MAINCROP
'Berlicum' Produces a uniform crop. The roots have good colour and flavour.
'Fly Away F1' Sweet flavour. Bred for carrot fly resistance.
'F1 Magno RZ' Vigorous grower with good colour. Stores well.

carrots

PEAS AND BEANS

RUNNER BEANS

Phaseolus coccineus

These climbing plants are often grown in ornamental gardens for their lovely red flowers and long green pods. They look wonderful growing up decorative supports or arches. New varieties offer flower colours in white or mauve. The production of the pods requires pollination by bees.

SOIL
Runner beans thrive in a deep, rich, moisture-retentive soil, but they will grow in relatively poor soil. Manure the previous autumn.

ASPECT
They like an open, sheltered, sunny position. Do not plant in windy areas as this will make pollination difficult and the support structures for the crop will be prone to blowing over.

SOWING/PLANTING
Runner beans are half hardy and therefore should not be planted or appear above ground until the risk of frost has gone. For an early start, sow the crop under glass in early spring. The beans are best sown individually in pots and then hardened off to be ready to plant out in early summer. Alternatively, sow directly outside in late spring. Before sowing, build a support for the crop. This is traditionally made up of a double row of canes tied at the top. For a more decorative effect, construct a tepee which can be placed in a vegetable garden or ornamental garden. Keep 25cm (10in) between each cane. Plant two seeds 50cm (2in) deep per cane and remove the weaker seedling after

Above: *A larger crop of beans will be produced if picked regularly. Select young pods and discard any old stringy ones.*

Above: *Many gardeners sow three beans at the base of each pole – "one for the crow, one for the slug and one for the kitchen".*

germination. Dwarf varieties are grown in single rows at 15cm (6in) apart and with 45cm (18in) between the rows. Sow direct or grow on under glass for an early start.

AFTERCARE
Keep the soil moist at all times, mulching with garden compost to help the soil to retain moisture. After harvesting leave the roots to rot down in the soil as the root nodules contain a valuable source of nitrogen. Turn in the roots when digging the soil during the autumn.

HARVESTING AND STORAGE
Pick the pods when they have reached 20–30cm (8–12in) in length and before they have become stringy and hard. It is important to pick regularly or the plants will stop flowering. Most plants will continue to flower until the first frosts. The only successful method of storage is to freeze any surplus beans.

PESTS AND DISEASES
One of the commonest problems with runner beans is their failure to set pods. This is often the case in periods of ho[...] weather. Regular watering will help[...]

and pod form[...]

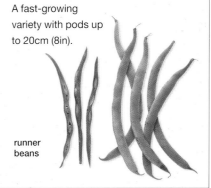

FRENCH (GREEN) BEANS

Phaseolus vulgaris

French beans are split into two distinct categories: dwarf and climbing. The dwarf varieties are by far the most popular as they do not take up much room. Both types are frost tender and need to be sown or planted out after any risk of frost has gone. Nowadays, there are many good varieties, which offer colourful pods in yellows and purples to liven up the vegetable garden.

SOIL
They thrive in fertile, free-draining soil that has preferably been manured in the previous autumn.

ASPECT
French beans require an open sunny site.

SOWING
French beans can be sown early under glass in pots in late spring, but they are best sown outdoors in early summer in a single or double row 4cm (1½in) deep with 8cm (3in) between the seeds. Place the rows 45cm (18in) apart. Plant outside in early summer when the threat of frost has passed. Treat climbing varieties in the same way as non-dwarf runner beans.

Below: *The pods of French beans are now found in a variety of colours. This purple pod variety is often grown in decorative borders.*

Above: *Leave the pods that you want to treat as haricot (navy) beans until the pods have swollen and turned yellow.*

AFTERCARE
Water regularly when the crop is in flower. Keep the plot weed-free throughout the growing season.

HARVESTING AND STORAGE
Harvest when the seeds are still immature on the plant. Pick regularly to encourage new pods. The beans are best eaten fresh,

Above: *Harvesting can begin seven to eight weeks after sowing. It is best to pick while the seeds are still immature.*

but they can be frozen. French beans can also be dried and stored in airtight jars and named haricot (navy) beans.

PESTS AND DISEASES
Generally trouble free. Blackfly and fungal diseases can cause problems. Slugs and snails are the main problem, especially at the seedling stage.

CULTIVATION
Sowing time Late spring (under glass); early summer (outdoors)
Sowing/planting distance 8cm/3in (dwarf); 25cm/10in (climbing)
Sowing depth 4cm (1½in)
Distance between rows 45cm/18in (dwarf); 90cm/3ft (climbing)
Harvesting Late summer until first frosts

VARIETIES
CLIMBING
'Blue Lake' A heavy-yielding variety that is suitable for freezing. The stringless pods contain small white beans.
'Farba RZ' Pods are round and stringless, growing up to 12cm (5in) long.
'Mantra RZ' A good cropper that produces uniform pods 20cm (8in) long. This variety is resistant to common bean mosaic virus.

DWARF
'Annabel' A compact variety that is good for growing in pots or grow bags. A heavy cropper of thin stringless pods.
'The Prince' An early variety. The dwarf-growing flat pod is often used for exhibiting.

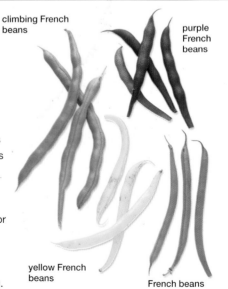

climbing French beans

purple French beans

yellow French beans

French beans

PEAS

Pisum sativum

There is nothing like the taste of freshly picked peas. This is because the moment that a pea is picked its natural sugars start to break down into starch, which affects the flavour. With careful planning and by using a range of varieties, peas can be freshly harvested from late spring until late autumn.

SOIL

Grow in a fertile moisture-retentive soil. Dig to a good depth in autumn and incorporate well-rotted manure or garden compost. Do not grow in soil that might get waterlogged, as this will cause basal rotting to the plants.

ASPECT

Peas thrive in an open sunny site, but will withstand light shade.

SOWING

Varieties are categorized as first earlies, which are smooth-skinned, and second earlies and maincrop, which have wrinkled skins. Sow first earlies outside in mid- to late autumn and overwinter the crop under cloches. For a slightly later crop, sow second earlies in late winter to early spring, starting them off under cloches to protect

Above: *Choose old seed varieties if you wish to harvest the crop at intervals, as many modern varieties mature at the same time.*

Above: *Wire netting can support smaller pea varieties, whereas the more decorative hazel sticks are used for larger ones.*

against frost. Maincrop varieties are sown at regular intervals from early spring to mid-summer without protection. Sow in flat-bottomed trenches, 23cm (9in) wide and 5cm (2in) deep. Sow the seed in a double row, 5cm (2in) apart, or in single rows with 60–90cm (24–36in) between trenches or rows.

AFTERCARE

Immediately after sowing protect the crop from birds by covering with wire netting, twiggy branches or tie black cotton thread over canes. Provide support, using pea sticks or plastic or wire netting, when the crop reaches 8cm (3in) high. For tall varieties place the supports on either side of the growing stems. Water regularly during dry spells, especially when the crop is in flower. Mulch with garden compost to improve soil-moisture retention.

HARVESTING AND STORAGE

Harvest when the pods are plump but not fully grown, starting from the bottom of the plant and working your way up. Keep picking to encourage production. Mangetouts (snow peas) need to be picked before the pods get tough. Fresh peas freeze well in plastic bags or containers. Dry peas by leaving them on the plant until they rattle about in their pods. Shell peas and store in an airtight container.

PESTS AND DISEASES

Peas are prone to a number of pests and diseases. Pigeons and sparrows can devastate young crops. Netting is the best protection. Mildew can also be a problem. Pea and bean weevil can cause checking of plant growth. The crop may be attacked by pea thrips in hot sunny weather. Silvery patches are seen on the pods and leaves, which will affect the yield. Sow early to avoid major attacks. The white-bodied caterpillar of the pea moth feeds on the peas inside the pods. The adults lay their eggs when the peas are in flower. Sow early or late to avoid the moth's flying period.

CULTIVATION

Sowing time Mid- to late autumn (first earlies); late winter to early spring (second earlies); early spring to mid-summer (maincrop)

Trench width 23cm (9in)

Trench depth 5cm (2in)

Sowing distance in trenches Sow a double row 5cm (2in) apart

Distance between trenches or rows 60–90cm (24–36in)

Harvesting Late spring until late autumn depending on variety

---

VARIETIES

FIRST EARLIES

'Feltham First' A vigorous grower suitable for autumn sowing.

'Meteor' Compact plants which produce heavy yields.

SECOND EARLIES AND MAINCROP

'Alderman' A tall variety with large pods. A high yielder, but needs support.

'Onward' Large peas with a superb flavour. Crops heavily and has good disease resistance.

MANGETOUT

'Carouby de Mausanne' Purple flowers and large pods. Tastes delicious.

'Oregon Sugar Pod' Superb sweet flavour. Fast growing and tall.

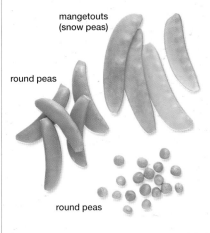

mangetouts (snow peas)

round peas

round peas

BROAD (FAVA) BEANS

Vicia faba

These are the hardiest and earliest of all the beans grown. Like many vegetables, the fresh or frozen produce that can be purchased from a shop does not do its flavour justice. Try growing this crop in your organic vegetable garden to experience the true succulent flavour. Varieties can be selected to grow green, white or red seeds.

SOIL

Grow broad beans in heavy soils that are well manured and have good drainage. Dig and incorporate manure during the autumn.

ASPECT

Broad beans thrive in an open sunny site that is sheltered from strong winds. This is essential if you are growing the crop over the winter.

SOWING

Overwintering varieties are sown in late autumn. Other varieties are sown from late winter to late spring. Sow in double rows in a shallow trench, 23cm (9in) wide and 4cm (1½in) deep with 23cm (9in) between the seeds. Alternatively, the crop can be started off under glass in late winter. Sow individually in pots to be planted out in spring.

AFTERCARE

Keep weeds down throughout the growing season. If there is a dry spell, give plenty of water throughout this period until the pods start to swell. Provide support for taller varieties. Place stakes or canes on either side of the crop, 25cm (10in) apart, and run

Left: *To grow a healthy crop of broad beans, choose an open sunny site which is protected from strong winds.*

string from stake to stake to support the stems. When the first pods start to form pinch out the top 8cm (3in) of growth. This will reduce the danger of blackfly attack and aid pod formation.

HARVESTING AND STORAGE

Pick the pods when they have become swollen. Do not allow the pods to be too mature because they will become leathery and tough. Continuous harvesting extends the cropping season. Broad beans are best picked and used fresh. Any surplus beans can be frozen or dried.

PESTS AND DISEASES

The most serious problem is blackfly. Removing the growing tips when the pods are starting to mature will help to deter this problem. The only other major problem is

chocolate spot, which can sometimes affect the crop. Avoid autumn sowings if this is a problem and destroy affected material.

CULTIVATION

Sowing time Late autumn (overwintering varieties); late winter to early spring (other varieties)

Sowing distance in trenches/ planting distance 23cm (9in)

Sowing depth 4cm (1½in)

Distance between trenches or rows 60cm (24in)

Harvesting Early to late summer

VARIETIES

'Aquaculce Claudia' Extremely hardy variety which is used for overwintering. Long pods containing white beans.

'Futua RZ' Early producer with compact pods. Tolerant of chocolate spot.

'The Sutton' Good compact plant at only 30cm (12in) long.

broad (fava) beans

Above: *Pinch out the tops of the plants when the first pods have begun to form. This aids pod formation and discourages blackfly.*

Above: *Taller varieties require support. Place canes at regular intervals on each side of the crop, tying string between each pole.*

MARROWS AND SQUASH CROPS

PUMPKINS

Cucurbita maxima

Pumpkins are popular with children because they look so impressive and can be carved out and used as lanterns. The flesh is cooked and makes good soups and pies. They are found in colours such as blue and green as well as the popular yellow-orange. Smaller varieties of pumpkin can be grown which are bred for flavour rather than size.

SOIL
Deep fertile soil that is rich in humus. Before planting dig out a planting pit 45cm (18in) deep and 60cm (24in) square. Fill half the dug-out pit with well-rotted manure or garden compost and fill back in again.

ASPECT
Plant or sow in a sunny position and protect from strong winds.

SOWING
Sowing can begin under glass in late spring at a temperature of 15–18°C (59–64°F). Soak the seeds overnight to speed up germination. Sow the seeds individually in pots. Plant out in early summer in the prepared planting pits after all threat of frost has passed. Plant at distances of 1.8m (6ft) apart. Alternatively, sow directly outside into prepared planting pits 1.8m (6ft) apart in early summer. Keep a distance of 1.8m (6ft) between the rows.

AFTERCARE
To keep the vigorous growth in check train the stems around the plant, pinning them to the ground with wire pegs. For larger

Above: *Pumpkins take up a lot a space, so careful thought is needed when siting them within the confines of a small garden.*

pumpkins, choose one to three good fruits when they are small and remove the rest. Watering needs to take place throughout the growing season. It is advantageous to feed every two weeks during this period. Pinch out the tips of trailing varieties towards the end of the summer. Stop watering and feeding once the fruits are mature.

HARVESTING AND STORAGE
It is best for the fruits to mature on the plant. Harvest the entire crop before the first frosts, leaving a stem on the fruit of about 5cm (2in) in length. Leave them in a sunny location for about a week for the skins to harden. Pumpkins store well. The popular orange-skinned varieties will store for several weeks whereas the blue-skinned type will last for up to three months.

PESTS AND DISEASES
Slugs are a problem, especially when the fruits start to grow. Mice can also cause damage. Destroy the plant if it contracts cucumber mosaic virus.

Left: *Harvest pumpkins when they have reached their mature colour. A good indicator is when the stems begin to split.*

Above: *Although pumpkins take time and patience to grow, they are ideal plants with which to encourage young gardeners.*

pumpkins

SQUASHES

Cucurbita maxima

Squashes are very closely related to marrows (zucchini) and pumpkins and there is very little difference in their cultivation requirements and culinary preparation. Squashes come in a diverse range of shapes and sizes. The outside flesh colour is also very varied, ranging from almost white to deep orange. They look delightful when used in the ornamental garden, climbing over trellis walkways and arches.

Squashes can be divided into two main groups: summer and winter types. The difference between the two groups lies in their storage qualities. Summer types will keep for two to three weeks, but are best used fresh from the plant, whereas winter types can still be used fresh but will also keep for long periods in storage.

SOIL

Squashes prefer a soil that is rich in organic matter. Dig over the soil in the autumn, incorporating copious amounts of well-rotted manure or garden compost. This not only enriches the soil with nutrients, but also helps to retain moisture in the soil, which is essential for healthy growth. Mulching with garden compost or straw will also help to prevent water evaporating from the soil.

ASPECT

Squashes thrive in an open sunny site that is protected from strong winds. These conditions are vital for successful growth because they are neither hardy nor robust.

Above: *Squashes undoubtedly have a culinary value, but they are often grown simply for their attractive looks. They look extremely ornamental if they are grown over archways or trellis.*

Left: *If you are growing squashes in a restricted space, cut off the trailing stems two leaves above a fruit.*

SOWING

Squashes can be started off by sowing individually in pots under glass in early spring. Sow individually in modules or fibre pots because they do not like their roots to be disturbed. Ideally, the temperature needs to be a constant of 18°C (64°F). Harden off and plant outside in early summer, after the risk of frost has passed. They need a lot of room to grow, so leave 1.8m (6ft) between the plants. If you do not have access to a greenhouse, sow directly outside in rows during early summer at a depth of 4cm (1½in). Keep 1.8m (6ft) between each seed and 1.8m (6ft) between rows. It is common to sow two seeds next to each other, removing the weaker seedling after germination. This ensures a plant at each station.

Above: *Squash fruits will quickly rot if left to mature on the bare soil. Support the fruits with straw to prevent damage.*

AFTERCARE

As the plants grow, train the trailing stems around the plant in a spiral to save space. When training the plants, pin the stems down with wire pegs. Alternatively, the size of the plants can be reduced by cutting off the trailing stems, two leaves above a fruit.

There are numerous varieties of climbing squash available. These can be extremely ornamental, especially when the growth is trained up ornate wire or wooden trellis supports. Keep the crop well watered throughout the growing season and give a high-potash feed every two weeks.

HARVESTING AND STORAGE

Harvest the summer squashes when the skin is tender and they are big enough to eat. Cut off the fruits, leaving 5cm (2in) of stem. Cut winter squashes in the same way if they are to be used fresh, otherwise leave them on the plant and harvest them just before the first frosts. Leave them in a sunny position for one week to harden the skins before storing.

Summer squashes have a relatively short storage life of up to two to three weeks. They are best used fresh from the plant. Winter squashes will keep up to two months if they are kept in a frost-free area. Store the squashes individually by hanging them in nets or boxing them and surrounding them with straw.

PESTS AND DISEASES

Slugs can cause serious damage to crops because they can eat completely through a stem if they are left unchecked. Cucumber mosaic virus is the most serious of the diseases to which squashes are susceptible. The leaves become mottled

and the fruit is distorted. Destroy any infected plants. Powdery mildew can cause problems in dry years. This can largely be ignored because the problem is normally not too serious. Keep the soil moist and plant at the correct distances to prevent overcrowding and allow for the free movement of air between the plants. This will help to prevent infections.

Left: *Squashes, like pumpkins, are ready to harvest when the stems begin to split. Cut them off with a small stem attached.*

CULTIVATION
Sowing time Early spring (under glass); early summer (outdoors)
Planting out time Early summer
Sowing distance 1.8m (6ft)
Sowing depth 4cm (1½in)
Distance between rows 1.8m (6ft)
Harvesting Late summer to early autumn

VARIETIES

SUMMER

'Custard Squash' White- and yellow-skinned varieties are available.

'Table Ace' A small, acorn-shaped fruit with dark green skin and orange flesh.

'Tender and True' Ball-shaped fruits with mottled green skin. Bush variety.

'Vegetable Spaghetti' An unusual squash. When cooked, the spaghetti-like strands can be scooped out.

WINTER

'Pompeon' Shiny dark green flat globe-shaped fruit. Golden flesh. Semi-bush habit.

'Turks Turban' A good ornamental variety that is also delicious to eat. A trailing variety.

'Vegetable Spaghetti' Fruits are cylindrical in shape. The flesh when boiled breaks up into strands similar to spaghetti. A trailing variety.

squashes

MARROWS AND COURGETTES (ZUCCHINI)

Cucurbita pepo

Marrows and courgettes are mainly grown for their delightful juicy fruits, although the young leaves, male flowers and small fruits are delicious to eat in summer salads.

SOIL

Marrows and courgettes thrive in soil that is rich in organic matter. To ensure optimum growth, dig in plenty of well-rotted manure or garden compost in the autumn. They grow extremely well on compost heaps.

ASPECT

An open sunny position. They are frost tender, so do not plant out until early summer after the risk of frost has subsided.

SOWING/PLANTING

You can start the crop off in late spring under glass by sowing individually into 9cm (3in) pots. Soak the seeds in water

Below: *The male flowers of marrows and courgettes (zucchini) can be eaten raw in salads or cooked.*

overnight because this will speed up the germination process. Grow on the seedlings and harden them off before planting out in early summer. Alternatively, you can sow direct outside in early summer to a depth of 4cm (1½in). Sow two seeds at one time and then remove the weaker one after germination. Covering with cloches will enhance the germination of the seedlings. Within the rows keep a distance of 90cm (3ft) between each plant for bush varieties and 1.2–1.8m (4–6ft) for trailing varieties. Leave the same distances between each of the rows.

AFTERCARE

Water marrows and courgettes regularly throughout the growing season. Trailing varieties will need to be trimmed in order to prevent them from taking over your vegetable plot.

CULTIVATION

Sowing time Late spring (under glass); early summer (outdoors)
Planting out time Early summer
Sowing/planting distance 90cm/3ft (bush varieties); 1.2–1.8m/4–6ft (trailing varieties)
Sowing depth 4cm (1½in)
Distance between rows 90cm/3ft (bush varieties); 1.2–1.8m/4–6ft (trailing varieties)
Harvesting Mid-summer onwards

Left: *When harvesting, use a sharp knife and cut through the stem 2.5cm (1in) away from the fruit.*

HARVESTING AND STORAGE

Courgettes taste delicious when they are young. Harvest them when they are approximately 10cm (4in) long. If left to grow much larger they are classed as a small marrow or they can be left to mature into a fully grown marrow. Harvesting can take place until the first frosts. Courgettes are best picked and used fresh. They can be frozen but will lose their firmness. Marrows store well, especially if left to mature on the plant. Store in a frost-free place in trays or hanging up in nets.

PESTS AND DISEASES

Cucumber mosaic virus is the most common problem. Destroy affected plants. Slugs love the vegetation. You can pick them off by hand at night or encourage natural predators such as frogs; or use a parasitic nematode.

VARIETIES

'All Green Bush' A heavy-yielding variety with mid-green courgettes.
'Jemma F1' An attractive variety with bright yellow courgettes. Has a slightly different flavour to normal green varieties.
'Kojac' Hairless and spineless for easy picking. A high-yielding variety.
'Nero Milan' This has dark-green fruits that are easily picked due to its open habit. A good variety for freezing.

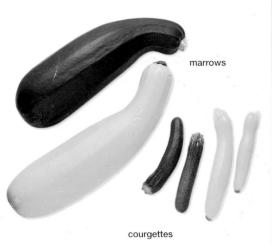

marrows

courgettes

CUCUMBERS

Cucumis sativus

There are two main types of cucumber: greenhouse varieties and outdoor or ridge varieties. Plants for growing under glass are tall climbing ones that bear long, tasty, slender fruits. Outdoor varieties are bushier in habit and produce shorter fruits. Those grown in the open are less prone to pest and disease attacks than when grown under glass. Many of the old outdoor varieties taste inferior compared with the greenhouse types. Choose a new outdoor variety as the taste has improved due to recent breeding.

SOIL

Grow outdoors in a well-drained soil that has been manured the previous autumn. Indoor varieties can be grown in large grow bags, large pots, soil borders or straw bales.

ASPECT

Outdoor cucumbers are a tender crop, so grow in a sheltered sunny location that is protected from strong winds.

SOWING

Start off indoor varieties under glass from late winter onwards at a temperature of 24°C (75°F). Sow individually in pots. Sow two seeds per pot and then remove the weaker seedling. Cucumbers do not like root disturbance, so plant into their final positions with care.

Sow outdoor (ridge) varieties under glass in late spring or directly outside in early summer. If sown outside, cover with a cloche or bell jar to raise the temperature until after germination. Sow or plant outside, leaving 75cm (30in) between the plants, with the same distance between the rows.

Above: *As the name suggests, greenhouse varieties need to be grown under glass.*

AFTERCARE

Indoor varieties will need supporting with poles and horizontal wires, tying in the climbing stems as they grow. Pinch out the tips when they reach the top of the supports. Tie in the side stems (laterals) along the horizontal wires. Pinch these out two leaves after the development of the first fruit. Greenhouse varieties taste bitter if fertilized, so remove any male flowers. Give a high potash liquid feed when the fruits start to develop. Keep well watered, taking care to water the soil around the plant, but not the plant itself. Misting the plants and watering the paths will help keep the humidity up. Shade the greenhouse with paint or netting to avoid strong sunlight.

Outdoor (ridge) varieties that are grown on the ground will need to be mulched with straw to keep the fruit clean and to stop them rotting. This also raises the soil temperature, helps retain moisture and suppresses weed growth. Pinch out the tips from the main shoots at 6–7 leaves. Mist plants in dry periods to increase humidity and keep well watered. Outdoor varieties need to be pollinated, so it is essential to leave the male flowers on the plant. Give a high potash feed every two weeks when the fruits start to develop.

HARVESTING AND STORAGE

Cut the cucumbers with a knife from the plant before they reach maximum size as

Left: *Ridge cucumbers are ideally suited for growing outdoors and can be grown as easily as courgettes (zucchini).*

CULTIVATION

Sowing time Late winter onwards (under glass); early summer (outdoors)
Planting out time Early summer
Sowing/planting distance 60cm/24in (under glass); 75cm/30in (outdoors)
Sowing depth 2.5cm (1in)
Distance between rows 75cm (30in)
Harvesting Mid-summer onwards

this encourages new fruits. Keep harvesting the crop until the first frosts. Cucumbers will keep in the refrigerator for about one week, but otherwise they do not store well.

PESTS AND DISEASES

Slugs and snails are a problem. Red spider mite and whitefly attack greenhouse varieties.

VARIETIES

GREENHOUSE
'Conqueror' An extremely old variety that tolerates lower temperatures than normal. Good-sized fruits.
'F1 Cumlaude RZ' A vigorous variety that produces heavy yields. Can be grown in an unheated greenhouse. An all-female variety.
'F1 Deltastar RZ' Delicious fruits that keep well. An all-female variety.

OUTDOOR (RIDGE)
'Bush Champion F1' Good compact variety. Fruits reach up to 25cm (10in). Resistant to cucumber mosaic virus.
'Marketmore' A high-yielding variety. Resistance is shown to cucumber mosaic virus.
'Stimora MIX F1' Can be used for gherkin pickling if harvested at 5cm (2in) or for slicing grown at 10cm (4in).

ridge cucumber

greenhouse cucumber

SHOOT CROPS

CELERY

Apium graveolens

Growing celery using the traditional trench method can be labour-intensive. The young seedlings are planted out in trenches and earthed up, a process that is called blanching. Earthing up makes the harvested stems white, less stringy and longer. The alternative is to grow self-blanching varieties which are planted closely together to carry out the blanching process. Self-blanching types are not as crisp and tasty as the trench type.

SOIL

There are two methods of soil preparation: the trench method and that for self-blanching varieties. For trench celery, dig out a trench that is 38cm (15in) wide and 30cm (12in) deep. Put an 8cm (3in) layer of rotted manure at the bottom of this and back fill with soil. This should be done in autumn or winter and allowed to settle before planting. Self-blanching celery is planted out in blocks and not rows. Dig over the soil in the autumn incorporating copious amounts of well-rotted manure or garden compost.

ASPECT

All celery varieties require a sunny site.

SOWING

Trench varieties are best started off under glass in module trays in early spring at a

Above: *When the stems are 30cm (12in) high a cardboard collar is fitted around the plant to blanch the stems.*

temperature of around 15°C (59°F). Harden off by placing them in cold frames two weeks before planting out in early summer. Plant out in trenched rows 30cm (12in) apart with 60cm (24in) between the rows. Self-blanching celery is started off under glass in the same way. Harden off the plants before planting out in blocks in early summer. Block planting at intervals of 23cm (9in) helps the process of self-blanching.

AFTERCARE

Water thoroughly in dry periods and feed with a liquid feed every two weeks. When trench celery varieties reach 30cm (12in), earth up over part of the stems. Repeat this process at three-week intervals until the soil is up to the lower leaves. An alternative to earthing up is to wrap cardboard around the celery stems when they are 30cm (12in) tall and again three weeks later. For self-blanching celery, place straw around the outside of the block to keep out the light. Green celery varieties do not need straw around the perimeter.

HARVESTING AND STORAGE

Trench celery is ready for harvesting from autumn onwards. Harvest as needed, but remember that the flavour is enhanced by the first frosts. Cover plants in the winter with straw if severe weather is expected. Lift self-blanching celery from autumn by the first frosts. Leave trench varieties in the

Left: *This form of celery, known as green or American celery, is popular because it does not require blanching.*

ground until required, but, in cold regions, lift and store in a frost-free area where the crop will last for weeks. Celery can be frozen, but may turn soft after defrosting, so use only in cooked dishes.

PESTS AND DISEASES

Slugs, snails, celery fly and carrot fly can all be a problem, as can diseases such as celery heart rot and celery leaf spot. Destroy affected plants. Irregular watering and feeding can make the celery stalks split.

CULTIVATION

TRENCH
Sowing time Early to mid-spring (under glass)
Planting out time Early summer
Planting distance 30cm (12in)
Distance between rows 60cm (24in)
Harvesting Autumn
SELF-BLANCHING
Sowing time Early to mid-spring
Planting out time Early summer
Planting distance in blocks 23cm (9in)
Harvesting Autumn

VARIETIES

TRENCH
'Giant White' Has a good flavour but requires good soil conditions. Stalks are white and tall.
'Solid Pink' An extremely old variety that will stand a number of frosts. Harvest in late autumn to early winter.

SELF-BLANCHING
'Golden Self-Blanching' Yellow dwarf variety with cream stalks which requires little or no earthing up.
'Tall Utah' Long green stalks that need no earthing up. Harvest in early autumn. Inner stalks self-blanch.

celery

FLORENCE FENNEL

Foeniculum vulgare var. *dulce*

This wonderfully decorative plant is grown for its white bulbous base that tastes of aniseed. It can be eaten raw in salads or braised as a vegetable. Its finely cut bright green foliage is attractive enough to grow as an unusual ornamental plant for the decorative garden. The leaves can also be used as a herb for flavouring dishes.

SOIL

Florence fennel thrives in light well-drained soils. If your soil is too heavy, incorporate grit or gravel before planting or build a raised bed. When digging in the autumn incorporate plenty of well-rotted manure or garden compost. This will increase water retention in the soil.

ASPECT

Requires an open sunny site with shelter from the wind.

SOWING

The best time of year to sow is early to mid-summer as crops sown earlier are likely to bolt. Sow thinly in rows 1cm (½in) deep with 45cm (18in) between the rows. After germination thin the seedlings to 23cm (9in) apart. Alternatively, the seeds can be started off under glass, but, as they do not like transplanting, it is best to sow in situ.

AFTERCARE

Water copiously, especially during dry spells. Earth up the soil around the bulbs, as they begin to swell, to around half of their height. Continue to draw up soil as the bulbs expand. This will blanch the bulbs resulting in a sweeter flavour.

HARVESTING AND STORAGE

Two to three weeks after earthing up check the bulbs. If they have reached the size of a tennis ball they are ready for harvesting. Pull the whole plant up or cut underneath the bulb and leave the root in the soil. This will re-sprout and offer new foliage, which can be used in flower arranging. Fennel does not store well and is best eaten fresh. It will keep for a few days in the refrigerator.

PESTS AND DISEASES

Bolting is the main problem. Do not sow too early or use resistant cultivars such as 'Argo RZ'. Other than that, generally trouble free.

CULTIVATION

Sowing time Early to mid-summer
Sowing distance Thinly
Sowing depth 1cm (½in)
Distance between rows 45cm (18in)
Thinning distance 23cm (9in)
Harvesting Autumn

Above: *When the bulbs begin to swell, draw up the soil around them. This will blanch the bulbs and make them taste sweeter.*

VARIETIES

'Argo RZ' Good uniform crop with white bulbs. Resistant to bolting, so good for using as an early crop.
'Romanesco' Lovely dark foliage with white bulbs that have a good aniseed flavour. Sow in late spring to mid-summer.

Florence fennel

Above: *The secret of growing successfully is to keep the soil moist and weed-free, thus ensuring fast healthy growth.*

Above: *Florence fennel is often planted in flower borders to display its decorative, finely cut foliage.*

ASPARAGUS

Asparagus officinalis

This perennial crop is a good long-term investment for the garden. After nursing the crop over the first two years in which no harvesting takes place, the crop will last for 20 years. The delicious tender young shoots (spears) are available from mid-spring to early summer. Asparagus is best picked and eaten fresh. The summer foliage is much prized by florists.

Left: *After harvesting the young asparagus shoots, the crop is left to grow to its full height, thus strengthening itself for producing next year's shoots.*

SOIL

Asparagus thrives in well-drained soil. Before planting or sowing, dig the soil in the autumn and incorporate plenty of well-rotted manure or garden compost. Lime the soil if the pH is acidic.

ASPECT

A well-sheltered, sunny spot to ensure optimum growth.

SOWING/PLANTING

SOWING

Soak the seed overnight before sowing to speed up the germination time. In spring, sow in rows 1cm (½in) deep keeping 30cm (12in) between the rows. Thin to 15cm (6in) between the plants and leave to grow on for one year. Lift the crowns in the following spring and transplant to a permanent site.

PLANTING

Asparagus plants are sold as crowns during the dormant season and are best planted out in early spring. To plant the crowns, dig out a trench 20cm (8in) deep with a ridge of 8cm (3in) running down the middle. Set out the asparagus in the centre of the ridge, placing the crowns 45cm (18in) apart.

Above: *Harvest the crop when the shoots have reached 15cm (6in). Cut the stems 5cm (2in) below the level of the ground.*

Cover the trenches over with soil to a depth of 8–10cm (3–4in). If more than one row is required, leave a space of 90cm (3ft) apart.

AFTERCARE

Keep the beds clean of weeds throughout the year, but do not use a hoe as this can damage the roots and newly emerging spears. An application of mulch can be given to keep the weeds down and retain soil moisture.

Once the foliage has turned yellow in the autumn, cut back to 5cm (2in) above the soil surface. Draw up a small ridge of soil over the plants before the new shoots emerge in the spring.

HARVESTING AND STORAGE

Newly planted crops will produce their first spears during the growing season, but do not cut any of them. Follow the same practice the second year. Harvesting is carried out in the third growing season in mid-spring to early summer when they have reached a height of 15cm (6in). Cut the spears 5cm (2in) below ground level. Stop cutting in early summer and let the remaining spears develop into foliage. This allows the food reserves to be built up for the following year. Asparagus does not store well and is best eaten fresh.

PESTS AND DISEASES

Asparagus beetle can attack the stems and foliage. This pest likes to overwinter in the foliage. Cutting stems back in autumn can help. New succulent spears are prone to damage by slugs. Violet root rot can cause severe problems. The roots are covered in purple mould and the leaves prematurely turn yellow. In bad cases, destroy plants and make a bed in a new site.

CULTIVATION

SOWING

Sowing time Spring

Sowing distance Thinly

Sowing depth 1cm (½in)

Distance between rows 30cm (12in)

Thinning distance 15cm (6in)

Transplanting time Following spring, same distances as for planting

PLANTING

Planting time Early spring

Planting distance 45cm (18in)

Planting depth 8–10cm (3–4in)

Distance between rows 90cm (3ft)

Harvesting (from the third year) In late spring for six weeks

---

VARIETIES

'Cito' A heavy cropper that produces long spears.

'Connover's Colossal' An old variety. Has delicious flavoured spears.

'Franklim F1' Heavy yields of thick spears. A small crop may be harvested in the second year.

asparagus

GLOBE ARTICHOKES

Cynara cardunculus Scolymus Group

This perennial is unusual in that it is the flower that is eaten and not the leaves or the roots, as with most vegetables. After harvesting, the flower bud is boiled or steamed and the various parts are eaten. Globe artichokes do take up a lot of room, so you might consider adding this ornate crop to a herbaceous border if you do not have space in the vegetable garden.

SOIL
As this crop will be in the same location for several years, you should prepare the soil to a high standard before planting. Dig deeply in the autumn, incorporating plenty of well-rotted manure or garden compost. Globe artichokes do not grow well on heavy clay as good drainage is essential.

ASPECT
An open sunny site in a sheltered location.

PLANTING/SOWING
Plant offsets of globe artichokes in the spring at 75cm (30in) apart with 90cm (3ft) between the rows. Alternatively, sow seeds thinly in spring in rows 2.5cm (1in) deep with 30cm (12in) between the rows. Thin the seedlings to 15cm (6in) apart ready to transplant the following spring. Plant in the permanent site as above.

Below: *It is easy to see why the globe artichoke is used by garden designers who are looking for architectural form.*

AFTERCARE
Water copiously throughout the growing season and feed every two weeks. Stems can be cut down in autumn and soil drawn around the crown of the plant. Protect the crowns in cold areas by covering with straw or bracken. Lift, divide and replant the crop every 3–4 years. Cultivate and incorporate organic matter to the soil during this process.

CULTIVATION	
Planting time	Spring
Planting distance	75cm (30in)
Distance between rows	90cm (3ft)
Sowing time	Spring
Sowing distance	Thinly
Sowing depth	2.5cm (1in)
Distance between rows	30cm (12in)
Thinning distance	15cm (6in)
Transplanting time	Following spring
Harvesting	Summer of second year onwards

Left: *Harvest the flower heads of the globe artichokes just before they open and while they are still green.*

Left: *Cut the stems down in autumn and draw the soil around the crown of the plant. The stems can be put on the compost heap.*

HARVESTING AND STORAGE
Begin harvesting in the second year. Cut the flower heads off just before they open and while they are still green. Leave on a stem of 2.5cm (1in) below the head. The heads are best eaten when they are fresh.

PESTS AND DISEASES
Generally trouble free, although they can be affected by blackfly, which is treated by spraying with insecticidal soap.

VARIETIES
'Camus de Bretagne' Large heads with a good flavour. It can be relatively tender compared to other varieties.
'Green Globe' Produces lovely green flower buds. Very popular variety and widely available.
'Purple Globe' Hardier than its green relative but the flavour is inferior.

globe artichokes

RHUBARB

Rheum x hybridum

Although rhubarb is classed as a vegetable, it is mainly used as a fruit. The leaves are extremely poisonous and no part of them should be eaten. Rhubarb looks superb in an ornamental border, being easy to mix in with other perennials and shrubs in the garden.

SOIL
Rhubarb grows well in soil that is rich in organic matter. Before planting incorporate plenty of well-rotted manure or garden compost into the soil when preparing the site. Remove any perennial weeds as they are difficult to eradicate after the crop has been planted.

ASPECT
A sunny location, away from shade.

SOWING/PLANTING
Sowing Rhubarb can be grown from seed, but the uniformity and quality of the plants cannot be guaranteed. Sow the seeds thinly in rows 2.5cm (1in) deep with 30cm (12in) between the rows. After germination thin out the seedlings to 23cm (9in). The crop is ready to transplant to its final destination during the following winter. Plant to the same specifications as described for planting below.

Above: *A bed of healthy rhubarb is an impressive sight. Rhubarb leaves are poisonous and cannot be eaten.*

Above: *Forcing should only be carried out every other year to prevent weakening the plants. This is a wicker rhubarb forcer.*

Above: *Harvest rhubarb sticks by pulling so that they come out of their "socket". Cut off the leaves and put on the compost heap.*

Planting Rhubarb plants can be bought in pots at any good garden centre or nursery. Alternatively, offsets can be divided off established plants during the dormant season. Plant the rhubarb plants that have been bought in pots throughout the spring. Offsets, on the other hand, are planted straight after being split in the winter. Space all the plants 90cm (3ft) apart.

AFTERCARE
Water well during dry periods. Mulch with well-rotted manure or garden compost in the spring and autumn to help retain moisture and suppress weed growth. Plants can be forced into producing shoots early if covered with a bucket or plastic bin in mid-winter. This crop will be ready to pick after six weeks. Do not force the same plants two years running or they will be weakened.

HARVESTING AND STORAGE
The red stems can be harvested from spring to early summer. Pull each stem from the base and it will come away with part of the base. Cut off the leaves and put on to the compost heap. Never strip a plant of all

its stems; it is best to leave at least four stems per plant. This enables the plants to recover and produce new growth, allowing the plant to be harvested the following year. Rhubarb will freeze for up to one year.

PESTS AND DISEASES
Sometimes prone to white blister. Cut off and destroy diseased foliage. Otherwise generally trouble free.

CULTIVATION
SOWING
Sowing time Spring
Sowing distance Thinly
Sowing depth 2.5cm (1in)
Distance between rows 30cm (12in)
Thinning distance 23cm (9in)
Transplanting time Following winter, plant as below
PLANTING
Planting time Winter (offsets); spring (pots)
Planting distance 90cm (3ft)
Distance between rows 90cm (3ft)
Harvesting From the second year onwards

VARIETIES
'Champagne Early' Beautiful red stems that are among the first to be harvested.
'Glaskin's Perpetual' Extremely quick growing and lasts for many years. Produces lovely red stems that can be cut in the first year.
'Victoria' A popular variety with thick stems that are ready in late spring.

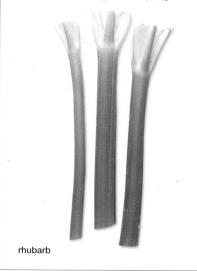

rhubarb

FRUITING VEGETABLES

PEPPERS

Capsicum species

Sweet or bell peppers (*Capsicum annuum* Grossum Group) are commonly used in salads and in many cooked dishes. Sweet peppers do not taste hot like their close relatives, cayenne or tabasco peppers (*Capsicum frutescens*) and chilli peppers (*Capsicum annuum* Longum Group). The plants bear fruits that are green when unripe, turning yellow, red and orange. Cayenne or tabasco peppers are exceptionally hot peppers that need to be used with care.

Chilli peppers are a little less hot than cayenne or tabasco peppers, but are still quite fiery (the seeds, which are the hottest part of the fruit, may be removed).

SOIL
Outdoor crops thrive in a well-drained, fertile soil. Greenhouse types need to be planted up in grow bags or large pots in peat-free potting mix.

ASPECT
Peppers require a sunny sheltered spot, otherwise they do well in a greenhouse, conservatory or on a vacant windowsill.

SOWING/PLANTING
Sow seeds in trays, modules or individual pots under glass in spring, at a temperature

of 18–21°C (65–70°F). If grown in trays, prick out the seedlings into small pots as soon as the seed leaves are large enough to handle.

Peppers have short root systems, so it is essential to pot up the plants gradually until they reach their final pot size of around 23cm (9in). Alternatively, pot up the young pepper plants until they are large enough to plant into grow bags or soil beds in mid- to late spring.

Plant outdoor peppers outside after hardening off in early summer. Plant in rows 50cm (20in) apart with the same distance between the rows. Peppers can be grown in a vegetable patch, in an ornamental border or in pots on the patio.

AFTERCARE
Keep the crop well watered, feeding once a week with a liquid organic fertilizer high in

Left: *Not all peppers are the evenly shaped fruits to which we are accustomed in supermarkets. These red peppers have reached the final stage of ripening.*

potash. Stake and tie the plants as they grow. Good ventilation in the greenhouse is recommended in hot weather.

HARVESTING AND STORAGE
Start to harvest sweet peppers from mid- to late summer. Pick the fruits when they are green, yellow, red, orange or purple. They are best eaten fresh although they will keep for up to two weeks in a refrigerator. Harvest hot or cayenne peppers when they are fully ripe and coloured. Use fresh or store in airtight jars after drying.

PESTS AND DISEASES
Grown under glass they suffer problems such as aphids, red spider mite and whitefly. Damp down the floor and mist the plants to increase humidity and deter red spider mite. Outdoors they may be attacked by aphids.

Above: *Chilli peppers, like sweet peppers, are green when they are unripe, turning yellow and then red when they are ripe.*

VARIETIES
SWEET PEPPERS
'F1 Mandy RZ' Produces large sweet tasting green fruits that turn red when mature. Resistant to mosaic virus.
'Red Skin' An F1 hybrid that produces uniform compact plants suitable for container growing. It has early maturing fruits.

CAYENNE AND CHILLI PEPPERS (HOT PEPPERS)
'Cayenne Large Red' Long, pointed, hot fruits that are produced in abundance.
'Habenero' An extremely hot chilli pepper. The green wrinkled fruits turn light orange when mature.

sweet peppers

chilli peppers

TOMATOES

Lycopersicon esculentum

Tomatoes are probably the most widely used vegetable for cooking. It is worth growing a few, either in the garden or in the conservatory (sun room) or greenhouse, so that you can experience the sweet juicy flavour offered by home-grown produce. Outdoor varieties look striking dotted among ornamental plants in borders or potagers. However, take care when siting tomato plants because they are closely related to the potato and suffer from several of the same pests and diseases. Include tomatoes on the same crop-rotation programme as potatoes or use grow bags to prevent the spread of soil-borne pests and diseases.

SOIL

Outdoor tomatoes like humus-rich soil. Dig over in winter, incorporating garden compost into the soil. Plant indoor varieties in grow bags or pots. If planted in a soil border in a greenhouse, change the soil every year to stop transference of diseases. Add garden compost to improve the soil structure.

ASPECT

Outdoor tomato varieties are tender, so choose a warm sheltered spot that receives plenty of sun.

SOWING/PLANTING

INDOORS These varieties can be started off under glass in temperatures of 18°C (65°F) in early to mid-spring. Sow seed in the same way as for outdoor varieties. Plant up into grow bags, pots or soil borders in mid- to late spring. Plants grown in borders need to be spaced 45cm (18in) apart.

OUTDOORS These varieties are best sown under glass in gentle heat or an unheated greenhouse in mid-spring. Sow thinly in seed trays if a large number of plants are required or sow individually in pots if only a few plants are needed. Seed sown in trays will need to be pricked out and transplanted into individual pots. Grow on and harden off, ready to plant outside in early summer. Plants need to be planted 45cm (18in) apart for cordon varieties and 60cm (24in) for bush varieties. Keep 75cm (30in) between the rows for both types. Alternatively, tomatoes can be planted into larger pots or grow bags before being placed outside. Harden off for 10 days before moving outside in early summer.

Above: *Tomatoes can be grown indoors or outside. Using grow bags in a greenhouse prevents the spread of soil-borne diseases.*

AFTERCARE

The tomato crop needs to be well watered. Feed every two weeks with a high-potash feed when the fruit begins to swell. If the crop is irregularly watered, causing wet and dry periods, this can cause blossom end rot. Support the crop using canes or suspended strings within the greenhouse and tie in the stems as they grow. Pinch out the top of the shoots when they reach the end of their supports. Side shoots need to be removed from cordon types.

Above: *Spiral supports are ideal for supporting cordon tomatoes because it saves you from having to tie them in.*

Left: *Plant outdoor tomato crops in a sunny sheltered spot. This will not only aid plant growth, but it is essential for fruit ripening.*

HARVESTING AND STORAGE

Harvest as they ripen and are fully coloured. A mature fruit is normally deep red in colour. Twist the fruit off the plant to avoid tearing the stem.

Tomatoes are best eaten straight from the plant. If you have a glut at the end of the season they can be frozen. Only use frozen fruits in cooked dishes as they will lose their firmness. At the end of the season there may be many green tomatoes left on the plants. Sever the plants at the base and hang upside down in a greenhouse or frost-free shed until the tomatoes ripen or put in trays into a drawer to ripen.

PESTS AND DISEASES

Tomatoes are prone to a number of pests and diseases. Aphids, potato cyst eelworm, whitefly and red spider mite are the main pests to which they are susceptible. Tomato blight, grey mould, potato mosaic virus, greenback, tomato leaf mould and scald are the diseases most likely to cause problems. Many of the problems listed here can be solved by undertaking good horticultural practices such as removing dead, decaying and diseased growth from the plants every day. Correct watering and good ventilation will also help to improve the health of the crop.

Above: *Do not throw away the remaining plants at the end of the season. Collect any that are left and hang them upside down under cover to ripen.*

Above: *Remove the side shoots from cordon tomatoes when they are small. Pinch or cut them out with a sharp knife.*

Above: *There is nothing better than to taste the warm sweet flavour of tomatoes harvested from home-grown plants.*

CULTIVATION

INDOOR VARIETIES

Sowing time Early to mid-spring

Planting time Mid- to late spring

Planting/sowing distance 45cm (18in)

Harvesting Summer onwards

OUTDOOR VARIETIES

Sowing time Mid-spring
(under glass)

Planting out time Early summer

Planting distance 45cm/18in (cordon); 60cm/24in (bush)

Distance between rows 75cm (30in)

Harvesting Late summer onwards

VARIETIES

GREENHOUSE

'Big Boy F1' Tall plant with large fruits that are good for stuffing and slicing. Nice bright red fruits.

'F1 Aromata RZ' Extremely productive variety with fruits averaging 100g (4oz). Resistance shown to tomato mosaic virus.

'Shirley F1' Popular variety that produces heavy yields. Resistant to fusarium, cladosporium and tomato mosaic virus.

'Super Sweet 100 F1' A tall and strong-growing variety, bearing many small red fruits which are rich in vitamin C.

OUTDOOR

'Gardeners Delight' Produces small cherry red tomatoes that have a superb sweet flavour. Can be grown under glass or outside.

'Red Alert' A high yielding outdoor variety with small delicious tasting fruits.

'Totem F1' Has a good compact habit. Ideal for pots and window boxes.

'Tumbler' A trailing variety that can be used in hanging baskets and containers. Has lovely, small, red fruits.

tomatoes "on the vine"

"beefsteak" tomatoes

standard-size tomatoes

cherry tomatoes

AUBERGINES (EGGPLANT)

Solanum melongena

Not so very long ago, aubergines were a rare sight on the shelves of our supermarkets and shops. Nowadays, they are more widely available and frequently grown by amateur gardeners in the garden or greenhouse. However, aubergines are tender and in temperate climates are best grown under glass rather than outside where they will struggle to thrive in anything but a hot sunny season. The large, conspicuous, shining fruits range in colour from purple through to white. They taste delicious when they are cooked, stuffed with meat, rice or vegetables, or when used to make ratatouille or moussaka.

SOIL

Grow under glass in grow bags or pots, using a peat-free potting mix. Plants grown outside require a fertile, well-drained soil and should have a general fertilizer applied before planting.

ASPECT

Aubergines thrive in a warm sunny spot that is sheltered from the wind. These conditions are ideally found in a greenhouse, cold frame or in barn cloches.

SOWING

Best conditions for growth are provided under glass. Soak the seeds overnight to

Above: *The aubergine is a tropical plant. The most commonly grown varieties produce magnificent purple fruits.*

improve the germination rate and then sow into individual pots in spring. Ideally the temperature within the greenhouse will be 21–25°C (70–77°F). Once the plants are large enough they can be planted into bigger pots or grow bags. Aubergines can be hardened off and planted outside if the temperature does not drop below 15°C (59°F). Plant to a distance of 50cm (20in) between plants in a row with the same distance between the rows.

AFTERCARE

Canes and string may be needed to support the plants once they have reached 45–60cm (18–24in). Pinch out the tips of the plants when they reach 38cm (15in) in height in order to encourage fruit formation. Water well throughout the growing season and feed once every two weeks with a high-potash liquid feed.

Left: *Aubergines can be planted up under glass in window boxes or tubs and then moved outside in early summer when the weather is warmer.*

CULTIVATION

Sowing time Spring (under glass)
Planting time Mid-spring (under glass); early summer (outside)
Planting distance 50cm (20in)
Distance between rows 50cm (20in)
Harvesting Mid-summer onwards

HARVESTING AND STORAGE

Cut each aubergine fruit from the plant when it is large enough – the flavour quickly deteriorates if they are allowed to become overripe. Harvest under glass from mid-summer and autumn for outside varieties. Aubergines are best used fresh from the garden although they can keep for up to two weeks once picked.

PESTS AND DISEASES

The usual greenhouse pests affect this crop if grown under glass. Aphids, red spider mite and whitefly are the main pests. Damping the floor down and misting the leaves will increase humidity, which will in turn discourage red spider mite.

VARIETIES

'Black Beauty F1' Produces dark violet coloured fruit that are oval to globe shaped. A very vigorous grower.
'Black Enorma' The largest fruit of all the varieties – up to 675g (1½lb).
'Easter Egg' A novelty fruit which is the colour and size of a large hen's egg. Taste is inferior to the traditional purple varieties.
'Long Purple' An old variety that has deep violet fruits that taste delicious. Not a heavy-yielding type.
'Money Maker' A popular new variety that produces good-sized purple fruits. Crops early.

aubergines (eggplant)

SWEETCORN (CORN)

Zea mays

This giant ornamental crop can reach a height of 1.5m (5ft) and needs a lot of room if it is to be grown in the vegetable garden. Sweetcorn is frost tender and is therefore best started off in the greenhouse and planted out in early summer in order to allow it the maximum growing season.

SOIL

Sweetcorn thrives on a free-draining soil that contains large amounts of organic matter. Dig the ground in the autumn and incorporate plenty of well-rotted manure or garden compost.

ASPECT

Requires a warm sunny location that is sheltered from strong winds.

SOWING

For an early crop, sow seeds under glass in mid-spring. For maximum germination the temperature should be around 13–15°C (55–59°F). Sow individually in pots, grow on and harden off before planting outside in early summer. Seed sown directly outside needs to be sown in late spring through to early summer after the danger of frost has passed. Crop protection is needed in the form of a cloche or cut-up plastic bottle.

CULTIVATION

Sowing time Mid-spring (under glass)
Planting out time Early summer
Sowing time Late spring to early summer (outside)
Sowing/planting distance 30cm (12in)
Sowing depth 2.5cm (1in)
Distance between rows 30cm (12in)
Harvesting Autumn

Sow in blocks, sowing two seeds 2.5cm (1in) deep every 30cm (12in) with 30cm (12in) between the rows. Remove the weaker seedlings after germination. Planting in blocks will ensure efficient wind pollination for the female flowers.

AFTERCARE

If cloche protection has been used to help get the crop off to a good start, remove the cloches when the leaves begin to touch the sides. Keep weeds down around the crop, but do not hoe as it is a shallow rooter. Water well throughout the growing season, especially during dry weather. Add liquid feed every two weeks when the cobs begin to swell.

HARVESTING AND STORAGE

The cobs are ready for harvesting when the tassels on the cobs turn brown. Test the cobs for ripeness. Pull back the sheath hiding the cobs, and squeeze one of the seeds. It is ripe if the liquid that oozes out is milky in colour. If the liquid is clear it is unripe. These are best eaten fresh because once they are cut the sugars change to starch. They will also keep well in the freezer.

PESTS AND DISEASES

Can be troubled by smut in hot dry weather. Large galls appear on the cobs which should be removed and destroyed. Destroy all plants after harvesting. Frit fly maggots can distort the growth of the crop at seedling stage.

Left: *The dying tassel of the female flower hangs from the developing cob. This indicates that it is ready for harvesting.*

Above: *To produce an early crop, start off the sweetcorn in a greenhouse and grow on before planting out in blocks.*

VARIETIES

'Golden Sweet F1' A sweet-tasting variety with bright yellow cobs. It has a high resistance to rust.
'Kelvedon Glory F1' An extremely heavy cropper with a good flavour.
'Minisweet' Produces mini cobs which are harvested at 10cm (4in) long.

mature sweetcorn

immature sweetcorn

FRUIT

Every garden has space for fruit. Even trees such as apples are available in compact varieties suitable for pots. Fruit trees can be trained into decorative shapes and also provide screens and boundaries. Larger gardens, however, may benefit from the cool tranquillity of an orchard of fruiting trees. Many people are reluctant to grow fruit because they are put off by what they see as the complex art of pruning. Fruit trees and bushes take two or more years before they start cropping and so give new gardeners time to learn their habits and master the intricacies of their culture.

Left: *Harvesting fresh, organically grown fruit is one of the greatest pleasures a gardener can experience.*

Above: *Ripening on the plant gives better sweetness and higher vitamin content than most shop bought fruit.*

Above: *Mouth-watering bunches of perfectly ripened fruit such as red currants provide colour during the summer.*

Above: *One of the delights of the fruit garden is the blossom that precedes the fruit. This is bramble blossom.*

STRAWBERRIES

Fragaria × ananassa

Strawberries are a popular fruit and also dependable for home production. The management of this crop is easier than that of tree fruits and even a small garden patch can yield a good crop of this delicious summer fruit.

OBTAINING PLANTS

While some strawberry varieties can be raised from seed, it is more common to buy plants. To be sure that your plants are true-to-type, vigorous and virus-free, purchase them from a reputable nursery. Always try to get registered virus-free plants as these can yield 50–75 per cent more fruit than ordinary stock plants. It is generally not advisable to transplant strawberries out of an old bed because diseases may be introduced.

SOIL AND PREFERRED ASPECT

Strawberries thrive on sandy loam soil, but will produce adequately on heavier soils provided they are well drained. A sloping site ensures good surface water drainage. The ideal soil pH is slightly acidic at between 6.0 and 6.5. The soil should contain adequate organic matter. Garden compost or manure is best dug in at the beginning of the season before planting. Alternatively, a green manure can be grown and dug in. When preparing strawberry plants for planting, never allow them to dry out. Cover the roots with moist peat moss or cloth, and keep the plants shaded at all times. Strawberries begin blooming in spring and can be subject to frost injury, so select a site that has good air movement. Avoid low-lying frost pockets and remember

Above: *Strawberries are so named because straw is placed under the ripening berries to keep them clean.*

that slopes facing the sun warm up faster in spring and stimulate earlier flowering, but can actually increase the danger of frost injury. In very frost-prone areas, a less sunny slope that delays blooming until after the seasonal danger of frost has passed can be to your advantage.

CULTIVATION

The goal during the first summer of growth after the spring planting is to establish healthy plants as early in the season as possible. In early summer, the parent plant sends out runners once it is established. Frequent, shallow cultivation between the rows, hand pulling of weeds and mulching with 5cm (2in) of hay, straw, or coarse sawdust two or three weeks after planting will greatly reduce the number of weeds.

Apply a fertilizer that is rich in potassium in late summer at the time flower buds are initiated for the next spring's fruit as this will help harden the plants for the coming winter.

Protect the crowns of plants during very cold periods in winter. Do not apply mulch too early in autumn as it can increase crown

rot and prevent the plants from completely going dormant, making them more subject to winter injury. Suitable mulches include newspapers, coarse sawdust, straw, hay or any loose mulch that does not compact.

Strawberry fruit is 90 per cent water and any moisture-stress during development will reduce yield. Always ensure that the crop is well watered while cropping.

HARVESTING AND STORAGE

Harvest when the berries are fully ripe. White areas indicate immaturity. Allowing the berry to reach full colour on the plant increases the sugar content and the size of the berry. Pick the berries with the stem and cap attached to allow the fruit to keep for a longer period. Berries that have their caps removed or are injured quickly go off.

The first harvest can occur about 30 days after the first bloom. Check every other day for ripe fruit. Place in shallow containers to minimize injury and chill promptly.

PESTS AND DISEASES

To avoid diseases, do not plant where tomatoes, potatoes, peppers or aubergines (eggplant) have been grown, or back into a site where strawberries have been grown in the last two years. Protect the fruit from birds with netting.

VARIETIES

'Baron Solemacher' Main cropper with a superb flavour and will tolerate a little shade. Tiny dark red fruits.

'Cambridge Favourite' Produces large red fruits that are mild in flavour. A good heavy cropper.

'Royal Sovereign' An early variety that has a superb flavour. Susceptible to pests and diseases.

'Trellisa' Really good-flavoured medium-sized fruit. Good variety for strawberry barrels.

strawberries

Above: *The developing fruit trusses can be protected from muddy splashes or soil borne rots with a mulch of straw.*

Above: *Removing the leaves and straw mulch after fruiting will prevent the build-up and spread of diseases.*

MELONS

Cucumis melo

Melons are popular with gardeners who have plenty of space to accommodate their spreading vines. They must be grown in a greenhouse or cold frame in cooler climates. Cantaloupes (muskmelons) do not tolerate cool temperatures or transplant very well, so wait until the soil is warm before planting seeds. Of the different types of melon available, cantaloupes are reputed to have the sweetest flavour, whereas honeydew melons store especially well.

OBTAINING PLANTS

Melons are grown annually from seed, which is sown from early to mid-spring, under glass in cooler areas. The seeds are sown about 1cm (½in) deep in pairs in a 7cm (2¾in) pot and the weaker one is thinned if both germinate. They can be potted on if outdoor conditions delay planting out. Greenhouse melons should be planted into their final position as soon as possible.

SOIL AND PREFERRED ASPECT

Melons can be grown outside in sheltered locations, but do better under cover in cooler areas. Melons require a fertile, well-drained soil that is not too rich and has a pH of 6.5–7. This should be cleared about three to four weeks before planting and the planting pit prepared. Each pit should measure 30 x 30 x 30cm (12 x 12 x 12in).

Above: *Melon vines are vigorous growers that must be restricted in order to ensure good-sized fruit.*

Place a good spade-full of well-rotted manure in the base before backfilling. Water the pit well and cover with plastic to warm up the soil in readiness for planting.

CULTIVATION

Seedlings are best planted out when they have developed four leaves and all danger of frost has passed. They should be planted with about 2–3cm (¾–1¼in) of the pot soil above ground level as a precaution against soft collar rot. Do not firm the soil but water each plant, keeping water off the stem. Plant the melons at 1–1.2m (3–4ft) intervals and place cloches and light shading over them for 7–10 days until they are established.

Melons should be stopped at the fourth or fifth leaf to encourage the production of side shoots. The four strongest side shoots should be kept and the rest removed after two to three weeks. Plants growing in cold frames should be trained into an "X"-shape.

Cantaloupes can also be grown on a trellis, but the fruit must be supported with a sling. Control the vigorous vines by pinching out the growing terminals once the melon crop has set. After this, pinch out all other lateral growths and flowers as they appear. Thinning may be necessary, particularly in areas with a shorter growing season. Bees are necessary for pollination and plants growing under cover may need pollinating by hand. One male flower should be sufficient for about four female flowers. Female flowers are easily recognized by the small embryonic fruit immediately behind them. Regular feeding and watering will aid the development of the crop. A good compost tea is especially useful for this.

HARVESTING AND STORAGE

The fruits are mature when there is a characteristic melon scent and circular cracking appears near to the stalk. When lifted they should part easily from the stalk. Melons do not store for more than a few days and are best eaten straightaway.

PESTS AND DISEASES

Melons are prey to relatively few diseases but a couple can be serious. Powdery mildew can be a problem as can soft collar rot if the stems are allowed to get wet. Verticillium wilt is a serious threat and affected plants should be removed. Many newer hybrid varieties are resistant to major diseases. Pests are generally less troublesome, red spider mite being the only potentially serious one in greenhouses and warmer areas.

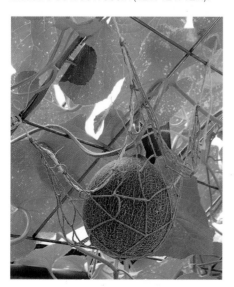

Above: *Melons can be trained to grow as greenhouse climbers, provided that the fruit is supported in a sling.*

VARIETIES

'Hero of Lockinge' Large fruits of a good flavour with a golden, fine-textured flesh. Good for forcing in cold frames.

'Ogen' Small fruits with a good flavour are borne on this early cropping variety. A good plant for cooler areas.

'Superlative' Large, almost round, green fruits with scarlet flesh. A good variety for greenhouses or cloche culture.

'Sweetheart' Medium-sized fruits with firm salmon-pink flesh. A hybrid variety suitable for colder areas.

cantaloupes (muskmelons)

water melons

APPLES

Malus domestica

There are currently numerous projects being undertaken worldwide to assess which varieties are best for organic garden culture. With such a wide choice of apples, this is a complex undertaking and the best advice is to grow a variety that is suited to your climate and taste. You may wish to consider those that are immune or quite resistant to apple scab. Others seem to be resistant to fireblight. If you choose a non-disease-resistant apple, you will have a very wide range of choice, but you will need to put more effort into controlling pests and diseases.

OBTAINING PLANTS

Propagation of apple trees is usually carried out by grafting a known variety on to a rootstock. This allows the grower to get the particular type of fruit that they want and the rootstock may confer other advantages such as disease resistance or dwarfing of the tree. It is possible to raise trees from seed but the results can be variable at best and at worst disappointing. This does not mean that a chance seedling would not produce a fine-tasting apple but most gardeners opt for the known variety and purchase stock for their gardens.

SOIL AND PREFERRED ASPECT

Apples are hardy in any open, sunny site, provided that it is not too exposed to strong winds. Apples tolerate a broad range of soils but thrive in a clay loam. They prefer a

Above: *Apples, restricted for growing in rows by hard pruning, will still yield large amounts of fruit.*

ROOTSTOCKS

The rootstock on an apple tree affects the size and rate of growth of the tree.

M27 An extreme dwarfing stock (bush, dwarf pyramid, cordon)

M9 Dwarfing stock (bush, dwarf pyramid, cordon)

M26 Semi-dwarfing stock (bush, dwarf pyramid, cordon)

MM106 Semi-dwarfing stock (bush, spindle bush, cordon, fan, espalier)

M7 Semi-dwarfing stock (bush, spindle bush, cordon, fan, espalier)

M4 Semi-vigorous stock (bush, spindle bush)

MM4 Vigorous stock (standard)

M2 Vigorous stock (standard)

MM111 Vigorous stock (half-standard, standard, large bush, large fans, large espaliers)

M25 Vigorous stock (standard)

MM109 Vigorous stock (standard)

M1 Vigorous stock (standard)

---

neutral to slightly alkaline soil that is rich, free-draining but moisture-retentive. Treat each newly planted tree with a general-purpose fertilizer such as fish, blood and bone and mulch with well-rotted organic matter to help the soil to retain moisture.

CULTIVATION

Apply mulch at regular intervals as the old mulch gradually breaks down. Keep the trees well watered in dry climates. Every spring, feed each tree with a general-purpose fertilizer. Some varieties only bear well every second year, with light crops every other year. Prevent this by thinning excess fruit in good years to give the tree strength for the following year. A light fall of apples is natural due to poor pollination. Excess fruit drop could be a sign of boron or magnesium deficiency or insufficient moisture.

PRUNING

Flower buds and fruit develop on the tips of the branches or on short two-year-old spurs along the branches. Train apples early in their life to the desired framework. As

---

PRUNING APPLES

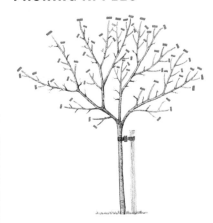

Spur pruning an apple bush tree
After planting, cut back the leader to about 75cm (30in) above the ground. Leave any side shoots that appear just below this cut and remove any others lower down. The following year, reduce all new growth by about half. This will form the basic framework. Subsequent pruning is restricted to reducing the length of new growth by about a third and removing overcrowded growth.

Planting and pruning an apple cordon *These are planted as feather maidens at 45° to the wirework. All side shoots are cut back to three buds on planting. Subsequent summer pruning (far right) consists of cutting back any new side shoots to three leaves and new growth on existing side shoots to one leaf. Winter pruning (right) consists of thinning out any of the older spurs if they have become congested.*

Left: *Growing apples as cordons is the ideal space-saving method if you only have a small garden and wish to grow some fruit.*

HARVESTING AND STORAGE

Harvest the fruit when fully matured and well coloured, according to the variety that you are growing.

PESTS AND DISEASES

If you are putting in trees for the first time, consider planting disease-resistant cultivars. Many new varieties will go a long way towards solving disease problems before they start.

Common diseases include apple scab, which shows as rough spots on fruits and leaves. Powdery mildew appears as a whitish powder on foliage. Both these diseases can be avoided by planting resistant cultivars or using sulphur spray in spring and summer. Fireblight is another problem, causing withering of branch tips, then entire branches, and sometimes, whole trees. Plant resistant cultivars and prune out infected wood. Codling moths create large tunnels to the core of the apples. Wrap tree trunks in corrugated cardboard to trap larvae that have left the fruits and are looking for a place to pupate. You can also use sticky pheromone traps to attract male codling moths.

To avoid some of these diseases, follow commonsense techniques. Prune trees for good air circulation, which lessens fungal problems, and clean up fallen apples.

trees mature, pruning mainly involves removing crowded branches. Annual pruning encourages new growth shoots and continual fruiting spur development. Large vegetative growth may indicate too heavy pruning. A large crop of small fruit indicates too little pruning.

POLLINATION USING CRAB APPLES

All apple varieties, whether they are cooking apples or dessert types, need pollination with another apple variety. This involves planting two trees near to each other. A good way to make sure that most varieties will be pollinated is to use a crab apple with a long flowering period. There are many of these and two of the best varieties for this purpose are listed below. Alternatively, you can purchase trees that have two (or more) varieties grafted on to the one rootstock.

Malus 'John Downie' has a long flowering period and thus pollinates most other apples. It is good for wildlife and very attractive, bearing bright red fruit.

Malus x *zumi* var. *calocarpa* 'Golden Hornet' is a spreading tree which has dark green leaves, white flowers and abundant golden-yellow apples. It is an excellent pollinator.

VARIETIES

'Braeburn' Large, green fruit with a red blush. Ripens very late but keeps well. Partly self-fertile although it will not pollinate with 'Fuji'. Developed in New Zealand from 'Granny Smith'.

'Cox Orange Pippin' An award-winning apple for taste that keeps up to three months. The fruit is multi-purpose. The tree is less ornamental than some apple trees. It prefers cold winters and requires pruning.

'Fuji' Round to flat apple with a very sweet yellow-orange flesh. Skin colour is red if given enough sunlight and cool temperatures. One of the best sweet eating apples. Stores well.

'Gala' Small- to medium-sized, conic-shaped red apple with excellent flavour and keeping qualities. Possibly the best variety for the early season although it will not cross-pollinate 'Golden Delicious'.

'Golden Delicious' Conic-shaped apple with a long stem, yellow to green skin, yellow flesh, and russet dots. Sweet, juicy, fine-textured. Stores well but susceptible to bitter pit and bruising. Erratic in self-fertility.

'Granny Smith' Round, green to yellow-skinned apple that is quite firm, has crisp flesh and keeps very well. If harvested early, it is green and tart, while later harvested fruit is yellow-coloured and sweet.

'Jonagold' The skin is yellow with red stripes; the flesh is sweet and mild and usually used fresh or baked. 'Jonagold' ripens in mid-autumn and keeps about three months. The tree is vigorous and productive but susceptible to mildew and scab. Its pollen is sterile, so it needs a pollinator although it will not return the favour.

apples

PEARS

Pyrus communis

Pears are among the easiest of the tree fruits to produce organically because their fertility requirements are not high. They are adapted to a wide range of climates and soils and pest problems are less than for other tree fruits. There are many varieties of pear. Asian and European pears can pollinate each other, but Asian pears often finish blooming by the time Europeans get started. For cross-pollination between pear species, avoid teaming early bloomers among the Asians, such as 'Seuri' and 'Yali', with late bloomers among the Europeans, such as 'Comice' and 'Ubileen.'

OBTAINING PLANTS

Pears can be grown from seed, but you cannot guarantee the quality of the resulting fruit. It is better to purchase known stock from a recognized nursery.

SOIL AND PREFERRED ASPECT

Pears are hardy in any open, sunny site, provided that it is not too exposed to strong winds. They can grow in most soils, but a moderately rich, well-draining soil that is neutral or slightly alkaline is usually best. Very rich soils will stimulate rapid leafy growth that can be disease susceptible and

ROOTSTOCKS

As with apples, the rootstock on which a pear tree grows affects the size and rate of growth of the tree.

Quince C Moderately dwarfing stock (bush, cordon, dwarf pyramid, espalier or fan)
Quince A Semi-vigorous stock (bush, cordon, dwarf pyramid, espalier or fan)
Pear Vigorous stock (standard, half-standard)

Right: *Most pears are ready for picking by the autumn, but they must be fully ripened off the tree.*

there is therefore no need to add lots of organic matter unless the soil is very poor or excessively free draining.

CULTIVATION

European pears Pears, like most other fruit trees, are grown by grafting the variety on to a rootstock. Seedlings of European pears (often from Bartlett pears) are usually used for rootstocks. Plant standard-sized trees about 5–8m (16–26ft) apart and dwarf trees about 3–4.5m (10–15ft) apart. Some varieties of pear always need cross-pollination, while others are reliably self-fertile.

Asian pears These are slightly less cold hardy than European types and may suffer tissue damage at temperatures below -20°C (-4°F). Most Asian pears also bloom slightly earlier than their European counterparts and may lose some blooms or buds to freezing in areas that are prone to late frosts. Growing Asian pears is similar to growing European types, but not identical. Asian pears tend to set too heavy a fruit crop, which requires hand thinning of young fruits soon after bloom to ensure a good crop. If heavy-bearing Asian pear varieties are not properly thinned, then the fruit size and quality will suffer.

PRUNING PEARS

Pruning an espaliered pear *After planting, cut back to two buds above the bottom wire. In the first summer, tie the central growth to a vertical cane and the next two shoots to canes at 45°. Cut back all other shoots to two leaves. In autumn, lower the two side shoots to the horizontal and tie the cane to the bottom wire. In winter, cut back the leader to two buds above the second wire and repeat the above until the espalier covers all the wires. When established, cut back all new shoots to three leaves each summer.*

Pruning a dwarf pyramid pear *After planting, cut back the leader by about a third. Cut back the side shoots to about 15cm (6in). In the first summer, cut back the new growth on the main side shoots to about five leaves and on the secondary shoots to three leaves. Thereafter, cut back new growth on the main stems to five leaves and reduce other new growth to one leaf. During the winter, thin out any congested spurs.*

PRUNING

Pruning pears is generally similar to that of apple trees and involves cutting off unnecessary branches so that light can reach all parts of the tree. Pear trees are also best kept quite low to make it easier to pick the fruit.

HARVESTING AND STORAGE

Bartlett pears ripen in summer, but most other varieties ripen later, usually in early autumn. European pears ripen to perfection only when they are removed from the tree and so are picked while they are still green and hard. The fruit will ripen in a cool place where the temperature does not exceed 24°C (75°F). Asian pears, however, will ripen on the tree and do not have to be picked and then cured like European pears. Pick them once they colour up, when they should be sweet.

PESTS AND DISEASES

Pears have most of the same pest and disease problems as apples, but usually to a considerably lesser degree. One problem that can cause serious damage is fireblight. Fireblight is greatly favoured by young, succulent tissues and it is better to try and limit the rate of growth to avoid this. Never try to compensate for rapid growth rates by pruning, as this will only stimulate the production of more susceptible soft tissue growth. Using less compost than for apples, never using manure, not applying large amounts of fertilizer and avoiding growing clovers and other legumes around the tree will ultimately yield better results.

Choosing fireblight-resistant pear cultivars is also a good start, but cultural controls are the best way to limit the spread of this disease. As a group, it is probably accurate to say that Asian pears are slightly more resistant to fireblight than European types. Once fireblight infection has occurred, there is no spray or other treatment (beyond quickly cutting out newly infected limbs) that will minimize damage. If cutting during the growing season, all blighted twigs, branches and cankers should be removed at least 10cm (4in) below the last point of visible infection, and burned. After each cut, the secateurs (hand pruners) should be sterilized in a disinfectant solution. During winter, when temperatures render the bacteria inactive, pruning out of fireblight-infected wood can proceed without sterilization.

The codling moth is probably the most important direct pest of the fruit. Capsid bugs and other "true" bugs will also feed on pears. Early feeding damage may result in a puckering or dimpling. Mid- and late-season feeding often leads to the development of so-called "stone cells" beneath the feeding site. The best way to deal with insect pests is to encourage natural predators such as lacewings around your pear tree.

Above: *Pear trees can be trained into a variety of decorative shapes such as this elegant cone.*

VARIETIES

EUROPEAN PEARS

'Bartlett' Ripens mid-season but stores poorly. Blooms early and so needs an early companion variety for pollination. Fruit tolerates intense sun better than average.

'Beth' An excellent, English-bred, self-fertile dessert pear that fruits in mid-autumn. A high-yielding and regular cropper, with white flesh that has a melting texture and excellent flavour. Will commence fruiting from early in its life.

'Comice' Juicy, yellow fruit with good flesh that ripens in mid-autumn, but will keep till mid-winter. Resists fireblight. Best in mild winters. Blooms very late, so not a reliable pollinator for early-blooming varieties.

'Conference' The large, yellow fruit is juicy and sweet, ripening in mid-autumn and keeping till mid-winter. Blooms early and will cross-pollinate with most Asian pears.

'Ubileen' An early ripener (but not bloomer), usually picked in mid-summer and ripening in late summer. The large fruit is yellow with a red blush and a buttery texture. This variety is quite disease resistant.

ASIAN PEARS

'Chojura' A late-blooming variety that has russeted fruit, with slightly astringent skin, which ripens in early autumn and keeps well.

'Seuri' This productive, fireblight-resistant and cold-hardy variety has very large orange fruit that ripens in mid-autumn and does not keep well. This variety blooms very early and is best planted with another early bloomer such as 'Yali'. It will not reliably pollinate any European pear.

'Shinsui' This variety forms a vigorous, upright tree with russeted fruit that is small, juicy and sweet.

'Yali' A hardy variety with deep red autumn foliage. The fruit is classically pear-shaped, yellow and ripens in mid-autumn. This early-blooming variety is a reliable pollinator only for 'Seuri' and other early-blooming varieties (not Europeans) and needs a fairly long cold season.

pears

APRICOTS

Prunus armeniaca

Apricots originally come from warm climates so will need a sunny sheltered spot in cooler regions. In temperate climates, they are best grown as fans against a sunny wall or in a greenhouse, although they can be grown as dwarf pyramid trees in warmer areas.

OBTAINING PLANTS

Apricots are propagated by budding them on to rootstocks. Most apricot plants are obtained as bought plants from specialist nurseries. Trees are usually planted during the dormant winter period. Only plant freestanding bush trees in warmer areas where the early flowers will not be damaged by early spring frosts.

SOIL AND PREFERRED ASPECT

Apricots require a moisture-retentive, friable and well-drained soil, rarely prospering in a stiff clay or heavy loam, and a sunny, sheltered site. A pH of 6–6.5 is desirable.

CULTIVATION

Water regularly in the first season and subsequently in dry spells as mature trees may wilt badly. Saturate greenhouse soils in late winter and mulch with well-rotted organic material. Protect the blossom of outdoor specimens from frost by draping horticultural fleece over the trees at night and removing it by day to allow pollinating

insects to work. It may be necessary to assist pollination in cooler areas and under glass by hand.

If the fruit set is heavy, then the crop may need thinning. This is done first at "pea-size" to one fruitlet per cluster, then again after stoning, and when the natural drop is over. Test for stoning by pressing a pin into a few fruitlets. The final spacing of fruit should be about 8–15cm (3¼–6in) apart.

Plants up to fruiting age should be fed in early spring with a general-purpose fertilizer such as fish, blood and bone to encourage growth. Once they reach fruiting age, mulch annually with well-rotted farmyard manure.

PRUNING

Fruit forms on both young wood and old spurs and so it is best to maintain a proportion of each. Shorten the leaders annually by one-third and tie in one healthy shoot per 25cm (10in) of main branch, remove ill-placed and upright growing

Left: *Apricots make fine specimens when trained as fans. Canes and wires help to maintain the shape.*

ROOTSTOCK

The rootstock will affect the size and rate of growth of the tree.

St Julien A Semi-vigorous stock (bush, fan)
Brompton A Vigorous stock (bush)

---

shoots. Pinch back the rest to four leaves from early summer onwards. Prune fan-trained specimens every year.

HARVESTING AND STORAGE

Leave to ripen on the tree to develop their flavour. The fruit is ripe when it comes away easily by lifting it with a twisting motion.

PESTS AND DISEASES

The main diseases are silver leaf, bacterial canker and brown rot diseases. Aphids, wasps and flies are the main pests.

PRUNING AN ESTABLISHED APRICOT FAN

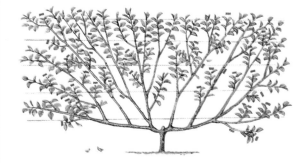

Once the fan has been established, the object of subsequent pruning is to maintain the shape. Cut out any shoots that are pointing in the wrong direction, especially those that point towards or away from the wall. Thin new shoots, leaving one every 15cm (6in). Prune the remaining shoots to five leaves in the spring and then again, after fruiting, back to three leaves.

VARIETIES

'Alfred' Produces fruit of a good flavour that is orange with a pink flush. Fruit ripens in mid- to late summer. A vigorous tree that flowers early and tends to crop biennially.

'Breda' This variety has fruit that is medium to large and orange with a dark red flush. It ripens against a wall in late summer or early autumn in the open. Heavy cropping, but tends to be short-lived.

'Moorpark' An extremely popular variety that has large fruit of a rich sweet flavour. It is a regular cropper that ripens in late summer. A moderately vigorous plant that is prone to dieback.

apricots

PLUMS

Prunus domestica and *P. salicina*

Plums are divided into two categories: the European plum, *Prunus domestica*, and the Japanese plum, *P. salicina*. European plums are usually self-fertile, but cross-pollination will ensure a better crop. Japanese plums are mostly self-infertile. There are many suitable cultivars but the most popular are the ones that provide fruit until late in the growing season.

OBTAINING PLANTS

Plums are almost always obtained as bought plants from specialist nurseries. There is no truly satisfactory dwarfing rootstock for plums, although trees are sometimes grown on rootstocks described as "semi-dwarf". Even these would be too large for a small garden, as a bush-type tree requires a spacing of 4–5m (13–16ft).

SOIL AND PREFERRED ASPECT

Plums need a well-drained soil, with plenty of organic material to hold moisture in the growing season, and a pH of 6.0– 6.5. An acid soil can be limed, but do not plant in an alkaline soil. Trees in thin soils over chalk often suffer from lime-induced iron deficiency. Grow fan-trained plums against a sunny wall.

Above: *While this cluster of plums growing against a sunny wall looks very appetizing, it could have been thinned earlier to ensure larger fruit.*

CULTIVATION

Plant plums between late autumn and early spring. Stake and mulch with well-rotted manure. An established plum needs plenty of nitrogen but, until good crops are being carried, it is usually sufficient to mulch with rotted manure or compost in spring. When crops are being borne, supplement the yearly mulch with a dressing of pelleted chicken manure.

PRUNING

Plums are not very amenable to training, and are seldom satisfactory as cordons or espaliers. They may, however, be grown as fans for wall-training or with the support of posts and horizontal wires. Root-pruning will probably be necessary every five years to restrain growth and maintain fruiting.

Plums may also be grown as semi-dwarf pyramids on a St Julien A rootstock. Such a tree requires a spacing of 3.5m (12ft).

HARVESTING AND STORAGE

Leave on the tree until ripe, then handle carefully. Pick when a bloom appears on the skin for cooking or preserves.

PESTS AND DISEASES

The main problems are aphids, red spider mite, plum sawfly, wasps and birds as well as rust, silver leaf and bacterial canker.

ROOTSTOCK

The rootstock chosen for a plum tree affects the size and rate of growth.

Pixy Dwarfing stock (bush, pyramid)
Damas C Moderately vigorous stock
St Julien A Semi-vigorous stock
(bush, fan, pyramid)
Brompton A Vigorous stock
(half-standard, standard)
Myrobalan B Vigorous stock
(half-standard, standard)

PRUNING AN ESTABLISHED PLUM FAN

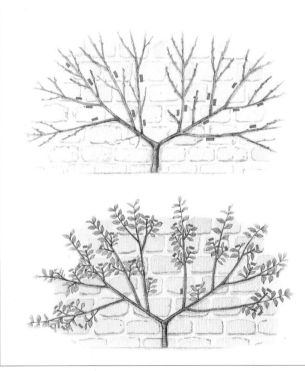

Pruning a plum fan in spring and summer
The main aim when pruning a plum fan is to maintain the fan shape. In spring (above left), cut out any new side shoots that are pointing to or away from the wall. If necessary, reduce the number of new shoots to about one every 15cm (6in). In summer (below left), cut back all new shoots to about six leaves, leaving any that are needed to fill in gaps in the framework. In autumn, after cropping, further cut back the shoots to three leaves.

VARIETIES

'Czar' A reliable bearer of juicy, blue-black fruit with yellow-green flesh in late summer. A fairly compact tree, hardy and usually frost-resistant. Succeeds in shade and fully self-fertile.
'Merryweather' A self-fertile damson, with large, blue-black fruit. Fruits well into the autumn.
'Victoria' Pale red, oval fruits with a greeny-yellow flesh. It can be a heavy cropper on a reasonably frost-free site and is fully self-fertile, bearing fruit in late summer to early autumn.

red plums   yellow plums

PEACHES AND NECTARINES

Prunus persica and *P. persica nectarina*

Peaches and nectarines are identical in all their cultivation requirements, although peaches are slightly hardier and more reliable in cooler areas. They both originate in warm climates and so need a sunny, sheltered spot. For this reason, they are best grown as fans against a sunny wall or in a greenhouse.

Both peaches and nectarines are self-fertile, so only one plant need be grown` if space is limited. They do not fruit until their fourth year of growing but will live for about 30 years once established.

OBTAINING PLANTS

Both peaches and nectarines are grown from stock bought from specialist nurseries. They are are normally planted during their dormant phase in winter. They are not particularly vigorous and dwarfing rootstocks are not essential. If you intend growing peaches or nectarines as a fan, use a plant that is grafted on to St Julien A or Brompton rootstock. If a very small bush is required for container growing, use a plant on Pixy rootstock.

SOIL AND PREFERRED ASPECT

Peaches and nectarines require very fertile, deep, well-drained loam, with a pH of 6.5–7.0. Full sun is essential if the bushes are to prosper. Only plant freestanding bush trees in warmer areas where early flowers will not be damaged by early spring frosts. If these are a problem grow as a fan against a sunny wall for protection.

Above: *Peaches, grown as fans, are both a decorative and productive way to cover a sunny wall.*

ROOTSTOCKS

The rootstock will affect the size and rate of growth of the tree.

Pixy Dwarfing stock (small bush)
St Julien A Semi-vigorous stock (bush, fan)
Brompton A Vigorous stock (bush)

CULTIVATION

Plants that have not reached fruiting age should be fed in early spring with a general-purpose fertilizer such as fish, blood and bone to encourage growth. Once they reach fruiting age, mulch annually with well-rotted farmyard manure. Protect the flowers from frost in the early part of the year with a horticultural fleece drape, ensuring that this is removed during the day to allow access for pollinating insects (smaller plants can be hand pollinated using a small sable brush). Never allow plants to become drought stressed once fruit has set, particularly when plants are growing against a sunny wall.

PRUNING

Like other stone fruit, never prune in the winter due to the risk of infection from silver leaf and bacterial canker. Prune freestanding trees in early spring by removing dead or diseased wood, crossing branches that can cause damage by rubbing and overcrowded branches. Prune fan-trained bushes every year. They are pruned by a renewal method in a similar way to that used for fan-trained cherries.

HARVESTING AND STORAGE

Allow to ripen fully before harvesting. The fruit is ripe when it comes away from the tree easily. Store for a few days once picked. Preserve for later use as freezing destroys much of the fruit's texture.

PESTS AND DISEASES

Both peaches and nectarines are prone to the same ailments. Common diseases include peach leaf curl, silver leaf, bacterial canker and mildew. Pests are only an occasional problem, the most serious ones being aphids and red spider mites. Scale insects can be a problem in the greenhouse.

PRUNING AN ESTABLISHED PEACH BUSH TREE

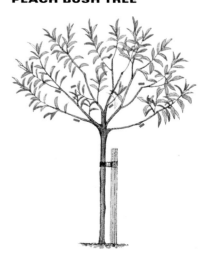

Not a great deal of pruning is required for a peach bush tree. In spring, cut back some of the older barren wood as far as a replacement new shoot. Also remove any awkwardly placed branches and keep the bush open and airy. Avoid making large cuts, as this is likely to allow canker to infect the tree.

VARIETIES

PEACHES

'Amsden June' Produces fruit with a good flavour. Ripens in mid-summer. Grow under glass or in the open.
'Peregrine' Large, round, crimson fruit with an excellent flavour. Crops well, ripening in late summer. Is suitable for growing in the open in warmer areas.

NECTARINES

'Early Rivers' Large yellow fruits with a rich flavour. Ripens in mid-summer.
'Lord Napier' Large yellow-orange fruits with a rich flavour. Ripens in late summer.

nectarines

peaches

CHERRIES

Prunus species

There are two main groups of cherry that are cultivated for their fruit: the sweet or dessert cherry (*Prunus avium*) and the acid or sour cherry (*Prunus cerasus*). The sweet is the type eaten as a raw dessert fruit, whereas the acid is usually cooked.

OBTAINING PLANTS

Named varieties are propagated on to rootstocks by budding in mid- or late summer or by grafting in early spring. There is currently no dwarfing rootstock available and a mature sweet cherry tree may grow up to 10m (33ft) in height. Bush Morello (acid) trees, on the other hand, rarely reach a height of 5m (16ft). Many varieties can be grown as fan-trained specimens.

SOIL AND PREFERRED ASPECT

Grow in a deep, very fertile, well-drained loam with a pH of 6.0–7.0. Sweet cherries need full sun, but acid cherries prefer light shade and can be trained as fans against a wall receiving little sun.

CULTIVATION

Plant at any time from mid-autumn to early spring. Mulch trees annually with manure or compost and feed fan-trained specimens regularly with a liquid feed.

Above: *Few fruits can rival fresh juicy cherries that have been ripened to perfection on the bush.*

PRUNING

Standard and bush trees need little pruning. Maintain an open, balanced habit and remove dead, crossing and rubbing branches. Sour cherries fruit on shoots formed the previous season. For fan training, after the basic fan of branches has been built up, annually replaced side growths are tied in parallel to the permanent branches. The replacement shoots are selected during late spring through to late summer.

HARVESTING AND STORAGE

Leave to ripen on the tree for as long as possible. Sweet cherries are best eaten at once but acid cherries can be stored for a few days. Freeze or preserve to store for longer.

SWEET CHERRY POLLINATION GROUPS

Cherries fruit best if grown near to another variety from the same group that flowers at the same time. This is not necessary for self-pollinating varieties such as 'Morello' or 'Stella'. Flowering period: (e) early; (m) mid-season; (l) late.

Group 1 'Early Rivers' (e), 'Bedford Prolific' (e), 'Knight's Early Black' (e), 'Roundel Heart' (m)

Group 2 'Bigarreau de Schrecken' (e), 'Waterloo' (e), 'Merton Favourite' (e), 'Frogmore Early' (m), 'Merton Bigarreau' (m), 'Merton Bounty' (m)

Group 3 'Bigarreau Napoleon' (m), 'Emperor Francis' (m)

Group 4 'Merton Premier' (m), 'Amber Heart' (m)

Group 5 'Merton Heart' (e), 'Governor Wood' (m)

Group 6 'Bradbourne Black' (l), 'Geante de Hedelfingen' (l)

Universal Donors 'Noir de Guben' (e); 'Merton Glory' (m), 'Bigarreau Gaucher' (l)

PESTS AND DISEASES

Bacterial canker and silver leaf, both of which are spread by pruning. The main pests are birds, blackfly (aphids) and winter moths.

PRUNING ESTABLISHED CHERRY TREES

Sour cherry fan *Once established, there are two purposes to pruning a cherry fan: to keep the fan shape and to ensure that there is a constant supply of new wood. To keep the shape completely, remove any shoots that are pointing in the wrong direction. For renewal, cut back in summer all shoots that have fruited, preferably as far back as the next new shoot. Tie these new shoots to the cane and wire framework.*

Sour cherry bush or tree *Once established, bush and full-sized sour cherry trees need little pruning other than to remove a third of the old fruiting wood, cutting back to a new growth. You should also remove any branches that are crossing.*

VARIETIES

DESSERT

'Bradbourne Black' A large, rich, dark crimson cherry that ripens in mid-summer and is a heavy cropper.

'Kentish Red' A bush of medium vigour that ripens in mid- to late summer. Good on a non-sunny wall. Fruits have a good resistance to bacterial canker.

'Stella' A vigorous variety with large, dark red fruits. A heavy-yielding variety that is also self-compatible.

ACID

'Morello' Juicy fruit with a bitter-sweet flavour when ripe. Crops regularly and is moderately vigorous, ripening in summer to early autumn.

cherries

BLACKCURRANTS

Ribes nigrum

Blackcurrants need a lot of space but are worth growing, as they are extremely high in vitamin C. Aside from this they are one of the true pleasures of summer and more than compensate for their space demands. They also have the advantage of being self-fertile, which means that you only need to grow one bush in order to get a good crop.

OBTAINING PLANTS

Blackcurrants can be propagated quite easily from hardwood cuttings during the dormant season. Choose healthy, blemish-free branches from the previous season's growth that are about 15–20cm (6–8in) long and about the thickness of a pencil. These will make good plants in about three years. More usually, however, plants are bought in.

SOIL AND PREFERRED ASPECT

Blackcurrants are heavy feeders that need a deep, fertile and well-drained soil. It is well worth while taking the time to prepare the soil properly prior to planting. The ideal soil pH is 6.5 and the site should be sheltered and sunny. Blackcurrants will tolerate light shade but the amount of fruit produced will be less.

CULTIVATION

Bare-rooted stock is planted in late autumn or early winter, whereas container-grown stock can be planted out at any time of the year. Plants should be spaced 1.8m (6ft) apart with 2m (6½ft) between rows.

Above: *Blackcurrants should be picked as whole trusses complete with the stalks to prevent damage.*

Blackcurrants grow as stooled bushes, which means that they send up new shoots from below ground level. When planting, set the plant 5cm (2in) lower in the ground than it was when grown in the nursery or pot, as this will encourage the formation of new shoots. Ensure that you cut back all the shoots to ground level after planting.

Blackcurrants have a high nitrogen requirement and need feeding with about 100g (4oz) fish, blood and bone or a similar organic compound fertilizer in spring. They benefit from a mulch of well-rotted manure or garden compost and, if growth seems poor, give a further feed in early summer.

PRUNING

Blackcurrants are always grown as freestanding bushes, so no support or training is needed. They produce fruit on wood made the previous year which means

that in the first year, little or no pruning will be needed, save removing dead, diseased or damaged branches. The second and subsequent years' pruning involves cutting the fruited wood back to ground level to encourage further strong growth. This is done in late summer after fruiting and, as the bushes get older, you may find that fewer shoots are produced from below ground level. If this happens, prune out all the old wood as low as possible just above a young shoot.

It is best to work on a three-year cycle, in the third year cutting out the first year's wood, in the fourth year cutting out the second year's growth, etc. This keeps the bush with a set of branches that will fruit and a set that will fruit the following year.

HARVESTING AND STORAGE

Pick the fruits as clumps when they are ripe. Some gardeners prefer to cut out the whole branch for convenience because this also prunes the bush at the same time. Blackcurrants are practically impossible to store fresh and are best eaten straightaway. They can be frozen or preserved as jelly.

PESTS AND DISEASES

Commonly encountered diseases include mildew, botrytis, leaf spot and reversion disease. The more commonly encountered pests are aphids, sawfly, big bud mite and birds. Provide netting in order to protect against marauding birds.

PRUNING A BLACKCURRANT BUSH

After planting, cut blackcurrant bushes back to a single bud above the ground. The following winter, remove any weak or misplaced growth. Subsequent pruning should take place after fruiting and consists of cutting out up to a third of two-year-old or older wood in order to stimulate new growth. Also remove any weak or misplaced stems.

RED AND WHITE CURRANTS

Ribes rubrum

Red and white currants are relatively easy to grow, even tolerating a little light shade. They can be grown as a bush or trained on walls. Currants fruit on wood that is one year old or off spurs on very old wood. The limited range of varieties belies their versatility as a culinary fruit.

OBTAINING PLANTS
Currants are usually bought in or raised from hardwood cuttings taken during the dormant period.

SOIL AND PREFERRED ASPECT
Grow in a deep, fertile and well-drained soil that has had well-rotted garden compost or manure worked in. The pH of the soil should be kept at about 6.5 to maintain healthy growth. The site should be sheltered and sunny to ensure the best cropping. Currants flower in early spring, so may need some form of protection against frost.

CULTIVATION
Plant bare-rooted stock in autumn or early winter and plants raised in containers at any time. Allow 1.8m (6ft) between plants and 2m (6½ft) between rows. When planting, set the plant at the same level as it was in the nursery or pot. Single cordons should be planted so that the arms are 30cm (12in) apart, double cordons 60cm (24in) apart and triple cordons 90cm (36in) apart.

All varieties of currant are self-fertile, making them ideal for even the smallest of

Above: *Red currants should only be picked when the fruit is fully ripe and has turned completely red.*

Above: *Red and white currants, grown here as cordons, are tied to vertical canes that are attached to lateral wires.*

gardens. They require a lot of potassium to flourish and will need feeding each spring. A browning on the leaf margins indicates a potassium deficiency, best countered with a liquid foliar feed of seaweed extract.

PRUNING
Freestanding bushes need training to produce a strong cup-shaped bush. Prune the bush in the summer, immediately after harvesting. Reduce the side shoots to five leaves and when the main stems have reached the desired height, treat these in the same way.

Train cordon-grown currants upwards rather than at an angle by pruning the main arms in winter. Cut back the leading shoot, leaving two-thirds of the last season's growth. The following summer, prune after harvesting by cutting any side shoots back to 7cm (2¾in) and any secondary shoots back to 2.5cm (1in).

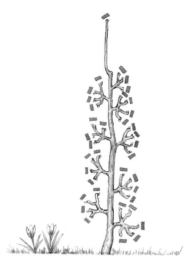

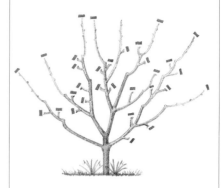

PRUNING CURRANTS

Pruning a red or white currant cordon *On planting, cut back the leader by half of its new growth and the side shoots to one bud. Thereafter, cut back the side shoots every summer to five leaves and, in winter, further reduce these to one bud.*

Pruning a red or white currant bush *After planting, cut back each shoot by about half. Subsequent pruning involves ensuring that the plant becomes an open bush. Cut back all new growth on the main shoots and reduce the new growth on all side shoots to one bud.*

HARVESTING AND STORAGE
Pick the sprigs of fruit whole when ripe. Eat straightaway, preserve as jelly or freeze.

PESTS AND DISEASES
Currants are generally trouble free if grown in good soil and well fed. Common diseases include mildew and leaf spot, while pests include aphids, sawfly and birds.

VARIETIES

RED CURRANT 'Red Lake'
Long trusses of large red berries in mid-summer. An excellent cropping variety.

red currants

WHITE CURRANT 'White Versailles'
A large currant in mid-summer. Excellent variety for making jams.

white currants

GOOSEBERRIES

Ribes uva-crispum

Gooseberries are one of the earliest soft fruits of the year. The traditional method of growing was as a bush but modern techniques include single, double and triple cordons. Cordons can take up as little as 15cm (6in) of growing space. All varieties are self-fertile, so only one plant can be grown if space is at a premium.

OBTAINING PLANTS
Gooseberry plants should be bought from a reputable organic supplier.

SOIL AND PREFERRED ASPECT
Gooseberries do best in a soil with a pH of 6.5 in a sunny, sheltered site. Fork over a wide area to break up the soil and remove weeds before digging the planting hole. Add garden compost or rotted manure to the soil at the base of the pit, along with about 50g (1¾oz) of fish, blood and bone or a similar general-purpose organic fertilizer.

CULTIVATION
Plant bare-rooted stock in autumn or early winter and container-grown plants at any time. Gooseberries are grown on a "leg" or stem so cut back all the side shoots before planting. Spread out the roots of bare-rooted bushes in the hole and cover with well-conditioned soil. Firm the soil around the roots. With container-grown bushes, keep the surface of the rootball level with the surrounding soil. Apply two handfuls of bonemeal to the soil when filling in and mulch with a well-rotted manure or compost. Plant bushes 1.2–1.8m (4–6ft) apart in rows, depending on the vigour of the variety. Allow a spacing of around 2m (6½ft) between each row. Plant single cordons

Left: *Gooseberries make excellent cordons. Train them up canes that are supported by lateral wires.*

Above: *Start picking gooseberries before the first berries are fully ripe in order to give the remainder an opportunity to ripen.*

30cm (12in) apart, double cordons 60cm (24in) apart and triple cordons 90cm (36in) apart, allowing 1.2m (4ft) between rows.

Keep well watered until established, and cover the soil around them with a 5–7.5cm (2–3in) thick mulch of compost or bark.

Freestanding bushes need no support. Cordons require wires, either attached to the fence or to posts. Gooseberries need high levels of potassium and feeding with a general-purpose fertilizer in spring as well as mulching with well-rotted manure or compost. If growth is poor, feed again in early summer. Browning of the leaves indicates a potash deficiency; apply a liquid foliar feed of seaweed extract. Cover the fruits with fleece to protect against frost.

PRUNING
Prune freestanding bushes after harvesting by reducing side shoots to five leaves. Treat the main stems in the same way when they reach their required height and cut out any damaged, dead or overcrowded stems. Prune cordons after harvesting by cutting any side shoots to 7cm (2¾in) and any secondary shoots to 2.5cm (1in).

HARVESTING AND STORAGE
Start picking heavy crops before they are fully ripe to allow remaining berries to ripen. Use the unripe berries in cooking. Eat straightaway, freeze or preserve.

PESTS AND DISEASES
Mildew and leaf spot are common. Pests are usually limited to aphids, sawfly and birds. Protect against birds with netting.

PRUNING A GOOSEBERRY

The basic aim when pruning gooseberries is to create an open framework. Establish a framework, first of all, by removing the basal shoots and cutting back the main shoots by about half in their first and second years. After this, cut back the new growth on the leaders in winter by about half and reduce the side shoots from these to two buds. Remove any damaged wood and any branches that cross or rub. Remove suckers and basal growth. In summer, prune the side shoots back to five leaves, but leave the main stems uncut.

VARIETIES
'Careless' Large green-skinned fruits ripening to white in summer. A reliable and heavy-yielding variety.

'Keepsake' Excellent flavoured fruits that are green-white in colour, transparent and slightly hairy. Can be picked early for cooking.

'Lancashire Lad' This bush produces large, dark red, oblong, hairy fruits that are extremely juicy. It has some resistance to mildew.

'Leveller' A fertile soil is required to ensure heavy cropping. This variety produces large, oval, yellow-green fruits with a slightly hairy skin and an excellent flavour.

gooseberries

RASPBERRIES

Rubus idaeus

Raspberries are unusual in that their roots and crowns are perennial, while their stems or canes are biennial. During the first growing season, the shoots of summer-bearing raspberries are strictly vegetative (non-fruiting). The following year, these canes flower, produce fruit, and then die. Autumn-bearing raspberries, on the other hand, produce fruit in the autumn at the tips of the current season's growth.

OBTAINING PLANTS

Raspberry bushes are almost always bought plants, although it is possible to raise them from seed. Existing bushes can be divided in winter and are usually available in late winter as bare-rooted plants in bundles.

SOIL AND PREFERRED ASPECT

Raspberries require an open sunny site, although they tolerate slight shade, and prefer a deep, well-drained but moisture-retentive soil with a pH of around 6.0. They suffer iron deficiency above a pH of 7.0.

CULTIVATION

Raspberries, whether bare-rooted or container-grown, should be planted out in late autumn or early winter. Plant them a little deeper than they were in the pot or nursery and space 45cm (18in) apart with 1.8m (6ft) between rows. Cut the canes to 15cm (6in) above ground and water thoroughly after planting. Winter-planted specimens will commence growth in the spring and produce tall canes. Raspberries need little or no feeding once they have been planted. Mulch, applied in the spring, will usually supply their nutrient needs.

Above: *Wires fixed to a sturdy wooden framework support this flourishing double row of raspberries.*

PRUNING

AUTUMN-BEARING RASPBERRIES

In early spring, prune back all canes to ground level and maintain the plants in a 30–60cm (12–24in) wide "hedgerow". No summer pruning is necessary.

SUMMER-BEARING RASPBERRIES

In early or mid-spring, remove all weak, diseased and damaged canes at ground level. Leave the most vigorous canes, those about 1cm (⅓in) in diameter when measured 90cm (3ft) from the ground. Space the remaining canes about 15cm (6in) apart and cut back the tips to live tissue if any have died back in winter. Maintain plants in a 30–60cm (12–24in) wide "hedgerow" and remove old fruiting canes at the soil surface after the last harvest of the summer, as this encourages the growth of new shoots the following year.

VARIETIES

EARLY AND MID-SEASON VARIETIES

'Glen Clova' Small- to medium-sized fruits that have a mild flavour. It is a heavy cropper with strong growth.

'Malling Jewel' Sweet-tasting, medium to large, red fruits.

'Malling Promise' Full-flavoured large red berries. A heavy yielding variety that is a vigorous grower.

AUTUMN FRUITING VARIETIES

'Fallgold' Produces yellow sweet-tasting fruits on vigorous canes. Ripens in early autumn.

'Heritage' Mild-flavoured round red berries. A prolific producer that requires a sunny location.

'Zeva' Dark red fruits that are prone to crumbling. A less vigorous variety that ripens in early autumn.

raspberries

HARVESTING AND STORAGE

Raspberries should be picked early in the morning before it gets too hot. They can be eaten fresh, preserved or frozen.

PESTS AND DISEASES

The main diseases that commonly affect raspberries are botrytis (fruit rot), mildew, late leaf rust (*Pucciniastrum americanum*) and *Phytophthora* (root rot) on wet sites. They may be affected by a number of pests including aphids, raspberry beetle, two-spotted spider mite, Japanese beetle, tarnished plant bug, cane borers and clipper beetle. Netting may also be needed as protection against bird damage.

GROWING RASPBERRIES ON POSTS AND WIRES

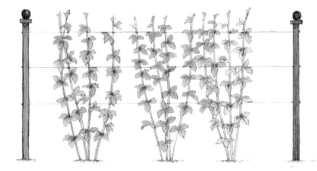

It is essential that raspberries have a strong supporting system of posts and wires. The plants are set at 45cm (18in) intervals. Each year, new raspberry canes are thrown up. When fruiting has finished on the old canes, these are cut out and the new canes are tied to the wires in their place. This sequence is followed every year. Raspberry plants put out suckers which can become established in the gangways between the rows. These should be dug up as soon as they appear.

BLACKBERRIES

Rubus fruticosus

Wild blackberries are gathered in late summer and early autumn in many areas. Growing blackberries offers the promise of high-quality fruit as well as ease of harvesting. The fruit of home-cultivated blackberries is usually much larger and often sweeter. Thornless varieties will make picking much easier.

OBTAINING PLANTS

Blackberries are usually propagated in late winter or early spring by planting root cuttings from healthy plants. Root cuttings should be 10–15cm (4–6in) long and about 1cm (½in) thick. Plant these cuttings 60cm (24in) apart in rows spaced 3m (10ft) apart for a "hedgerow". The root cuttings are best placed about 2–5cm (¾–2in) deep. Prepare the soil first by adding plenty of well-rotted compost and a generous base dressing of general-purpose fertilizer such as fish, blood and bone. Add more fertilizer about one month after planting and again in early to mid-summer.

SOIL AND PREFERRED ASPECT

Blackberries are hardy in any open, sunny site, provided that it is not too exposed to strong winds. They grow on a wide range of soil types. A soil pH of 6.0–6.5 is best, but blackberries will grow in soils ranging from a pH 4.5–7.5. A deep, fine, sandy loam is ideal, but blackberries grow well in heavier soils if they are well drained.

Above: *Blackberries often fruit over a long season, starting in late summer and lasting until late autumn.*

CULTIVATION

Canes from erect blackberries will be semi-erect or almost trailing in the first growing season. They should be kept in the row area since they will produce fruit the next year.

PRUNING

Blackberry canes are biennial. Vegetative canes develop the first year, bear fruit the second year, and die after fruiting. New canes produced in the second and later years will be erect and should be cut to a height of 1–1.2m (3–4ft) in mid-summer to encourage lateral branching. Prune hedgerows to a width of about 1–1.2m (3–4ft).

HARVESTING AND STORAGE

Blackberries need to be harvested when fully ripe, as they will not ripen after harvesting. Harvested fruit should not be allowed to sit in the sun and needs to be chilled as soon after harvesting as possible. Most blackberry varieties do not freeze particularly well and are best eaten fresh. Alternatively, they can be made into jelly or stewed before freezing.

PESTS AND DISEASES

While most blackberries are trouble free, spur blight, mildew, botrytis and cane spot are occasional disease problems. Pests are also mercifully few but can include wasps, aphids and raspberry beetle. Birds also love this summer treat and the plants may need protection with netting during their fruiting period.

VARIETIES

'Himalayan Giant' Sharp-flavoured blackberry that is a heavy cropper. Vigorous growth in stems and strong thorns.

'Oregon Thornless' A cut-leaved, thorn-free form of the blackberry. Berries are small, mild and sweet, ripening in early autumn.

'Smoothstem' Large shiny fruits that are rather sharp in taste. Enjoys a sunny location.

blackberries

METHODS OF TRAINING BLACKBERRIES

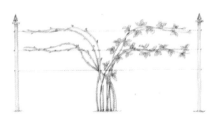

Alternate bay *One way in which you can train blackberries is to tie all the new growth to one side of the wirework. After fruiting, remove the previous year's growth from the other side and then use this for the next year's new growth. Repeat each year.*

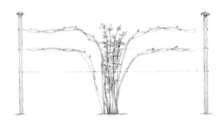

Rope training *A second way to train blackberries is to temporarily tie in all new growth vertically to the wirework and along the top wire. The current fruiting canes are tied in groups horizontally. These are removed after fruiting and the new growth tied into their place.*

Fan training *The new canes are temporarily tied vertically and along the top wire, while the fruiting canes are tied in singly along the wires. Any excess canes are removed. After fruiting, these canes are taken out and the new growth tied into their place.*

BLUEBERRIES

Vaccinium corymbosum and *V. ashei*

Blueberries are divided into two main groups: lowland blueberries (*Vaccinium ashei*), which include the whinberries or bilberries, and the better known blueberries (*V. corymbosum*). Despite some differences between the plants, the berries are essentially the same. Highland blueberries are self-pollinating, but set more fruit if they are grown with other varieties. Bilberries need another variety for successful pollination so at least two bushes of different varieties will have to be grown. The varieties listed in the panel are derived from *V. corymbosum* and will set fruit with their own pollen. For maximum crops at least two varieties should be planted together.

Above: *Pick blueberries when they are ripe – approximately ten days after they turn blue – and use immediately.*

OBTAINING PLANTS

Blueberries can either be propagated from cuttings taken in spring or purchased as plants in containers or as bare-rooted plants. Take 10–15cm (4–6in) softwood cuttings in late spring from the tips of the current season's growth. Alternatively, hardwood cuttings are taken during the dormant season after sufficient chilling has occurred, usually in mid- to late winter.

SOIL AND PREFERRED ASPECT

Blueberries are hardy in any open, sunny site, provided that it is not too exposed to strong winds. They need a very acidic soil, with a pH of 5.0–5.5. The soil should be consistently moist but never waterlogged. It should not be too rich in nutrients prior to planting.

CULTIVATION

Before planting, cut plants back to a height of 15–30cm (6–12in) or remove at least 50 per cent of the top, including all flower buds. Do not allow newly set plants to flower and fruit the first year.

Set the plants at the same depth they grew in the nursery or 1cm (½in) deeper and mulch with a well-rotted manure or compost.

Blueberries are grown as freestanding bushes, so no support or training is needed. They are not heavy feeders, but an annual application of about 100g (4oz) of fish, blood and bone and an annual mulch in late winter will ensure good growth. Blueberries require from 2.5–5cm (1–2in) of water per week. Newly established plants have the most critical water needs and can be damaged by either over- or under-watering. Short periods (one to three weeks) without rain can stress blueberry plants severely. Irrigation during dry periods is required for them to establish properly.

Bilberries require cross-pollination between different varieties for good fruit set and two or more varieties should be planted close by each other. Highland blueberries are self-fertile, but planting with other

PRUNING AN ESTABLISHED BLUEBERRY BUSH

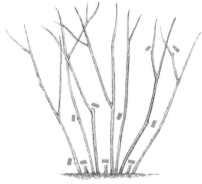

Blueberries fruit on older wood, so no pruning is needed for several years. Thereafter, cut out any weak or misplaced shoots as well as the old wood that has ceased fruiting in order to stimulate new growth.

varieties may increase fruit set and size. Insects, especially wild bees and honeybees, are necessary to pollinate blueberries. For this reason, efforts to attract these insects into your garden will be rewarded by a good fruit set.

PRUNING

In the first few years after planting blueberries, remove the tips of the branches in autumn. As the bush gets larger, cut out any old, weak or damaged growth and ensure a free air supply by allowing about 15cm (6in) between each branch.

Prune bilberries immediately after harvesting because this permits shoot regrowth and flower bud formation before plants become dormant.

HARVESTING AND STORAGE

Blueberries should be picked when they are ripe, approximately ten days after they have turned blue. They are best used immediately as they do not store well, but can be stewed and then frozen.

PESTS AND DISEASES

Bilberries are generally more resistant to both pests and diseases than Highland blueberries. Where diseases do occur, they are mainly limited to mildew and botrytis, while pests are usually restricted to an occasional outbreak of aphids. Birds are a more common problem and the bushes may need netting to protect against them.

CRANBERRIES

Vaccinium macrocarpon, *V. trilobum* and *V. vitis-idaea*

True cranberries (*V. macrocarpon*) grow in low-lying bogs. Many cranberry varieties exist, most of which are wild selections and not the product of breeding programmes. They are generally only available in the USA and are mostly grown as a commercial crop. The easiest of the three to grow is the highbush cranberry (*V. trilobum*), a deciduous shrub that grows up to 3m (10ft) high. Highbush cranberries require no special soil conditions and tend to be grown from the species and not varieties. Lingonberries (*V. vitis-idaea*) are relatives of cranberries that are grown in many Scandinavian countries and can only be cultivated in cooler locations. There are only a few lingonberry varieties available.

Above: *Cranberries should be harvested fresh from the plant once they redden but are still firm.*

OBTAINING PLANTS

Cranberries and lingonberries are propagated from cuttings and are available from a few specialist growers. The highbush cranberry can be propagated by hardwood and softwood cuttings, layering, crown division and by seed.

SOIL AND PREFERRED ASPECT

Cranberries grown in open soil will need a certain amount of soil modification. They need an acidic soil, ideally with a pH of 4–5, and should be grown in full sun. If your soil is sandy remove topsoil to a depth of 20cm (8in) and add a heavy-duty plastic liner. Pierce the liner and add about one-tenth of the volume of the excavated soil with well-rotted, but acidic, compost. Mix in about 50g (1¾oz) of bonemeal, rock

phosphate and dried blood per square metre (yard). Wet the planting mix thoroughly before planting.

If your soil is clay or silty, dig out an area 20cm (8in) deep and add the compost without a plastic liner, adding fertilizer and watering as above.

The highbush cranberry is tolerant of a wide variety of soil types, but it will do best where the soil is consistently moist and well-drained.

CULTIVATION

Cranberries can be planted in mid- to late autumn or in mid- to late spring. Highbush cranberries are best planted in late autumn

or early spring. The growing mix needs to be moist to the touch, but does not need to be saturated. Apply a general-purpose fertilizer such as fish, blood and bone in the early summer of each year.

Weed the cranberry bed regularly during the summer. Mulch the plants with pine needles or leaves in late autumn in order to protect against the drying effects of winter winds.

PRUNING

Once the cranberry bed is established, pruning is restricted to the removal of excess runner growth and older uprights as needed. Lingonberries rarely need pruning.

Pruning of a highbush cranberry should also be kept to a minimum and light renewal pruning should be all that is needed.

HARVESTING AND STORAGE

Harvest berries of all types by hand when red. Pick before a hard frost or protect them with covers.

PESTS AND DISEASES

Cranberries and lingonberries have few insect predators or diseases in domestic settings. Highbush cranberries will occasionally suffer with bacterial leaf spot, powdery mildew, shoot blight, plant bugs or thrips.

CUTTING BACK CRANBERRIES

Cranberries have no specific pruning requirements and any pruning should be restricted to the removal of excess runners and older uprights as and when it is needed. Use a pair of sharp shears to cut off any semi-erect or wispy stems in early spring and top-dress with 50g (1oz) fish, blood and bone per square metre (yard) in order to encourage new growth.

GRAPES

Vitis vinifera

In high and low latitudes, where hot summers cannot be guaranteed, grapes are usually grown in a greenhouse. Modern breeding practices have yielded a few varieties that can be grown outdoors in these regions but these are really only suitable for wine-making.

OBTAINING PLANTS

Vines can be propagated from cuttings, commonly referred to as "vine eyes". These cuttings should be 30cm (12in) long and inserted to half their length in good soil in late autumn to early winter. Plant out rooted cuttings in autumn or early winter of the following season. Prune the young plant to within 30cm (12in) from its base. Mulch with well-rotted manure or compost.

SOIL AND PREFERRED ASPECT

Despite being hardy, in cooler places vines can only be grown in a sheltered position that remains warm and sunny while the fruit is ripening. They thrive on a poor soil as long as it contains plenty of organic matter. The pH of the soil should be around 6.5–7.0. Soils should be free draining but not prone to drought, especially in the fruiting season.

Above: *Grape vines, grown over an arch or pergola, provide an ideal decorative feature for the small garden.*

CULTIVATION

Grow out of doors in favourable areas, preferably given the protection of a warm wall. Mulch annually in spring with well-rotted manure or compost and, if growth seems poor, feed with fish, blood and bone.

PRUNING

Plants grown outdoors can be grown as cordons, espaliers, fans or bushes. The bush method is the simplest, although the straggly habit of the bush form makes it a nuisance in the garden and trailing on the ground may spoil the berries. The cordon consists of a rod trained to a wire framework about 1.2m (4ft) high. The laterals from the rod are cut back each winter to one bud. Espaliers are grown by developing pairs of branches 30cm (12in) apart from the main stem.

HARVESTING AND STORAGE

The fruit is ready for picking when the stems turn brown. Cut the stem on either side of the bunch to leave a small "T"-shaped handle.

PESTS AND DISEASES

There are a multitude of pests and diseases that can affect grape vines. The main diseases in domestic settings are botrytis and mildew. Pests are few, but include red spider mites, wasps and birds. Use netting to protect against bird damage.

PRUNING ESTABLISHED GRAPES

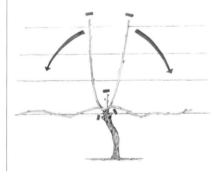

Established double guyot, winter pruning *Each year remove the horizontal branches that carry fruiting stems, leaving three vertical central shoots. Pull two of these down on each side of the central shoot, so they are horizontal, and tie in place on the wire. The third shoot should be cut back to leave three strong buds which will form the three verticals for the following year. Mulch the plants with a generous layer of well-rotted compost.*

Established double guyot, summer pruning *Train the new shoots from these buds vertically, removing any side shoots that develop on them to one leaf. Allow the vertical fruiting shoots to grow on the horizontal branches, removing any side shoots that appear. Cut back above the top wire to three leaves. After fruiting, remove the horizontal branches and train the remaining three central shoots as described above.*

HERBS

Herbs have been an important part of human culture for thousands of years. Before the advent of modern medicine they were widely used as a cure for many ailments and indeed are still used for medicinal purposes to this day. However, the majority of people grow herbs for culinary purposes, either as a small collection of favourite herbs in pots or in a herb garden. Every garden has some space for herbs and many are highly decorative or have great value as companion plants. Whichever way you grow them, herbs are an invaluable addition to the both the garden and kitchen.

Left: *A well-maintained herb garden will reward the keen organic gardener with a wealth of fragrances and textures.*

Above: *Chives* (Allium schoenoprasum) *have pungent hollow stems as well as attractive mauve flowers.*

Above: Ocimum basilicum *'Dark Opal' is a reliable basil cultivar with purple leaves and bright cerise-pink flowers.*

Above: *Marjoram* (Origanum) *is an aromatic, sun-loving herb which can be grown at the edge of a border.*

CHIVES

Allium schoenoprasum

Chives are bulbous herbaceous perennials which can grow to a height of 70cm (28in) or more. Smooth, slim, hollow, green leaves are produced in thick tufts. Small white bulbs appear in clumps on the base of the plant below the surface of the soil. Rose-purple or mauve flowers are carried on leafless stalks, making this an attractive herb for the ornamental garden. Garlic chives (*A. tuberosum*) are slightly smaller, growing to 50cm (20in), and their main storage tissue is a rhizome rather than a bulb. The leaves are similar to chives but are flat instead of hollow and the flowers are white. They are one of the kitchen herbs that few gardeners would want to be without.

SOIL AND ASPECT

Chives need a well-drained, fertile soil with a pH of 6–7. They are equally at home in full sun or partial shade, although shade can produce stragglier plants and fewer flowers.

Nitrogen is important and a regular application of composted manure is also recommended.

PROPAGATION

Chives can be grown as an annual or a perennial. Space plants 10cm (4in) apart in rows 30cm (12in) apart. They grow better if cut down to 10cm (4in) in summer. Chives are readily propagated from seed which can be sown under glass in early spring and transplanted or sown directly outdoors. Germination takes 10–14 days. Several cuttings can be obtained each year but the number may be limited by rust disease as the season progresses.

HARVESTING AND STORAGE

The leaves are cut as needed. Although best used fresh, they can be frozen or dried. *A. tuberosum* is sometimes blanched to soften the leaves before eating.

CULINARY USES

The fresh and dried leaves can be used in a variety of dishes. The bulbs can be pickled and the flowers can be used fresh or dried.

CULTIVATION
Sowing time Early spring (under glass); spring (outside)
Planting out time Spring
Thinning and planting distance 10cm (4in)
Distance between rows 30cm (12in)
Harvesting Any time the plant is in growth
Storage Frozen or dried

Above: *The pretty flowers of chives make a tasty and colourful addition to summer salads as well as to the herb garden.*

DILL

Anethum graveolens

This annual, with its round, erect stem, grows 30–60cm (12–24in) tall and has finely divided, thread-like, blue-green leaves. The flowers are yellow and, although the fruit is commonly called a "seed", it is actually a dry half-fruit. This herb exists as two general types: the familiar garden dill (*A. graveolens*), which is known as American or European dill, and Indian or Japanese dill (*A. sowa*). European dill is the most common type and is grown in temperate and subtropical countries around the world. There are a number of different varieties of *A. graveolens*, each with their own fragrance or growth properties.

SOIL AND ASPECT

Dill is adaptable to many soils, but a slightly acidic soil (with a pH of 5.6–6.5) and good drainage is preferred. Germination can be poor in drought-prone, sandy soils or on clays where surface capping is a problem. Position dill in full sun.

Dill can be grown outdoors or in a greenhouse. It can be invasive if it is allowed to go to seed.

PROPAGATION

Sow seed in spring to early summer in shallow drills 3–5mm (⅛–¼in) deep. Germination takes approximately 7–14 days; successional sowing can provide a season-long supply. Thin to 23cm (9in).

HARVESTING AND STORAGE

Harvest the dill leaves or cut back the entire plant once it reaches approximately 30cm (12in) in height. Harvest the seed when it begins to turn brown.

CULINARY USES

Fresh dill leaves are used in a wide range of dishes such as soups and salads. The seed can be used in the preparation of pickles and condiments. The immature or mature seed-heads are also used whole in pickles.

Right: *The tall stems and graceful feathery leaves of dill make this herb a decorative addition to the kitchen garden.*

CULTIVATION
Sowing time Spring to early summer
Sowing depth 3–5mm (⅛–¼in)
Thinning and planting distance 23cm (9in)
Harvesting As required (leaves); when it begins to turn brown (seed)
Storage Dried (leaves and seed)

ANGELICA

Angelica archangelica

Angelica can be grown as an aromatic biennial or a short-lived perennial (for about four years). It grows to 1.5–2.4m (5–8ft) tall. It has upright, ridged, hollow stems and large bright green leaves. The small, white or greenish flowers are borne in summer.

SOIL AND ASPECT

Prefers moist, fertile soil in partial shade and will grow in a wide range of pH from 4.5–7.3.

PROPAGATION

Propagate by seed or root division. Seeds germinate in 21–28 days. The viability of seed decreases quickly so fresh seed is best. It can be sown directly outdoors in the summer or started indoors and planted out later. Space plants 30cm (12in) apart in a row with 60–90cm (24–36in) between rows. Angelica may live up three years before flowering.

> **CULTIVATION**
> **Sowing time** Late summer
> **Sowing depth** 1cm (½in)
> **Thinning and planting distance** 30cm (12in)
> **Distance between rows** 60–90cm (24–36in)
> **Harvesting** Until flowering (leaves); while young (stems); when ripe (seed); early autumn (roots)
> **Storage** Dried (leaves); crystallized (stems); dried (seed)

HARVESTING AND STORAGE

Pick angelica leaves before flowering takes place, and use fresh or dried. Cut the stems while young for crystallizing and storage. The seeds should be picked when ripe and dried. Harvest the roots in early autumn and dry them at 38–60°C (100–140°F).

CULINARY USES

Stems can be steamed and eaten like a vegetable or candied. Dried leaves can be made into a tea and fresh leaves added to salads, soups or stews.

Above: *Although less commonly used than it once was, angelica still makes a striking plant in the herb garden. It can also be a feature in the ornamental garden.*

CHERVIL

Anthriscus cerefolium

This tall, hardy biennial plant is often best grown as an annual. Chervil reaches a height of 30–60cm (12–24in). It has large white flower heads. The delicately cut leaves make it a valuable addition to the ornamental garden as well as the herb and kitchen garden. Although it is more often grown as an ornamental plant, many people use the seed to make herb teas and crystallize the young stems. The leaves can also be used to flavour fish dishes and fruit desserts.

SOIL AND ASPECT

Chervil should be grown in a well-drained, fertile soil with a good organic content and a pH of 6–7. The plants do best in full sun or partial shade. Growing chervil in an open, hot, sunny site may result in the plants going to seed quickly if not kept well watered.

PROPAGATION

Chervil seed should be sown in a sunny position in the spring and then again in

> **CULTIVATION**
> **Sowing time** Spring to early summer
> **Sowing depth** 1cm (½in)
> **Thinning and planting distance** 20cm (8in)
> **Harvesting** Late spring onwards
> **Storage** Dried

early summer. Sow the seed in drills 1cm (½in) deep. A successional sowing every three to four weeks will extend the life of this crop. The seedlings should be thinned or transplanted to 20cm (8in) apart.

HARVESTING AND STORAGE

If you wish to use fresh chervil, pick the tips of the stems once a month. If the leaves are to be used dry, then harvest the leaves just before the blossoms open and dry them on trays in a warm room or cool oven.

CULINARY USES

Chervil leaves are used as a condiment and in salads and have a flavour reminiscent of both aniseed and parsley. Chervil combines well with parsley and chives.

Above: *The delicately cut leaves of chervil make it ideal for both the kitchen and ornamental garden.*

HORSERADISH

Armoracia rusticana

This rather large plant has leaves that are reminiscent of a dock (*Rumex*) and is used as a herb and a vegetable. The plant has a strong taste and is consequently used only in relatively small quantities. Horseradish is easy to grow and the main problem may be preventing it from spreading too much.

SOIL AND ASPECT

Thrives in any light rich soil, although it will prosper in most soils, particularly those that have been well prepared. If you intend to lift plants completely that are growing on lighter soils then you must remove all the roots to prevent dense regeneration of deep-rooted horseradish plants all over the vegetable garden. Contain plants by planting in a plastic bucket with lots of small holes punched in the bottom. Horseradish is usually best given its own growing area and is not recommended for growing among rows of other crops.

PROPAGATION

Mature horseradish plants are divided and clumps or root sections are planted out in the autumn or spring. You will probably find that one plant is enough but if more are needed they should be planted 30cm (12in) apart.

HARVESTING AND STORAGE

Horseradish is best harvested as it is needed throughout the growing season. For winter use, the roots can be lifted and stored in trays of moist sand for up to two months. The leaves are best harvested when young.

CULINARY USES

The roots are the principal harvest from this plant. They can be simply peeled and grated for use in salads or mixed with other ingredients to make a sauce. Horseradish greens can also be diced and used in various dishes.

Right: *Horseradish is a large and vigorous plant that needs careful placing in the garden if it is not to take over.*

FRENCH TARRAGON

Artemisia dracunculus 'Sativa'

This is a half-hardy perennial plant that grows up to 60cm (24in) tall. Tarragon will need winter protection in colder areas or annual replacement. The closely related Russian tarragon (*A. dracunculus dracunculoides*) has a more bitter taste, but is considerably hardier and often grown as a substitute for French tarragon in colder areas. The taste of Russian tarragon improves with age.

SOIL AND ASPECT

Tarragon grows in any well-cultivated soil. The less hardy French tarragon may be best "plunged" into the ground for the summer growing season and lifted before the winter cold sets in. Divide frequently (every two to three years) or the plant will become root-bound. You should overwinter some plants indoors even in mild areas.

PROPAGATION

French tarragon cannot be grown from seed and so plants will need to be purchased.

Once established, clumps can be divided in order to increase stock. The hardier Russian tarragon can be grown successfully from seed and can be raised in pans or shallow drills outside. Both types should be planted out in spring at a distance of 30cm (12in).

HARVESTING AND STORAGE

Harvest tarragon in early summer for steeping in vinegar. For drying, harvest in mid-summer. Harvest fresh tarragon by picking off leaves or tips of branches with multiple leaves.

CULINARY USES

The leaves are widely used for flavouring and seasoning and it is an essential ingredient in French cooking. The French sometimes refer to it as *herbe au dragon*, due to its reputed ability to cure snake bites. It is often used in various sauces, such as tartare and white sauce, and for making herb vinegar.

Above: *Tarragon is an excellent plant for herb gardens, but it must be protected in winter in cool areas.*

BORAGE

Borago officinalis

Borage is an annual that grows to 45–60cm (18–24in) high. The fresh leaves and the sky-blue flowers have a spicy, cucumber-like taste and an onion-like smell. The plant attracts bees and is also a useful companion plant for tomatoes. It is very attractive and worth including in both the ornamental and herb garden.

SOIL AND ASPECT

Borage thrives in average and poor dry soils (pH between 5–8). The plants usually do best in full sun, although they will grow in partial shade. To encourage leaf growth, supply rich moist soil, but if flowers are the object, restrict the use of organic fertilizer and make sure that the plants get plenty of sun. Borage is difficult to transplant once it is actively growing because of its tap root. Transplantation should therefore be done at the seedling stage. Ideal for container culture, borage can be planted in a large tub with smaller herbs around the edge.

PROPAGATION

Sow the seeds 1cm (½in) deep in the spring to early summer. The seeds will germinate in about 7–14 days. Thin or transplant the seedlings so that they are approximately 30cm (12in) apart.

HARVESTING AND STORAGE

The fresh leaves of borage are best, but they can also be dried. Harvest leaves for drying as the plant begins to flower. Dry the leaves quickly, ensuring good air circulation and with no overlapping of leaves. The flowers can be frozen in ice cubes for summer drinks.

CULINARY USES

Borage is primarily used in herb teas but the young leaves or peeled stems can also be chopped and used in salads or boiled as a pot-herb. The flowers make a colourful addition to salads and summer drinks and can also be candied.

Right: *Borage flowers can be used dried in potpourri, but leave on some of the flowers so that you can collect the seed.*

CULTIVATION
Sowing time Spring to early summer
Sowing depth 1cm (½in)
Thinning and planting distance 30cm (12in)
Harvesting Any time (flowers); when young (leaves)
Storage Frozen in ice cubes or crystallized (flowers); dried (leaves)

CARAWAY

Carum carvi

Caraway has aromatic, feathery, finely cut leaves and a thick, tapering root. During the second year, tiny white or pink flowers and reddish brown, crescent-shaped fruits develop. Caraway plants generally grow 75–150cm (30–60in) high when they are in flower. This biennial herb has a variety of uses but is mostly grown for its small aromatic seeds. The leaves can also be used.

SOIL AND ASPECT

Caraway should be grown in full sun in fertile, well-drained soil with a pH of 7.5. It will tolerate most soil types but seed germination can be poor on clay if the soil surface is prone to capping. Caraway needs a position that it can occupy for two seasons, as it will not produce seed until the second. A dressing of garden compost or well-rotted manure should be applied in the first year before planting with an additional mulching in the second year. It will tolerate light frost.

PROPAGATION

Sow seed 1cm (½in) deep in late spring to late summer in rows 40–50cm (16–20in) apart. Germination takes about 10–14 days. Thin to 15cm (6in) between plants. To grow caraway as a root crop, thin to 20cm (8in) apart. Caraway will easily self-seed around the herb garden if a few of the flower heads are left.

HARVESTING AND STORAGE

Harvest the seeds when they are ripe and before the first seeds fall. Harvest the roots in the autumn of the second year. Harvest the leaves when young. The seed can be dried and then stored.

CULINARY USES

Caraway seeds can be used in a number of different dishes, while the shoots and leaves can be added to vegetable dishes and salads. The roots, which are like a small, thin parsnip, are sometimes eaten as a vegetable.

Right: *Caraway produces pretty white or pink flowers before seeding and dying in the second year.*

CULTIVATION
Sowing time Late spring to late summer
Sowing depth 1cm (½in)
Thinning and planting distance 15cm/6in (leaf crop); 20cm/8in (root crop)
Distance between rows 40–50cm (16–20in)
Harvesting While young (leaves); when ripe (seed); autumn of second year (roots)
Storage Dried (seeds)

CORIANDER (CILANTRO)

Coriandrum sativum

This hardy annual, which is a member of the parsley family, grows to 60–90cm (24–36in) in height and occasionally survives into a second year. Its erect slender stems are branching and bright green. The small pink, pale blue or white flowers are borne in compound umbels. The seeds are used as a condiment and as a component of beverages.

SOIL AND ASPECT

Coriander grows on most soils, but it does demand a sunny situation. If the plant is to be raised for its leaves, then a rich, free-draining soil with good organic content is recommended. For seed, the soil can be less nitrogen-rich and must be in full sun.

PROPAGATION

Coriander is best sown fresh each season, but it will self-sow in a favourable situation. Plants can also be raised from seed in a greenhouse during the colder winter months for a year-round supply of leaves. Alternatively, the seed is sown outside in autumn or spring in shallow 1cm (½in) drills. Germination can be slow, but once the plants emerge they should be thinned to about 15cm (6in). Plants that are grown for their leaves will benefit from successional sowings every three to four weeks throughout the summer.

HARVESTING AND STORAGE

Coriander seed is usually ready for harvesting just as the seeds are ripe and before they drop. The leaves are gathered when young throughout the summer. The seeds can be stored if they are dried and the leaves can be dried or frozen.

CULINARY USES

The dried powdered seeds are used as a flavouring in dishes such as curries. The aromatic leaves can be used dried or fresh.

Right: *The young succulent leaves of coriander are ideal for both cooking and summer salads.*

CULTIVATION
Sowing time Autumn or spring
Sowing depth 1cm (½in)
Thinning and planting distance 15cm (6in)
Harvesting When ripe (seed); while young (leaves)
Storage Dried (seed); dried or frozen (leaves)

FENNEL

Foeniculum vulgare

Fennel is widely used as a culinary herb. It is a biennial or perennial plant that will grow as an annual if it is not protected. Fennel reaches 1–1.5m (3–5ft) in height. The roots, stalks and leaves are all edible, with the spice coming from the dried seeds. The tiny yellow flowers and finely cut leaves, which can be bronze in some varieties, make it a highly decorative plant for the ornamental garden.

SOIL AND ASPECT

Thrives in a sunny position and a well-drained, rich soil though it will do quite well in poorer conditions. Applying a mulch of well-rotted compost will favour the development of the leafy growth, whereas a poorer site will encourage flowering. Fennel resembles dill, with which it can cross-pollinate, so keep these two apart.

PROPAGATION

Fennel can be grown from seed that is station sown in the spring at intervals of

CULTIVATION
Sowing time Spring
Sowing depth 1cm (½in)
Thinning and planting distance 45cm (18in)
Harvesting Before seeds ripen (flower heads); while young (leaves); when ripe (seeds)
Storage Dried (seed); frozen (leaves)

45cm (18in) in 1cm (½in) drills, although one or two plants are usually sufficient. Can become invasive if allowed to self-seed.

HARVESTING AND STORAGE

The flower heads are collected before the seeds ripen and the seeds are threshed or bashed out when completely dried. The leaves are collected fresh when young and used as needed. They can also be frozen for use during the winter.

CULINARY USES

Fennel leaves are used in salads and sauces and the seeds can be used in sausages and cakes.

Above: *All parts of the fennel plant are edible, making this both a useful and handsome garden plant.*

HYSSOP

Hyssopus officinalis

Hyssop is a shrubby perennial that grows up to 1.2m (4ft) high. It is used as a pot herb and as an ornamental addition to the edible landscape or potager garden. It is particularly useful for creating low hedges in parterres and knot gardens.

SOIL AND ASPECT
Hyssop thrives in a sunny position in free-draining soil. Wet soils will considerably reduce the life of the plant. A light mulching of rotted garden compost and dried blood in spring will promote good leafy growth. The plant will benefit from regular trimming, which will also provide the new leafy growth that is most suited to culinary use.

PROPAGATION
Despite being a shrubby perennial, hyssop is not particularly long lived, especially on heavier, wet soils, and may need replacing every three to four years. It can easily be raised from seed, either sown in a seedbed and transplanted or sown directly where it is needed. Sow seed in spring in 1cm (½in) drills, thinning to about 30cm (12in). Purchased plants and those raised from cuttings taken in early summer are also planted out at the same distance in spring.

HARVESTING AND STORAGE
Hyssop leaves can be harvested as required and may be dried for later use.

CULINARY USES
Hyssop is used to flavour various liqueurs, including Chartreuse. The leaves, which have a rather bitter taste, are used sparingly to counter fatty dishes.

CULTIVATION
Sowing time Spring
Sowing depth 1cm (½in)
Thinning and planting distance 30cm (12in)
Planting and transplanting time Spring
Harvesting Any time
Storage Dried

Above: *The shrubby nature of hyssop makes it ideal for use as a low hedge in a potager.*

BAY

Laurus nobilis

A hardy evergreen tree or shrub that grows widely in the Mediterranean region. In warm areas bay can grow as tall as 18m (60ft). Inconspicuous white flowers appear in clusters in late spring. Bay can be grown in cooler locations but it must be sited in a sheltered spot and may only make a relatively small tree. Alternatively, bay trees make good pot specimens for a patio and can be overwintered in a cool greenhouse or conservatory (sun room). The leaves are best used when they are fresh or within a few days of picking.

SOIL AND ASPECT
Bay trees appreciate a moist, rich but free-draining soil, although they are surprisingly tolerant of poor conditions, especially if sited in a hot sunny position.

PROPAGATION
Take semi-ripe cuttings from the current season's shoots in mid- to late summer.

CULTIVATION
Planting time Spring
Planting distance 1.2m (4ft) or more
Harvesting Any time
Storage Dried

Purchased plants and those raised from cuttings can be planted out in spring at a distance of 1.2m (4ft) or more.

HARVESTING AND STORAGE
Bay leaves can be harvested at any time; the mature leaves have the best flavour. The leaves can also be dried and stored in an air-tight container.

CULINARY USES
Bay is a very popular culinary herb, with one or two leaves at a time being included in a large number of dishes. The leaves are widely used in bouquets garnis or added to soups, sauces or stews. Bay leaf is often included as a pickling spice. It is settling to the stomach and has a tonic effect, stimulating the appetite and the secretion of digestive juices.

Above: *Bay makes a highly decorative specimen shrub for cool conservatories or a warm place outside.*

LOVAGE

Levisticum officinale

Lovage is a hardy perennial with ribbed stalks similar to celery and hollow stems that divide into branches near the top. Yellow flowers, about 3cm (1¼in) across, are borne in summer. The leaves have a strong taste, whereas the roots have a nutty flavour. Lovage is very robust and can grow as tall as 2m (6½ft) and spread to form a clump several yards wide.

SOIL AND ASPECT

Lovage prefers a well-drained soil rich in organic matter with a pH of 6–7.5. It can tolerate heavy clay soil, but grows best in a more loamy soil.

PROPAGATION

Lovage is easily propagated in autumn by seed, which can be slow to germinate (about 10–28 days), or by root division. Plant seed in rows in autumn at a depth of 1cm (½in) and thin to 60cm (24in). However, as it is such a vigorous plant, you may only want one plant. If more are required, then plant them 60cm (24in) apart in spring. Lovage is hardy but mulching assists winter survival.

HARVESTING AND STORAGE

Leaves are usually harvested twice a season starting in the second year, although large specimens will support a limited harvest continually through the season. The stems are cut in spring and the roots are dug in the autumn of the third year and can be used fresh or dried. Seeds can be harvested in late autumn or when ripe and dried for use.

CULINARY USES

Use the fresh leaves in salads, soups, stews, stir-fries and potato dishes and the seeds whole or ground in cakes, biscuits, sauces, pickles or salad dressings or with meats. Use the dried root as a condiment and cook the grated fresh root as a vegetable. The fresh root can also be used raw in salads, in herbal teas or preserved in honey.

Right: *Lovage is a splendid architectural plant, but it must be prevented from spreading too much.*

CULTIVATION
Sowing time Autumn
Sowing depth 1cm (½in)
Planting time Spring
Thinning and planting distance 60cm (24in)
Harvesting Any time (leaves); when ripe (seed); from autumn of third year (roots); spring (stems)
Storage Dried (leaves and seed)

LEMON BALM

Melissa officinalis

This herbaceous perennial has lemon-scented leaves and clusters of small, white or yellowish, tubular flowers. It grows to a height of 1.5m (5ft) and can be invasive if not regularly cut back to prevent self-seeding. The foliage is a welcome addition to the herb garden and is best sited near to a path so that the fragrance is released when brushed against. Bees are attracted by the scent.

SOIL AND ASPECT

The ideal soil for lemon balm is moist but well drained and with a pH of 4.5–7.5. It will grow in sun or partial shade but should not be planted in very dry conditions.

Apply a good dressing of composted manure and a fertilizer such as fish, blood and bone annually to encourage good leafy growth. It is an attractive plant for the first part of the year but can become straggly. It is best cut back to stimulate new, fresh and attractive growth. Cutting back also prevents self-seeding around the garden.

PROPAGATION

Propagate from seeds, root divisions or stem cuttings. The seeds can be planted directly outside in 1cm (½in) drills in the spring or started off in a greenhouse in late winter. The plants should be thinned to 30–45cm (12–18in) apart.

HARVESTING AND STORAGE

Plants should be cut as flowering begins by cutting off the top growth, leaving a 5cm (2in) stubble for regrowth. Lemon balm can be susceptible to frost and so mulching is recommended if hard frost is likely. The leaves can be dried and then stored for later use.

CULINARY USES

The fresh leaves give a lovely lemon flavour to salads, vegetable dishes, chicken dishes, poultry stuffing and drinks. The dried leaves can be used to make herbal tea and are also added to potpourri and herb pillows.

Right: *Lemon balm is beautifully scented but like all members of the mint family can spread rapidly.*

CULTIVATION
Sowing time Winter (indoors); spring (outside)
Sowing depth 1cm (½in)
Thinning and planting distance 30–45cm (12–18in)
Harvesting When the leaves are still fresh-looking
Storage Dried

MINT

Mentha

Mint is an aromatic herb, with square, erect stems and flowers in the leaf axils. It is an invasive perennial or annual. Most mints grow to about 30–90cm (12–36in) in height. Spearmint (*M. spicata*) leaves are green, slightly crinkled and almost hairless with a very pungent lemony mint aroma and bitter taste. Peppermint (*M. × piperita*) has flat, smooth, shiny, pointed green leaves and reddish-lilac to purple flowers. Peppermint and spearmint spread rapidly by stolons and rhizomes and can become a weed problem.

SOIL AND ASPECT

A well-drained, fertile soil with a pH of 5–7 in full sun is preferred, although mints will prosper in a wide range of soil types in sun or partial shade. Mint can become invasive and it is a good idea to plant it in a below-ground container in most garden situations. Plants can suffer from mildew and rusts and a wilt disease caused by the soil fungus verticillium. Despite this, they have a tendency to spread rampantly through borders if left unchecked. Where mint is regularly cut back, apply a nitrogen- rich fertilizer such as dried blood or pelleted poultry manure and top-dress with well-rotted compost.

PROPAGATION

Mints are usually propagated from cuttings of stems, stolons and root divisions. Plant out propagated or purchased plants in spring, 30cm (12in) apart.

HARVESTING AND STORAGE

Mint can be harvested twice a season, leaving a stubble of at least 10cm (4in), although it is more usually collected as needed, picking the leaves when they are young and fresh. Cutting back stimulates new growth that is perfect for picking. The leaves can be dried or frozen.

CULINARY USES

Mint leaves are added to beverages, jellies, soups, stews, sauces, vinegar and used to flavour meats such as lamb.

CULTIVATION
Planting time Spring
Planting distance 30cm (12in)
Harvesting While leaves are young
Storage Dried or frozen

Above: *Mint is a must for the herb garden but take care not to let it spread unchecked in open ground.*

BERGAMOT

Monarda didyma

Bergamot is not widely used as a culinary herb today, but its whorled flower heads make it worthy of inclusion in the herb garden. There are various colours to choose from, including bright red. The leaves release an aromatic fragrance when they are brushed against which makes weeding among these herbs an absolute pleasure.

SOIL AND ASPECT

Bergamot thrives in a rich, moist soil. Soils with a tendency to dry out will quickly kill the plant unless watered. The plants are best replanted in a fresh patch every three years or so and clumps benefit from a light mulching of well-rotted garden compost after a dressing of fish, blood and bone or similar general-purpose organic fertilizer. *M. didyma* can spread by means of flat stems near the surface, resulting in it needing to be divided and re-situated every two to three years or so. It is also prone to mildew. Other species are much less prone to mildew (and also grow and flower much better) in a moist soil, or at least in a place where they do not get too dry in summer.

PROPAGATION

Bergamot can be raised by division, cuttings or by seed in spring. The seed can be sown in spring in rows at a depth of 1cm (½in), but plants tend to look better in drifts or clumps. In either case the plants should be spaced about 45cm (18in) apart.

HARVESTING AND STORAGE

The leaves should be harvested when they are still young. The flowers can also be picked as they are just opening and both can be dried and then stored.

CULINARY USES

The leaves of bergamot dry well and can be used to make a herbal tea. This is not the same as the bergamot in Earl Grey, which is a tropical citrus. Both the leaves and flowers can be used.

Right: *Garden bergamot is most commonly grown for its looks, rather than for using in the kitchen.*

CULTIVATION
Sowing time Spring
Sowing depth 1cm (½in)
Planting time Spring
Thinning and planting distance 45cm (18in)
Harvesting While young (leaves); as they are opening (flowers)
Storage Dried

SWEET CICELY

Myrrhis odorata

Sweet cicely, an early-summer-flowering perennial, is something of a rarity these days and usually only grown by devotees. It is reminiscent of cow parsley and the seed-heads produced later in the summer are quite attractive in their own right. The leaves are a pretty mottled green, and are large and fairly deeply cut. It grows to a height of 60–90cm (24–36in) and can become invasive when it likes the conditions. Sweet cicely is a good choice for including in a wild garden.

SOIL AND ASPECT

Sweet cicely likes a moist humus-rich soil and, unusually for a herb, will thrive in shade. It is perfectly at home at the base of a hedgerow and provides a pretty effect in late spring and early summer. Like many of its close relatives, the individual plants are short lived, but it self-seeds prolifically and must be prevented from becoming a weed in a herb garden.

PROPAGATION

Sweet cicely can be slow to germinate and difficult to transplant, so it is best sown in situ using freshly ripened seed. Sow seed in autumn in drills 1cm (½in) deep. The seedlings should be thinned to 60cm (24in). Plants should have their seed removed before it gets the chance to self-seed.

HARVESTING AND STORAGE

The leaves of sweet cicely are harvested from spring to early summer, and can be dried. The seeds taste of aniseed only when they are still greenish, so collect them when they are still unripe. The seeds have no taste if they are completely black.

CULINARY USES

Sweet cicely has a mild aniseed flavour that can be used to counter the acidity of sharp-tasting fruit. It was used as a sweetening agent for stewed soft fruits and rhubarb. The leaves make an attractive garnish.

Right: *Sweet cicely is something of a rarity in that it is ideally suited for both herb and wild gardens. It can be used in potpourri.*

CULTIVATION
Sowing time Autumn
Sowing depth 1cm (½in)
Thinning and planting distance 60cm (24in)
Harvesting Spring to early summer (leaves); unripe, when green (seed)
Storage Dried (leaves and seed)

BASIL

Ocimum

The height, leaf colour, flower colour, and growth habit of basil can vary a great deal depending on the variety. Sweet basil (*Ocimum basilicum*) has smooth, bright green leaves and small, white flowers. It can grow 60–90cm (24–36in) high and has an erect and branched habit. Cinnamon basil (*O. basilicum* 'Cinnamon') has a similar habit but is smaller, growing only 30–40cm (12–16in) tall. This type has smaller, purplish leaves, pink flower spikes and an anise-cinnamon-like odour. Lemon basil (*O.* × *citriodorum*) has a growth habit resembling cinnamon basil but has smooth, bright green leaves and small white flowers. Purple basil (*O. basilicum* var. *purpurascens*) is noted for its strongly scented purple leaves.

SOIL AND ASPECT

Basil requires a minimum temperature of 10–15°C (50–59°F) and pH of 5–8 in order to thrive. The growing area should be in full sun with light, fertile, well-drained soil. The application of garden compost or well-rotted manure can aid growth. Avoid applying too much nitrogen, as this will decrease the essential oils in the growing tissue, resulting in weak-flavoured leaf and stem tissue. Keep well watered. Basil is a good companion plant for tomatoes.

PROPAGATION

For an early supply, sow seeds in plug trays in a greenhouse and transplant outside in warm weather. Seed can be sown outdoors in 1cm (½in) drills in the late spring, provided that the soil is kept moist. Thin or plant out at 20–23cm (8–9in) intervals.

HARVESTING AND STORAGE

Pick frequently to avoid the development of woody stems. Regular picking is advised as the leaves become bitter if the plant is allowed to flower. Take care when harvesting as the leaves bruise easily.

CULINARY USES

The fresh or dried leaves are used in tomato dishes, pasta sauces, vegetables and soups. Basil is useful in Mediterranean dishes and is always best used fresh.

CULTIVATION
Sowing time Late spring
Sowing depth 1cm (½in)
Thinning and planting distance 20–22cm (8–9in)
Harvesting Any time
Storage Dried or frozen

Above: *Basil combines well with tomatoes both as a companion plant in the garden and as an ingredient in cooking.*

SWEET MARJORAM AND OREGANO

Origanum majorana, O. vulgare

Sweet marjoram grows to a height of 30cm (12in) and makes a good companion plant for aubergines, pumpkins and courgettes. Oregano can grow to a height of 60cm (24in) and is generally hardier than marjoram. It is a sprawling herb and, unlike sweet marjoram, is not suited for growing indoors. Oregano makes a good companion plant for cauliflower, but should not be planted with broccoli or cabbage. Many plants are classified as oregano and their flavour depends on where they are cultivated. In general, the hotter the sun, the stronger the flavour.

SOIL AND ASPECT

Sweet marjoram and oregano thrive in full sun and prefer a light, fairly rich, well-drained, slightly alkaline soil, with a pH of 7–8. Poorer soils result in a more pungent taste and can stimulate early flowering. As it is not entirely hardy, pot up sweet marjoram in autumn and overwinter indoors or sow seed each year.

PROPAGATION

Sweet marjoram is easily grown from seed sown in spring in 1cm (½in) drills or by cuttings taken in summer. Thin or plant out at 30cm (12in) intervals. In cooler areas, marjoram can be overwintered indoors in pots. Oregano can be grown from seed sown similarly to that of marjoram or by taking stem cuttings or root divisions. The seed can be slow to germinate and the resulting plants may not be true to the parent plant, or may even be flavourless, making vegetative propagation the preferred option.

HARVESTING AND STORAGE

Harvest and dry the leaves before flowering occurs. Dry by tying the stems together and hanging in a warm, dry, well-ventilated place. Both herbs can also be frozen.

CULINARY USES

These flavourful herbs are used in many dishes, especially in Italian recipes.

CULTIVATION
Sowing time Spring
Sowing depth 1cm (½in)
Dividing time Spring
Thinning and planting distance 30cm (12in)
Harvesting While young
Storage Dried or frozen

Above: *Marjoram is a good companion plant for pumpkins, courgettes and aubergines as well as a culinary herb.*

PARSLEY

Petroselinum crispum

Although it is a biennial plant, parsley, which grows up to 45cm (18in), can only be cropped in the first year and is usually grown as an annual. In its first year, it develops plenty of leaves, on fairly long stems that come from the crown of the plant. In the second year, the plant produces only a couple of leaves and a long bloom stalk that will self-sow if you allow it. Parsley is one of the most popular and versatile culinary herbs and can be grown indoors or outdoors. It makes an excellent subject for a container or as an edging to paths. There are two forms: curly-leaved parsley (*P. crispum*) and French or flat-leaved parsley (*P. crispum neapolitanum*).

SOIL AND ASPECT

Parsley does best in a sunny spot, but will also prosper in light shade. It should be grown in a moist fertile soil and benefits from the addition of well-rotted garden compost or manure and a nitrogen-rich fertilizer such as dried blood or pelleted chicken manure. Keep well watered in long hot, dry spells.

PROPAGATION

The seeds should be soaked in water and then sown either under cover or outside in 1cm (½in) drills. Thin or plant out at 20–25cm (8–10in) intervals. A spring sowing will provide leaves through summer while a second sowing in late summer will provide winter leaves. These will need protection with a cloche.

HARVEST

Young leaves should be snipped just above ground level as needed. The harvested leaves can be dried or frozen for later use.

CULINARY USES

The leaves and stem are used to flavour and garnish a wide variety of dishes. Curly-leaved forms have a subtle flavour whereas the flat-leaved types have a stronger taste.

Right: *Parsley is one of the most popular and versatile herbs for use in the kitchen. It also looks decorative in the herb garden.*

CULTIVATION
Sowing time Spring or late summer
Sowing depth 1cm (½in)
Thinning and planting distance 20–25cm (8–10in)
Harvesting Any time
Storage Dried or frozen

ROSEMARY

Rosmarinus officinalis

This greatly valued herb, which is native to southern Europe, grows up to 1.2m (4ft) tall. As well as a being a useful culinary herb, rosemary is also a beautiful, drought-resistant plant that can be used in landscaping. It has attractive blue flowers that are a good source of nectar for bees. There are two basic types: the trailing or prostrate type and a bush type that will, in time, become large enough to be considered a shrub. Prostrate rosemary makes an excellent groundcover plant.

SOIL AND ASPECT

Rosemary thrives in a well-drained soil in a sunny position. It is slightly tender and will suffer if it is planted in a wet soil during the cold winter months. It is an excellent plant for use in coastal areas. Rosemary is a plant that actually thrives on neglect and will die if you fertilize or water it too much or plant it in very rich soil.

PROPAGATION

Rosemary is best bought as an established plant or raised from cuttings. Plant out in the eventual position in spring to late summer. One plant is usually enough for most culinary requirements, but, if you do want to grow more than this, space the plants 75cm (30in) apart.

HARVESTING AND STORAGE

Harvest the young, tender stems and leaves, taking off no more than one-third of the plant at one time. For drying, harvest just before the plant flowers. After drying, the leaves can be stored for later use.

CULINARY USES

Rosemary leaves can be used for making tea, in sauces or for flavouring many meat (especially lamb) and vegetable dishes. It may also be used in herb breads and is excellent for including in potpourri. It can be used either fresh or dried.

Right: *Rosemary, which is native to southern Europe, will thrive in coastal areas or in a dry sunny spot.*

CULTIVATION
Planting time Spring to late summer
Planting distance 75cm (30in)
Harvesting Any time
Storage Dried

SAGE

Salvia officinalis

Sage is a long-lived, hardy, shrubby perennial with grey, felted leaves. It can reach 80cm (32in) in height. It has a distinctive flavour that combines well with a variety of meats and vegetables. Sage is an excellent decorative specimen for use in the ornamental and kitchen garden. There are coloured-leaved forms, including deep purple and bright yellow, as well as the culinary grey-leaved form. The spikes of blue-purple flowers appear in late spring and will attract bees.

SOIL AND ASPECT

Sage is very easy to grow in the right conditions. It prefers full sun and a reasonably fertile, well-drained soil that does not get too dry. The main problem with sage is to keep it under control. Pinch small plants to make them branch, then let them grow to harvesting size and avoid letting the stems get so tall that they lie down or you will end up with a twisted, woody tangle in a couple of years.

PROPAGATION

Sage is best grown from cuttings taken in early to mid-summer or purchased as young plants. They can also be raised from seed. Seeds require 20 days at 20°C (68°F) for germination to take place and are best raised under cover. Sow seed in trays or shallow pans or under cloches in spring in 1cm (½in) deep drills. Plants should be thinned out, transplanted or planted 60cm (24in) apart in their required position.

HARVESTING AND STORAGE

Sage is best harvested when it is just starting to flower and used either fresh or dried. Harvest after the dew dries in the morning, cutting the stems so that there are one or two leaves remaining at the bottom. Air-drying sage will result in a leathery rather than a crisp product that should be stored in airtight jars. Chop or rub the leaves into a powder when you need to use them.

CULINARY USES

The leaves are used to flavour soups, stews, stuffings, sausages and roast meats as well as to make tea. The coloured leaf forms taste the same as the grey-leaved form.

CULTIVATION
Sowing time Spring
Sowing depth 1cm (½in)
Cuttings Taken early to mid-summer
Thinning and planting distance 60cm (24in)
Harvesting Any time
Storage Dried

Above: *The pungent leaves of sage are ready for harvesting when the handsome flowers appear.*

SAVORY

Satureja

Summer savory (*S. hortensis*) is an annual that grows to about 45cm (18in). It has a less tidy appearance than winter savory (*S. montana*). Winter savory is a perennial that also grows to about 45cm (18in) high, but is much hardier in cultivation. It can be treated in the same way as common thyme, which it closely resembles, although it is slightly more compact, with darker leaves and white flowers. Like thyme, winter savory makes a good edging plant and will benefit from a light pruning in spring to keep it compact. Both winter and summer savory can be grown in containers and are occasionally raised as rock garden plants.

SOIL AND ASPECT

Both types of savory are Mediterranean herbs that need a warm sunny site with free-draining soil. In colder areas winter savory may need some form of winter protection.

PROPAGATION

Summer savory is an annual that needs reasonably warm, damp conditions for germination, but only a little water thereafter. Both types of savory grow well from seed that should not be sown too deeply. They are best station sown at 30cm (12in) intervals in mid-spring in 1cm (½in) drills. Thin to 30cm (12in).

HARVESTING AND STORAGE

You can gather the young stem tips early in the season but when the plant begins to flower, harvest the entire plant and then dry. The dried leaves can be stored for later use.

CULINARY USES

Although these are among the oldest of herbs, they are not widely grown or used today. Summer savory is sometimes called the bean herb because it goes so well with green beans and is used in a range of bean dishes. Both types of savory have a spicy, peppery flavour and are used to flavour fresh garden beans, vinegar, soups, stuffings and rice.

CULTIVATION

Sowing time Mid-spring
Sowing depth 1cm (½in)
Thinning distance 30cm (12in)
Harvesting Before flowering (stem tips); on flowering (whole plant)
Storage Dried

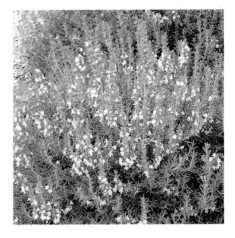

Above: *Savory thrives in warm sunny conditions and provides a spicy addition to many dishes.*

THYME

Thymus vulgaris

Thyme is a perennial plant that reaches 30–45cm (12–18in) in height. It can be grown indoors or outdoors and in sun or partial shade. There is a very wide range of thymes that can be grown in the herb garden. Most are similar in terms of their culinary value, although the broad-leaved forms have a slightly stronger flavour. The wide range of colours available makes them excellent subjects for ornamental gardens and edible landscaping.

SOIL AND ASPECT

Thyme likes a sunny situation and a well-drained soil. It is not particular about the soil type and will even grow in poor "gravelly" soils. Thymes are excellent plants for edging borders and can be grown in containers and between the cracks in the paving in patios. They are durable and will even withstand being walked on. They can get straggly after a few years, although a light trimming will help maintain a good habit.

PROPAGATION

Thyme can be grown from seed in spring, although this does not allow for the propagation of particular forms or varieties. Seeds require 25 days at about 16°C (61°F) for germination and are best raised under cover and transplanted out later. Plants can also be raised vegetatively from cuttings or layers taken in early to mid-summer. Plants should be spaced at 30cm (12in) intervals.

HARVESTING AND STORAGE

Nip off leafy stem ends and flowers as and when they are needed when the plants are at the full-flowering stage. These can be used fresh or dried by hanging a bunch in a warm place. They can also be frozen.

CULINARY USES

The leaves can be used with meats, soups, sauces and egg dishes. Thyme improves digestion, destroys intestinal parasites and is a good antiseptic and tonic. Its leaves can be used as a condiment and a tea.

Right: *Despite the wide range of cultivated thymes that are available, most have similar uses in the kitchen.*

CULTIVATION

Sowing time Spring
Cuttings or layers Early to mid-summer
Thinning and planting distance 30cm (12in)
Harvesting Any time
Storage Dried or frozen

WINTER

THE KITCHEN GARDEN

VEGETABLES

EARLY WINTER
- Hoe between crops on fine days.
- Examine stored onions and potatoes for any sign of disease and discard second-class seed. Any potatoes that are sprouting should be placed apart in dry trays.
- Protect more tender plants with leaves or cloches.
- Begin forcing rhubarb and seakale under a light-proof cover.
- Order seed catalogues and plan the new season's crops.

MID-WINTER
- Tidy up and put vegetable waste on the compost heap.
- Hoe between growing crops when dry.
- Sow broad (fava) beans and peas in warm sheltered positions.
- Sow early vegetables under glass or cloches.
- Start potatoes in a frost-free shed.
- Plant rhubarb in well-manured beds.

LATE WINTER
- Hoe weeds when the weather allows.
- Clear old beds ready for new season.
- Cut pea and bean sticks.
- Sow early vegetables under glass or cloches.
- Plant artichokes, garlic, shallots, lettuce (winter), potatoes (early), rhubarb and seakale.
- Plants overwintering under cloches should be hardened off and only protected when the weather is frosty.

FRUIT

EARLY WINTER
- Finish pruning fruit trees and bushes on frost-free days. Large standard trees will need pruning every second or third year.
- Firm newly planted trees where the frost has been at work.
- Do not plant any more trees until the spring; just prepare the ground.
- Currants and gooseberries should be pruned if not already done.
- Prune outdoor vines.
- Remove unwanted suckers from raspberry stools but do not prune until early spring.

MID-WINTER
- Start pruning hardier trees such as apples. Do not prune apricots, cherries, figs, nectarines and peaches.
- Prepare grafting material.
- Plant container-grown trees and cover soil with well-rotted manure.

LATE WINTER
- Prune damsons, pears, plums and quince.
- Spread manure around fruit trees and dig it in.
- Prepare new strawberry beds.
- Fertilize by hand the blossom of fruit trees grown under glass.

HERBS

EARLY WINTER
- Prepare ground for planting when conditions allow.
- Protect tender herbs under cloches.
- Continue to remove dead stems from herbaceous types.

MID-WINTER
- Prepare ground ready for planting.
- Force early growth under cloches.
- Make early sowings under glass.

LATE WINTER
- Remove dead stems from herbaceous types.
- Continue forcing under cloches.
- Continue sowing under glass.

SPRING

EARLY SPRING
- Hoe weeds when the weather allows.
- Prepare seedbeds.
- Protect early crops from birds.
- Begin sowing in sheltered places in the open.
- Sow early vegetables under glass or cloches.
- Plant out early crops raised under glass and early potatoes.
- Plant early broad (fava) beans out in the garden under glass.

MID-SPRING
- Hoe weeds regularly.
- Prepare beds for planting out.
- Feed cabbages with high-nitrogen fertilizer such as chicken manure.
- Potatoes need the soil drawn over their leaves to protect them from frost.
- Begin sowing remaining summer crops outdoors.
- Continue sowing more tender crops under glass.

LATE SPRING
- Hoe weeds regularly.
- Cut asparagus when shoots reach 15cm (6in).
- Maintain the succession of seed sowing to give salad throughout the summer season.
- Continue planting out summer crops.
- Sow late crops such as broccoli and plant out winter crops previously sown under cover.
- Last chance to plant late potatoes.
- Plant out cucumbers, pumpkins and melons in beds previously used for protected early crops.

EARLY SPRING
- Protect blossom with fleece on cold nights.
- Last chance to plant container-grown fruit bushes.
- Graft apples, cherries, pears and plums that were prepared in mid-winter.
- Finish pruning fruit trees and bushes.

MID-SPRING
- Continue protecting blossom.
- Wall trees will need moisture from now on.
- Watch for pests and diseases.
- Grapes will require thinning in order to swell their size.

LATE SPRING
- All fruit will benefit from a mulch.
- Apricots, peaches and Morello cherries should have fruiting spurs shortened back to three to four leaves.
- Limit raspberry suckers to around four to six to each stool.
- Put straw around strawberries to protect the fruits from the ground.

EARLY SPRING
- Continue sowing under glass.
- Plant out hardy herbs once hardened off.
- Prune shrubby types.
- Lift and divide herbaceous types until late spring.

MID-SPRING
- Continue sowing under glass.
- Continue planting out.
- Take basal cuttings.

LATE SPRING
- Sow herbs like parsley (*Petroselinum crispum*) and chervil (*Anthriscus cerefolium*) for winter use.
- Continue sowing under glass and planting out.

SUMMER

EARLY SUMMER
- Hoe weeds regularly throughout summer.
- Water all salad crops regularly.
- Feed heavy feeders like cauliflowers with liquid manure or compost tea.
- Keep picking peas to stimulate flowering.
- Harvest early potatoes and replace with winter turnips or late celery.
- Support runner beans.
- Sow the last of the outdoor salad crops and continue sowing seed of late or winter crops.
- Thin out seedlings.
- Plant late-season crops raised under cover.

MID-SUMMER
- Water all salad crops regularly.
- Remove debris, following harvest, to the compost heap until late summer.
- Potatoes and other crops may need earthing-up.
- Pinch out and stop tomatoes and marrows.
- Maintain the succession of seed sowing for late or winter crops.
- Thin out the beetroot crop so that the roots can form properly.
- Plant late-season crops raised under cover.

LATE SUMMER
- Water all crops regularly.
- Remove debris, following harvest, to the compost heap.
- Harvest seed from French (green) beans and onions.
- Garlic and onions can be harvested this month and then ripened.
- Potatoes for next year's seed should be dug up and dried in the sun.
- Maintain the succession of seed sowing for late or winter crops.

EARLY SUMMER
- Continue mulching trees and bushes to conserve moisture.
- Cut back untidy vigorous growth.
- Over-laden trees may need support. Aphids will appear, so take appropriate action.
- Throw nets over fruiting trees and shrubs to prevent the birds getting the fruit first.
- Peaches and apricots may need some thinning.
- Strawberries should have regular watering.

MID-SUMMER
- Thin trees and remove unnecessary growth.
- Hoe round the roots of fruit trees and water them.
- Fruit trees may be budded when the weather is moist.
- Espalier and dwarf fruit trees will need training and protection from birds.
- Strawberries should be layered and clipped to the soil to secure their position.

LATE SUMMER
- Protect fruit on walls from wasps and birds as it ripens.
- Pruning can be started and trees budded.
- Apples, pears and plums may need the fruit thinning out if the crop is heavy.
- Cut down the old canes of raspberries after harvesting.
- Cut off unwanted runners from strawberries and remove the old straw from round the crowns.

EARLY SUMMER
- Continue sowing under glass.
- Continue planting out until late summer.
- Harvest herbs for storing before they flower.
- Plant out tender herbs.
- Dead-head unless seed is required until late summer.
- Cut back herbaceous types to stimulate growth until late summer.

MID-SUMMER
- Cut mint (Mentha) and other sweet herbs for drying.
- Pull out parsley (Petroselinum crispum) unless it is being kept for seed.
- Propagate sage (Salvia) or savory (Satureja) from cuttings or division.

LATE SUMMER
- Harvest herbs as required.

AUTUMN

EARLY AUTUMN
- Hoe weeds regularly throughout autumn.
- Water all crops regularly.
- Harvest onions and bend down the necks of the remainder to prevent seeding.
- Continue to lift potatoes.
- Expose the fruit of outdoor tomatoes to the sun by removing the covering leaves.
- Maintain the succession of seed sowing for late or winter crops.
- Plant late season crops raised under cover.

MID-AUTUMN
- After beans and peas have been harvested, turn the soil over and leave it fallow over the winter.
- Lift root vegetables when their tops fade.
- Cut down asparagus foliage when mature.
- Onions and turnip beds should be thinned.
- Clear the last of the potatoes and store them.
- Earth up celery and leeks.
- Plant out late-season crops and protect tender types such as cauliflower.

LATE AUTUMN
- Get the soil ready for spring sowing.
- Protect crowns of tender crops with a mulch of leaves.
- Lift the last of the beetroot and carrots.
- Earth up celery and leeks if not already done.
- Spinach will continue to crop as it is thinned.
- Dry off the late potatoes for seed stock next year.
- Continue to plant out late-season crops and protect tender types such as cauliflower.

EARLY AUTUMN
- Wall fruit that has ripened will need protecting.
- Fruit trees may be budded and light pruning continued.
- Early varieties of apples and pears that do not keep well should be gathered.
- Prune currants and gooseberries to keep them in shape. Raspberry canes that have fruited should be removed to make room for the new growth.
- Strawberries should have unwanted runners removed to give space to the main plants.

MID-AUTUMN
- Look though the nursery catalogues and order fruit stock, then prepare the ground and remove stock to be replaced.
- Move any trees or bushes that are in the wrong place.
- Apples and pears can now be gathered.
- Apricots, cherries, currants and gooseberries should be pruned and the cuttings burnt.
- Loganberries and raspberries should be planted now.

LATE AUTUMN
- This is the time to plant fruit trees in well-prepared ground.
- Begin winter pruning of fruit trees.
- Plant currants and gooseberries.
- Figs will need thinning.
- Spread manure between rows of new strawberry plants.

EARLY AUTUMN
- Harvest seed as it ripens.
- Harvest leaves and stems as required.
- Cut back herbaceous types to stimulate new growth.

MID-AUTUMN
- Harvest seed as it ripens.
- Tidy away dead material.
- Protect tender herbs.
- Plant shrubby and herbaceous types until late autumn.
- Move tender container herbs under some protection.
- Divide herbaceous herbs until late autumn.

LATE AUTUMN
- Prepare ground for planting when conditions allow.

INDEX

ACKNOWLEDGEMENTS

Authors' Acknowledgements
We would like to thank the following people who worked as models for the photography: Joe Lovell. Debbie Hart for her willow weaving skills, Jane Dobson for her graft unions and Ian Gandy and Stewart Brown for the lawn maintenance shots. A big thank you to Writtle College and their staff for allowing the use of their grounds and glasshouses to take many of the photographs.

Publisher's Acknowledgements
The publisher would like to thank the following for kindly allowing photography to take place in their gardens:

t = top   b - bottom   l = left   r = right   c - centre

The Centre for Alternative Technology, Wales 9bc and br; 10t; 18t; 29bl; Edmondsham Manor, Dorset 11b; 17tl; 25bl;110; Fardel Manor, Devon 28c; 30bl; Valerie Ferguson, Bath 13b; 17tr; 17b; 21b; 34t; HDRA, the Organic Organisation, Coventry 10b; 11t; 13t; 18b; 29t; 44bl; 109; RHS Rosemoor, Devon 14; 16t; 16b; 40br; 37br; 38t; 84t; RHS Wisley, Surrey 8; Writtle College, Chelmsford 20t.

The publisher would also like to thank the following for kindly allowing their photographs to be reproduced for the purposes of this book:

The Garden Picture Library 54bl (Howard Rice); 57cr (Jerry Pavia); 57b (Sunniva Harte); 58t (Sunniva Harte); 58b (Brian Carter); 63t (David Askham); 107 (John Glover).